THE BASEBALL CODES

THE
BASEBALL
CODES

Beanballs, Sign Stealing, and Bench-Clearing Brawls:
The Unwritten Rules of America's Pastime

Jason Turbow

with Michael Duca

PANTHEON BOOKS NEW YORK

Library of Congress Cataloging-in-Publication Data
Turbow, Jason.
The baseball codes : beanballs, sign stealing, and bench-clearing brawls : the
unwritten rules of America's pastime / Jason Turbow and Michael Duca.
p. cm.
Includes bibliographical references and index.
ISBN 978-0-375-42469-4
1. Baseball. 2. Baseball—Rules. I. Duca, Michael. II. Title.
GV867.T78 2010
796.357—dc22   2009022253

www.pantheonbooks.com
Printed in the United States of America
First Edition
2 4 6 8 9 7 5 3 1

CONTENTS

CONTENTS

THE BASEBALL CODES

Introduction

With apologies to Joe Carter, the most memorable moment of the 1993 baseball season didn't even happen while a ball was in play. It began the moment that Robin Ventura charged Nolan Ryan on the Arlington infield, causing many of the 32,312 jaws in attendance to drop at the spectacle. Ryan was as close to a personification of the term "battle-hardened" as baseball had ever seen, at forty-six a big-leaguer longer than his would-be assailant had been alive.

If pitting a strapping twenty-three-year-old against a graying veteran more than two decades his senior seems like a mismatch, it was—in reverse. Ryan quickly put Ventura into a headlock and rained blows upon his forehead, providing the season's most enduring visual and a source of endless jokes about his own toughness and Ventura's lack thereof. In 2001, ESPN rated it the No. 1 televised baseball fight ever.

"The way [people] carry on," said Ventura, "you'd think [Ryan] was a combination of Clint Eastwood, Bruce Lee, and [rodeo star] Larry Mahan."

The most interesting thing about the fight, however, isn't the fight at all—it's what led up to it. The genesis of the moment occurred years before the fateful pitch left Ryan's fingertips, long before Ventura's head ended up in the crook of the pitcher's left arm. It was less an ill-placed fastball that drove Ventura to the mound than an ongoing dispute over baseball's code of conduct, informally known as the "unwritten rules." Less strategic than moral, these rules collectively drive the game, form-

3

ing not just a code but the Code, the ultimate measure used to shape ballplayers' attitudes toward themselves, each other, and the game they play.

Ryan and the White Sox had been going back and forth about a variety of perceived Code violations for years. Ventura, in fact, was only tangentially involved with most of it; it was just on his unfortunate watch that the pot happened to boil over.

America saw an apparently calm Ventura start toward first base after being hit on the elbow with a Ryan fastball, then spin toward the mound, drop his helmet, and charge. Ryan, a part-time rancher, referred to the treatment he dished out as "cow-mugging," and although the punches were purely superficial—one account called it an "atomic noogie"—the humiliation was profound. The young All-Star was helpless against a man on the verge of retirement, unable to do more than absorb whatever it was Ryan decided to dish out. The lack of severity only added to the fight's comic overtones, said Mike Leggett of the *Austin American-Statesman*, making Ventura "the first guy ever to get five straight hits off Nolan Ryan."

For Ryan, it was the final season of a splendid twenty-seven-year career, during which he compiled stats that completely transcended those of his peers. He was the all-time strikeout leader by a wide margin, had started the second-most games ever, and allowed the fewest hits per nine innings. His seven no-hitters were as many as the next two guys on the list, Sandy Koufax and Bob Feller, combined.

He was also unquestionably a throwback to a different era, and no one in history better served to illustrate the evolution of the Code from one generation to the next. Ryan came up in the time of Gibson and Drysdale, pitchers who, when feeling beneficent, allowed batters to vie for offerings over the inner portion of the plate, but who ferociously discouraged anyone with the guts to reach for a pitch outside. They treated a number of canons as gospel:

- If you dig in, you'll be brushed back or hit.

- If you hit a home run, you'll be brushed back or hit.

- If you watch your home runs, you'll be brushed back or hit.

These were the rules that Ryan grew up learning, and as his career progressed—and as the older generation gave way to the new—he became their foremost champion. Ryan was, according to Jack McDowell, whose twelve-year big-league tenure included five seasons as Ventura's teammate in Chicago, the "last guy standing from that head-hunting era."

"If you were digging into the batter's box [against Ryan] . . . you were digging yourself a grave," said Craig Grebeck, who played alongside Ventura for six seasons. Grebeck learned an early lesson about Ryan's rules in 1992, when he made the mistake of questioning the great pitcher by naïvely asking the umpire to check the baseball after a pitch with fastball rotation broke on him like a slider. Players on the White Sox bench howled at the audacity—check a ball on *this* guy? Grebeck's own coaches were yelling that he'd soon be on his backside . . . or worse. That Rangers catcher Ivan Rodriguez had already returned the ball to Ryan only inflamed matters, because the pitcher then had to toss it back to the umpire. Terrified, Grebeck tried to stay light on his feet for the rest of the game, looking at every pitch he saw from Ryan as a potential weapon to be used against him. He still doesn't know why Ryan held back, figuring only that the pitcher laughed at the third-year player's impudence and chose to pitch *to* him, not *at* him. Perhaps it was respect for the fact that in 1990, Grebeck, then a rookie, crushed the first pitch he ever saw from Ryan for his first home run as a big-leaguer. Whatever it was, virtually the entire White Sox clubhouse was surprised when the pitcher didn't so much as knock him down.

Ryan's old-school tendencies seemed to grow in stature over the course of his career, even as the rest of baseball relaxed around the inside corner through the eighties and nineties. It started at the game's lowest levels, as youth-league pitchers began to learn their craft against the enlarged sweet spots of aluminum bats, which trained them early not to try to dominate the plate's inner half. At the major-league level, the newfound power of the steroid era gave pitchers ever more reason to stay outside, as pitches that could once be counted on to jam even the strongest players were hit over outfield fences with regularity.

At the same time, two more phenomena took shape. The first was that umpires began working from the assumption that most pitchers who hit batters did so intentionally, and as a result many batters followed suit. The second was that as salaries skyrocketed, newly minted millionaires became more protective of their ability to maintain earning power, and took increasingly more offense when pitchers came inside with potentially career-threatening fastballs.

The result was that intimidation tactics were slowly but certainly abandoned by huge numbers of pitchers. This starts to explain why some players began to have a problem with Nolan Ryan, who hadn't changed a bit over all those years.

The series of events that culminated with Ryan's fist bouncing atop Ventura's forehead illustrates how long baseball grudges can last. It began during the second game of a doubleheader between the Rangers and White Sox on August 10, 1990, almost three years to the day before Ventura's misbegotten charge. In that game, Ryan allowed back-to-back home runs; the first was the aforementioned shot by Grebeck, the second to the equally diminutive Ozzie Guillen. They would be the only home runs either player would hit that season. Ryan lasted just five innings, and Chicago swept the twin bill.

When the same clubs met seven days later, it wasn't difficult to predict what would happen the first time Grebeck stepped to the plate. "My first two at-bats ever against Ryan, I hit the ball hard, and he wasn't going to allow me to have that edge," said Grebeck, who, after his home run, had smashed a ball into the right-center-field gap that was tracked down by outfielder Ruben Sierra. "His unwritten rule was that he wanted that edge. And if someone had some good at-bats against him, he was going to get that edge back on his side. And back then, the way you did that was by knocking a guy down."

Ryan did more than that—he hit Grebeck in the back. "That," said Chicago All-Star Frank Thomas, "was what really started it all."

In the same game, Ryan knocked down Scott Fletcher one pitch after the White Sox second baseman asked umpire Tim McClelland to examine the ball for scuff marks. Chicago pitcher Greg Hibbard responded by hitting Rangers third baseman Steve Buechele in the arm, igniting a brawl between the teams.

That was the first part of the bad-blood equation. The second was

Texas's propensity for coming back big against the White Sox. On June 20, 1991, Texas scored five runs in the ninth to beat Chicago 7–3. Eleven weeks later, on September 8, the Rangers scored four runs in the ninth to win 7–6. On May 1 of the following season, Texas scored two in the sixth and three in the ninth for an 8–4 victory. The following day, the Rangers scored three in the eleventh for a 4–1 win.

This sort of trend is not easily forgotten by an opponent. Eventually the White Sox became inured to certain baseball mores when facing Texas, such as displaying compassion when holding a big lead. On August 3, 1993—the day before the famous fight—the White Sox built a 10–0 advantage by the sixth inning, led in part by a three-hit day from Ventura, who was riding a ten-game hitting streak. The third baseman also happened to skirt the unwritten rule mandating cessation of aggressive tactics during a blowout when he tallied the team's ninth run by scoring from second on a single by Lance Johnson in the second inning. In most corners that's too early to alter tactics, no matter what the score. It was enough, however, to tick off a Code adherent such as Ryan.

True to form, Texas scored six runs in the final innings of an 11–6 loss, but Ventura's slight had already registered.

"We didn't even think anything about it, but the next morning in the paper they were all talking about how we were trying to run up the score," said McDowell. "We're thinking, 'Fuck you. You stop scoring six runs in the ninth and we'll stop running with a nine-run lead in the sixth.' "

Ryan took the mound for Texas the next day.

In their clubhouse, Chicago players discussed their collective beef with Ryan and came to the conclusion that they'd taken enough abuse. "The whole world stops when that guy pitches, like he's God or something," McDowell said at the time. "He's been throwing at batters forever, and people are [too] gutless to do anything about it." The White Sox set out to change that trend, coming to the collective conclusion that only an extreme measure—like, say, charging the mound—had a chance to effect measurable change.

With little voice in the matter, Ventura found himself at the center of it all the instant he was hit on the elbow. "Robin really didn't want to charge him," said Thomas. "It was just one of those things where we all knew he was going to drill him, and once it happened he reacted. He wasn't angry, he was just saying, 'You can't be doing that for no reason.' . . . He really, wholeheartedly didn't want to do it."

"That was the problem," said McDowell. "When he went out there, he didn't know what to do, because he wasn't mad."

Ryan had been charged exactly once before, thirteen years earlier, by Dave Winfield. In that brawl he actually took a step backward as Winfield lit out toward the mound, and ended up paying for it—Winfield got in the only blows of the fight before the pair tumbled to the turf and were buried beneath a pile of players. The pitcher was not about to make that mistake again. "When someone comes out to the mound, they're coming out there with the intent to hurt you, and I'm not going to be passive about it," he said shortly after the fight.

Thus, the unwitting Ventura found himself in a place he very clearly did not want to be. He'd charge Ryan again, he said at the time, if he "felt it was necessary," but he never got the chance—Ryan made only six more starts that season, none against the White Sox, then retired. And because of a series of events triggered by the Code that dated back at least three seasons, a two-time All-Star who drove in more than ninety runs eight times is remembered primarily for one thing—the atomic noogie administered to him by Nolan Ryan.

Ryan and Ventura are just two participants in baseball's long history of Code-fueled disputes. For more than a century, ballplayers have built the unwritten rules to cover everything from trivial clubhouse interactions between teammates to all-hands melees between bitter rivals. The rules are in a constant state of development and evolution, and nearly every section of the proverbial codebook has both supporters and detractors. When enough players and coaches eschew a given rule for a long enough period of time, it simply falls by the wayside, often to be replaced by something new. (Take digging into the batter's box; once forbidden, it's now a common occurrence.)

Because they're unwritten, the rules must be picked up through experience. "You learn what's acceptable and not acceptable and where you fit and where you don't fit, and the only way you can learn is by basically fucking up," wrote eight-year major-leaguer-turned-psychologist Tom House in *The Jock's Itch*. This can lead to painful lessons, either from irate teammates or from opposing pitchers, many of whom revel in the opportunity to offer seminars to young players, using as their instructional tool of choice a fastball to the rib cage.

As filled with minutiae as the unwritten rulebook can be—"Don't walk in front of the catcher on the way into the batter's box? I've never heard of that," said Davey Lopes—at its essence is basic sportsmanship.

"I can break it down into three simple things," said Bob Brenly, who followed a nine-year big-league career by managing the Arizona Diamondbacks to a world championship in 2001. "Respect your teammates, respect your opponents, and respect the game."

If this sounds simple, there's a wild diversity of philosophies on just how to go about it. For example, though it's commonly acknowledged that running up the score on an opponent is discourteous, the definition of "running up the score" not only has evolved over time, but is far from universally accepted within the modern game. Additionally, when and how to retaliate for Code violations is as complex as what constitutes a violation in the first place.

Further complicating matters, at least from an outsider's perspective, is that the more stringently a ballplayer adheres to these tenets, the less likely he is to talk about them to people outside the game. He's secretive because he's insulated, and he's secretive because the outside world doesn't truly have a handle on the politics of his particular office. Mostly, though, he's secretive because he can be. It's the way the system's set up. Without any explanation of what's happening and why, outsiders tend to become baffled at what they often consider to be extreme reactions.

A case in point can be taken from the angry response Giants broadcaster Mike Krukow received from a number of Bay Area parents after praising pitcher Tyler Walker on the air for launching a retaliatory strike against Mark Mulder after the A's ace hit two Giants, including Barry Bonds. "They're pissed off that they have Little Leaguers and I'm teaching them the wrong baseball," Krukow said. "But I'm not teaching Little League baseball. Their fathers teach them Little League baseball. I'm explaining what goes on here at the major-league level. And if Walker doesn't do what he did, then he's got to answer to Barry Bonds. And Barry Bonds has every right to get in his face, and every other pitcher's face, that doesn't protect him."

If these comments seem at all inflammatory, it must be pointed out that Krukow is an ex-pitcher, a baseball man, whose opinions reside in the mainstream of the sport. He understands how baseball as an institution is improved by the Code, and, just as important in his role as a broadcaster, he understands how those who don't pay close attention might fail to comprehend that fact. It makes for a tough balancing act.

Generally speaking, the more fans know, the more they're likely to misconstrue. So the wall effectively becomes its own set of rules: Don't expect outsiders to understand baseball's world, or even give them the chance to form a wrong impression. To talk about the unwritten rules is to violate the pre-eminent one: *Keep your mouth shut.* Some things do leak out—not everyone possesses the same sense of insularity, and some people simply have trouble filtering their thoughts—but for many active players the notion of discussing most parts of the Code is tantamount to revealing state secrets. Take the following excerpt from an interview with All-Star pitcher Jason Schmidt, conducted in the fall of 2006:

How does a pitcher or team know when it's time to get someone?
SCHMIDT: [Answer off the record, and not very revealing at that.]

Has anything like that ever crossed your experience?
SCHMIDT: No doubt. Totally.

What was it?
SCHMIDT: I don't remember.

Have you ever been ordered to hit someone?
SCHMIDT: I wouldn't say ordered. Sometimes you just know. You can't say that in a newspaper.

This is for a book.
SCHMIDT: You can't say it in a book.

The point being that Jason Schmidt is no different from the majority of his colleagues. Unlike Jim Bouton, who drew scorn from teammates and opponents alike when his groundbreaking *Ball Four* was published, depicting for the first time the major-league ballplayer as he truly lived and worked, most modern players avoid similar treatment not just by avoiding topics of potential embarrassment but by refraining from saying anything remotely interesting.

"The first thing they teach you is that what goes on in the clubhouse stays in the clubhouse," said Dusty Baker. "That's not so anymore. Now everybody wants to know what the team meeting was about. Well, that's the *team* meeting. If you're on the team, we'll tell you. It's not being anti-press, it's not being secretive—it's just how it is. [While managing the Chicago Cubs], I wanted to put up a sign, just like in the locker rooms in the old days, that says 'What goes on in here stays in here.' I wanted to put it in the kitchen, because if you put it in a public area it would be construed as anti-press, which it's not."

Perhaps, but this still makes it difficult to write about the unwritten rules. House described it like this:

> Baseball protects its own, no matter what the offense, as long as the offense stays within the confines of the baseball world. You may have a serious gambling problem, and the team may know about it, but they'll keep your secret as long as you perform, and as long as you keep your problem to yourself. Someone may take you aside and tell you to watch yourself, but no one is going to talk to the press or the commissioner's office until you do something to warrant it.
>
> . . . There are many things that baseball manages to keep quiet about. In fact, players who are foolish enough to discuss what went on in a closed clubhouse meeting, or reveal that two players almost killed each other after the game, often turn up on other teams the next year. That kind of behavior just isn't acceptable. You must be loyal to your teammates, even though you may hate every last one of them.

That such potential for discord exists within a clubhouse is hardly a secret—any group of twenty-five guys that spends as much time together as does a baseball team is bound to have conflicts—nor is it a secret that any leaks from within spell open season for the media. For proof of this, one has only to look at the rare instance when tempers boil over in the open, such as Jeff Kent pushing Barry Bonds in the Giants dugout, or Darryl Strawberry and Keith Hernandez coming to blows in front of a phalanx of reporters during Mets spring training. Stories deconstructing team strife followed each of those incidents for weeks; years after combatants have put their differences aside the press continues to look at any reconciliation with skepticism.

This was the case long before the existence of the twenty-four-hour news cycle. After a tough, 2–1 loss in the opening game of the 1939 World Series, Cincinnati's starting pitcher, Paul Derringer, and right fielder, Ival Goodman, fought in the clubhouse over a fly ball that Derringer thought Goodman should have caught. As teammates raced to separate the two, Reds manager Bill McKechnie ordered the doors to the clubhouse closed and all reporters kept at bay until the mess was straightened out. To reinforce his instructions, he threatened a thousand-dollar fine—slightly less than a month's pay for the average player—to anyone who leaked the information. When reporters were admitted about ten minutes later, team members, true to their manager's wishes, acted as if nothing was amiss, and not a word was written about it the next day. It wasn't until Reds third baseman Bill Werber wrote a book more than sixty years later that a description of the affair came to light.

Even more dramatic was the hotel-room brawl between Davey Johnson, then a star second baseman for the Braves, and his manager, Hall of Famer Eddie Matthews, in 1973. The way Johnson tells it, after an initial verbal disagreement the manager invited him into his room and challenged him to a fight. Johnson, reluctant at first, changed his mind when Matthews wound up for a roundhouse punch, then knocked the older man down. Matthews charged back, and as the sounds of the scrape flooded the hallway, players converged on the scene. In the process of breaking things up, several peacemakers were soon bearing welts of their own.

"The next day at the ballpark we looked like we had just returned from the Revolutionary War," wrote House (a member of the team, who, true to the code of silence, left all names out of his published account). "Everybody had at least one black eye, puffed-up lips, scraped elbows, and sore hands. It had been a real knockdown battle."

This was something that couldn't be hidden from the press. Matthews called the team together, and as a unit they came up with a story about a game that got carried away, in which guys took good-natured beatings. Flimsy? Maybe. Accepted? Absolutely.

"You can ask Hank Aaron and others on that team," Johnson said, laughing. "Eddie said his biggest regret [in his baseball career] was not having it out with me again. That one never got out. It never made the papers."

"You might not like everybody on your team, but just because you don't like a guy, it doesn't mean you talk about them . . . ," said Yankees closer Mariano Rivera. "If someone is doing the wrong thing, you should address the problem but not bring it into the world. You don't have the right to publish it. If it's a problem, go and attack it and try to fix it, but not by telling everyone."

Look no further than Robin Ventura for proof. After suffering one of the most humiliating beatings in baseball history, he had every right to shout from the rooftops about the injustices visited upon his team by Nolan Ryan, baseball's premier badass, and how he wanted only to put an end to the bullying. Instead, he adhered to the Code and basically kept quiet about the situation. It might not have done much to win respect outside baseball's inner circle, but the guys in clubhouses around the league expected no less.

PART ONE

ON THE FIELD

1

Know When to Steal 'Em

In July 2001, Rickey Henderson was forty-two years old and, by an enormous margin, baseball's all-time stolen-base leader. The San Diego Padres outfielder was well over two decades into his major-league career and had long since been anointed the greatest leadoff hitter of all time. Then he stole second base against the Brewers, and Milwaukee manager Davey Lopes exploded.

It wasn't just any steal that set Lopes off—it happened in the seventh inning of a game in which the Padres led 12–5, after Milwaukee's defense had essentially cried "uncle" by positioning first baseman Richie Sexson in the hole behind Henderson instead of holding him on. The play was so borderline, as far as stolen bases go, that it was ruled defensive indifference, and Henderson wasn't even credited with a steal. That wasn't his goal, however. Henderson was approaching Ty Cobb's all-time record for runs scored (which he would ultimately best in the season's final week), and he had just put himself into scoring position.

Lopes could not have been less interested in the runner's motivation. As soon as Henderson reached second, Lopes went to the mound, ostensibly to talk to pitcher Ray King but really to direct a tirade up the middle. At top volume and with R-rated vocabulary, Lopes informed Henderson that he had just become a target for the Brewers pitching staff.

"I didn't appreciate what he did," Lopes told reporters after the game. "I know he's trying to obtain a record for most runs scored, but do it the right way. If he keeps doing stuff like that he's going to get one of his players hurt. I just told him to stay in the game because he was going on his

17

ass. We were going to drill him, flat out. I told him that. But he chose not to stay in the game; I knew he wouldn't."

Henderson was removed after the inning by Padres manager Bruce Bochy, which the skipper insisted had to do with the lopsided score, not Lopes's threats. Afterward, Henderson said that he was reluctantly following green-light orders given to him by third-base coach Tim Flannery and sanctioned by Bochy, and that showing anybody up was the last thing on his mind. "Davey and I argued, but I told him that on my own, in that situation, I wouldn't go down and steal that base," he said. ("Rickey said I gave him the sign?" said a surprised Flannery when he heard Henderson's take. "Rickey didn't even *know* the sign.")

"To be blunt, what he did was bullshit," said King after the game. "We weren't holding him on. If he's going to break the record that way, he doesn't deserve it. The guy's probably going in the Hall of Fame, but to try to get to second base just to score a run, that's sorry. When he took off I said, 'You've got to be kidding.' "

What Henderson had done was break one of the cornerstone entries in baseball's unwritten rulebook: Don't play aggressively with a big lead late in the game. It's tantamount to running up the score in football, and no tenet of the Code is more simultaneously revered and loathed. It means the cessation of stolen-base attempts, sending runners in search of extra bases, swinging at 3-0 pitches, and an assortment of other tactics aimed toward scoring at all costs.

"There is no excuse that can be made up to justify trying to show someone up," said Hall of Fame manager Sparky Anderson, one of the Code's staunchest practitioners in his twenty-five years at the helm of the Cincinnati Reds and Detroit Tigers. "There's no excuse, and you can't invent one."

Though many baseball minds hew to this rule, there's a group of firm believers who call it hogwash. Bochy in particular took up the opposite side of Lopes's argument, pointing out that by playing Sexson back and failing to hold Henderson on, Milwaukee's manager effectively gave his team a defensive advantage it wouldn't have had if the first baseman had been tethered to the bag. "[In a blowout game a team] will make moves to improve its defensive situation, yet it wants the team hitting not to do anything to try to improve its offensive situation," said Hall of Fame baseball writer Tracy Ringolsby. "If you're not going to hold the runner on, the runner has the right to take the next base, because you're saying it's not that important—and you're taking away an offensive opportunity from the ball club by not playing your normal defense."

Lopes wanted no part of the second-guessers. "All of those people that took shots at me, they don't know nothing," he said a week after the incident. "Unless you've played this game, you have no clue. You can say what you want as an outsider and criticize me, because that's your right. But you have no idea what you're talking about because you didn't play the game. They're ignorant when it comes to that. . . . The people in baseball, they know. I've had people here, old-timers, come up to me and say, 'We'd drill the guy at second base [if he did what Henderson did].' " Never mind that Bochy was effectively an old-timer himself, having caught in the major leagues for nine seasons before becoming a manager.

It was the same reason Yankees third-base coach Larry Bowa got so upset in 2006 when Baltimore's Corey Patterson stole second base, then third, when his team held a 10–4, eighth-inning lead, screaming, "Play the game right!" at the startled runner. But here's the rub: The Orioles led 10–0 just a half-inning before, and New York possessed the best offense in baseball, as it showed during its four-run seventh. Patterson said after the game that he checked with people in his dugout and got the green light to run. At the very least, he displayed a cognizance of the Code and was doing his best to straddle the line between propriety and victory.

Patterson's dilemma illustrates a common conundrum: What's a big lead, and when exactly is late in the game? As evidenced by the difference of opinion between Bowa and Patterson, one man's idea of running up the score is another man's idea of reasonable insurance.

Baseball's semi-official "closing time" used to be four runs after six innings—the reach of a grand slam—but that's no longer a universal notion. When players started getting bigger and pitching started getting softer and the designated hitter was invented and home runs started flying out of ballparks more frequently, what was once considered a big lead was no longer so.

"Five runs in the fifth inning in the American League is nothing," said manager Jim Leyland. "That's only one half-inning away from having someone tie up the game."

The best way to illustrate a diversity of opinions, of course, is with the opinions themselves:

- "It used to be that [running with] anything more than a four-run lead was wrong, and you've got to be careful with that."—Tony La Russa

- "When I was playing, if you had a four-run lead it was a courtesy not to run. But you can do that now."—Ozzie Guillen

- "Once I had you by five runs and you couldn't tie me with a grand slam, that was it."—Sparky Anderson

- "I was always taught you shut it down at five runs after six."—Dusty Baker

- "Five runs in the sixth, I'm not stopping there. We get into the seventh inning, then I'll start chilling a little bit."—Ron Washington

- "We play [to shut it down] if you're up seven runs in the seventh inning."—Jim Slaton

- "From the seventh inning on, if one swing of the bat can tie you up, it's game on," said ex–first baseman Mark Grace in 2006. "If it's 4–0, you have Jason Schmidt on the mound, and he's only given up one hit, you still go for it if Ray Durham gets on base in the eighth inning. Now, if it's 6–0, you're in territory where you might get a player hit in the brain in response."

"There's always going to be fights arising from those situations where you have one side thinking one way and the other side thinking another," said ex-outfielder Von Joshua. "I guess that's why they call them the unwritten rules."

At least the game's most prominent minds share the same general vicinity of opinion, largely because most of them come from the old school. With many modern players insisting that the run differential be as many as eight before shutting things down, however, it's easy to see how arguments occur. Look to the base Arizona's Craig Counsell stole while his team held a 6–0, sixth-inning lead over the Rockies at home in 2005. Colorado pitcher Jamey Wright disagreed with Counsell's philosophy and voiced his displeasure by sending a pitch toward the head of the next hitter, Chad Tracy. According to traditional opinions, Wright had a point—

but a half-inning later, the Rockies scored three times and had the tying run on deck, lending credence to Counsell's attempt to steal his way into scoring position. "With one hit that game's tied, so that stolen base was not out of line," said Diamondbacks hitting coach Mike Aldrete. "In my opinion they were wrong, but there was a lot of screaming and yelling."

For Counsell, this was standard procedure. He had done the same thing against Philadelphia in 2003, when he swiped second in the seventh inning while his team held a six-run lead. In that instance, Phillies pitcher Joe Roa took it out on Counsell himself, aiming a fastball at his chin during his next at-bat, which served to empty both dugouts.

"It's getting harder and harder to know when to draw the line, because of the frequency of the big inning," said Dusty Baker. "That's something that, I think, is going to be more and more wrestled with, more than any of the other unwritten rules in modern baseball." (To Baker's point, the day before Lopes exploded at Henderson, the Pirates scored seven runs with two outs in the ninth inning, to beat Houston 9–8.)

The most glaring modern example of such a comeback came in 2001, when Seattle led Cleveland 12–0 midway through the fourth inning, and 14–2 in the top of the fifth. Even after a three-run Indians rally, Seattle still led by nine in the bottom of the seventh, and Mariners manager Lou Piniella removed three of his stars, Ichiro Suzuki, Edgar Martinez, and John Olerud. (Indians skipper Charlie Manuel countered by replacing Roberto Alomar, Juan Gonzalez, Ellis Burks, and Travis Fryman in his own lineup.)

Things, however, didn't play out as expected. Cleveland put up three runs in the seventh, four in the eighth, and five in the ninth to tie the game, then won it in the eleventh, 15–14, becoming just the third team in history—and the first in seventy-five years—to come back from as many as a dozen runs down to win. After the game, Manuel talked about his own team's resilience, but he may as well have been directly addressing both Piniella and the Code. "The biggest message is, never give up," he said. "Keep swinging."

Which is the whole point. Even Lopes, whose run-in with Henderson preceded Cleveland's historic comeback by just a few weeks, had an opinion on the Mariners' collapse. "There's a difference in trying to manufacture runs," he said. "What if Lou Piniella said, with a 12-run lead, that he's going to bunt a runner over to second? Would he do it? No. . . . You don't stop playing to win. You don't stop trying to score runs. But you don't hit and run, you don't steal bases and you stop trying to manufacture runs. That's the difference."

On the flip side of the argument, do a handful of examples like Cleveland's comeback (which happens once every several generations) really undermine baseball's need for this unwritten rule? Does the notion that a team might once a season stage that type of rally offer adequate justification for a player or manager fiercely tacking runs on to an already intimidating lead?

Part of the beauty of the Code is that there is no truly correct answer. Piniella may have erred in removing his stars too early that day against the Indians, but he hit it on the screws in his post-game comments. "You never know about baseball," he said. "That's for damn sure."

Even without strategic certainty, informed guesses can be made about when to shut things down, based on a variety of factors:

Where are we playing? It used to be only the bandboxes of Wrigley Field and Fenway Park that blurred the line ("You can never have enough runs in Boston," said longtime Tigers catcher Bill Freehan), but, with new homer-friendly ballparks in places like Arlington, Houston, Philadelphia, and Cincinnati, the notion of how much is enough has never been so muddy. The poster child for this consideration is Coors Field, where, in the thin air of Denver, the *losing* team scored at least ten runs ten times in 1998 alone—a rate of nearly once a week. (On May 19, 1999, the Rockies scored twelve runs and still lost by a dozen to Cincinnati, 24–12.)

What's the status of the bullpen? When Los Angeles manager Grady Little heard complaints about Kenny Lofton's steal of second while his Dodgers held a 5–1, ninth-inning lead over San Francisco in 2006, his response was simple: "Has anyone here seen our bullpen? We have to keep doing that." Sure enough, the very next night San Francisco scored four runs in the ninth to beat the Dodgers, 6–5.

"The other team doesn't know what I've got in the bullpen," said infielder-turned-coach Jose Oquendo. "If my closer or two or three of my relievers aren't available that day, we might have to play the game more aggressively."

How well is my team hitting? After Counsell stole second against Philadelphia with a 7–1 lead in 2003, Diamondbacks manager Bob Brenly justified it with the sentiment that his offense was not exactly a powerhouse. "We weren't trying to incite them or rub it in their faces," he said. "We've been scuffling to score runs all season and it was still early enough where we couldn't [assume a victory]."

How good is the starting pitcher, and how well is he holding up? This supersedes the bullpen question, should the starter be throwing well enough to remove the relief corps from the equation. A four-run lead behind Sandy Koufax contrasts starkly with a four-run lead behind a middle-of-the-road starter.

What does the matchup look like? When Phil Garner took over as manager of the Brewers in 1992, only one of his players, Greg Vaughn, ended up with more than twelve homers. Garner did, however, have a group of guys who could run. With that in mind, he put on a perpetual green light, sending runners whenever and wherever he could. Milwaukee ended up leading the majors with 256 stolen bases, and their ninety-two wins were good for second place in the American League East. Garner finished second to Tony La Russa in manager-of-the-year balloting.

His freewheeling style was not universally appreciated, however, especially by Tigers manager Sparky Anderson, who was outspokenly critical of Garner's run-at-all-costs style.

"Ping and run, ping and run—that was our game," said Garner of his team, which finished behind all but one AL club in home runs. "Sparky's old-school," he added. "I stole one night with a five-run lead in about the sixth inning, and one of [Anderson's] coaches said that our running game bordered on ridiculous. One of my coaches had a nice comment on that, saying, 'We have to get on base, steal second, and steal third before we're in scoring position. Detroit's in scoring position when they walk to the plate.' " Indeed, Detroit—led by thirty-homer hitters Cecil Fielder, Rob Deer, and Mickey Tettleton—led the league in longballs, more than doubling Milwaukee's output on the season.

The volume of the conversation grew so loud that Garner sought out Anderson to explain himself before the teams played one day in Milwaukee. "Sparky, God only knows, you're the dean of baseball," he recalls saying. "I would not try to do anything to embarrass you. But I need to tell you that I'm not going to go home at night thinking I shut a ballgame down and let you guys get back in to win it. I can't sleep with myself that way. I understand the way the game's been played. I played it that way for a number of years myself. But it's a different era."

Anderson responded that in his book, such tactics were considered to be disrespectful and inflammatory.

Garner's comeback was unequivocal. "It's your job to stop me," he said. "If you can't stop me, then I'm playing until I feel comfortable. And if I don't feel comfortable with a ten-run lead, then by God I'm running. And if you take exception, fine, you take exception. You do what you have to do and we'll do what we have to do."

For what it's worth, the Brewers finished seventeen games ahead of Detroit that season.

In a game in 1996, the Giants trailed Los Angeles 11–2 in the ninth inning, and decided to station first baseman Mark Carreon at his normal depth, ignoring the runner at first, Roger Cedeno. When Cedeno, just twenty-one years old and in his first April as a big-leaguer, saw that nobody was bothering to hold him on, he headed for second—by any interpretation a horrible decision.

As the runner, safe, dusted himself off, Giants third baseman Matt Williams lit into him verbally, as did second baseman Steve Scarsone, left fielder Mel Hall, and manager Dusty Baker. Williams grew so heated that several teammates raced over to restrain him from going after the young Dodgers outfielder.

The least happy person on the field, however, wasn't even a member of the Giants—it was Dodgers hitter Eric Karros, who stepped out of the batter's box in disbelief when Cedeno took off. Karros would have disapproved even as an impartial observer, but as the guy who now had a pissed-off pitcher to deal with, he found his thoughts alternating between anger toward Cedeno and preparing to evade the fastball he felt certain was headed his way. ("I was trying to figure if I was going to [duck] forward or go back," said Karros after the game. "It was a 50–50 shot.") Giants pitcher Doug Creek, however, in a display of egalitarian diplomacy, left Karros unmarked, choosing instead to let the Giants inflict whatever retribution they saw fit directly upon Cedeno. (Because it was the ninth inning, nothing happened during that particular game.)

At second base, Scarsone asked Cedeno if he thought it was a full count, and the outfielder responded that, no, he was just confused. "If he's that confused, somebody ought to give him a manual on how to play baseball," said Baker after the game. "I've never seen anybody that confused."

In the end, it was Karros who saved Cedeno. When he stepped out of the box, as members of the Giants harangued the bewildered baserunner, Karros didn't simply watch idly—he turned toward the San Francisco bench and informed them that Cedeno had run without a shred of institutional authority, and that Karros himself would ensure that justice was administered once the game ended. Sure enough, as Cedeno sat at his locker after the game, it was obvious to observers that he had been crying. Though the young player refused to comment, it appeared that Karros had been true to his word. "Ignorance and youth really aren't any excuse," said Dodgers catcher Mike Piazza, "but we were able to cool things down."

This happens more frequently than one would expect. Said pitcher Jack McDowell: "It's amazing, but there are actually guys [in the major leagues] who still just don't know." There are many reasons for this. Fifty years ago, even star players spent up to six years in the high minors before reaching the big leagues, during which time they were initiated into the ways of the Code. These days, the minor leagues are a one- or two-year stop for top players. Because the minors serve mainly as a training ground, coaches have players do things like steal bases at inopportune times, simply to provide extra learning opportunities. Though blatant Code violations are still noted, the gray areas (a lead of between four and seven runs, for example, during the seventh inning or earlier) are almost uniformly glossed over.

"My first year in pro ball was in Grand Forks, North Dakota [in 1962], and that was just about the first thing our coach, Bob Clear, talked about," said former Tigers catcher Jim Price. "Today, it's just not as strong, and players have to pick up that stuff wherever they can."

Aggressive behavior on the base paths isn't limited to steals, of course; taking an extra base on a hit to the outfield can be just as damning. Nobody faults standard station-to-station baseball in the late innings of a blowout game—runners advance one base on a single, two on a double, and score on a triple—but going first-to-third or second-to-home on a single won't win many friends in the opposing dugout. Rangers manager Ron Washington had a firm rule for these situations during the decade he spent directing traffic as the third-base coach for the Oakland A's: If a play was close enough to force a slide—even if Washington thought the runner would be safe—that runner didn't go. "But if he can walk across home plate and there won't be a play on him, I'm not stopping him," he said. "That's baseball."

Not everyone is restricted by such limits. In a 2003 game against the Marlins at Fenway Park, Boston's Todd Walker raised hackles on the Florida bench by tagging up from third base on a shallow fly ball by catcher Doug Mirabelli. His team led 21–5 at the time. Though Walker defended his actions after the game—"I lose respect for [the Marlins] if they're upset that we're tagging," he said—Boston third-base coach Mike Cubbage was a bit more contrite. "I can see why they would [be upset] . . . ," he said. "[But] if I don't send the guy, [Red Sox hitters] are not going to be happy. It's a fine line."

If there was a mitigating factor for Boston, it came in the first inning, when the Red Sox set a record by scoring ten runs before Florida pitchers could record an out. Eighteen batters into the frame, three Marlins hurlers had given up thirteen runs, twelve hits, and four walks; a base hit by Johnny Damon in his *third* at-bat of the inning brought home Boston's fourteenth run. At that point, Cubbage decided to stanch the bleeding. Despite its being a shallow single, and even though the runner at second, Bill Mueller, was among the slowest men on the team, Cubbage sent him chugging toward home, where he was thrown out by several steps. As Mueller headed back to the dugout, the inning finally, mercifully, over, Marlins catcher Ivan Rodriguez patted him on the back in a "Hey, thanks" kind of way.

That's the unpredictable nature of the unwritten rules—while one person feels he's doing something appropriate, even benevolent, his opponent may well feel the opposite way. Rodriguez's apparent appreciation for Mueller's kamikaze dash for the plate could have easily turned into something much darker had he mistaken it for another slap in the face in an inning already full of them. Had Mueller tried to take Rodriguez out by slamming into him during the play, it would likely have precipitated a brawl. It's not like that hadn't happened before.

Just two weeks earlier, in fact, Reds third-base coach Tim Foli waved home Adam Dunn from second on a Ken Griffey, Jr., single while Cincinnati held a 10–0 lead over Philadelphia. Foli, however, was playing strictly by the Ron Washington rulebook—Dunn was going to score standing up, and to hold him would have deprived Griffey of an RBI. In fact, as Foli watched the play unfold, he couldn't see any option but to send the runner: The outfielder's throw missed the cutoff man, and the second baseman had to scamper to get to the ball. There was no way his throw would come close to beating Dunn.

Except that Dunn, sensing Foli's lack of urgency, slowed down considerably, allowing the defense time to recover. By the time he recognized his mistake, he was just steps away from catcher Mike Lieberthal, who was standing in the base path, ball in hand. At that point, Dunn—a six-foot-six, 240-pound former football player for the University of Texas—reacted instinctively, putting everything he had into a brutal collision. And though he didn't succeed—Lieberthal held on for the second out of the inning—when Dunn next came to bat he was thrown at by reliever Carlos Silva, and charged the mound.

"I don't know what I'm supposed to do there," said the slugger after the game. "Stop and let him tag me out? Slide? I think I did the right thing." That, though, is the essence of the Code: Even the best-intended plays can go awry, and the next thing a pitcher knows, there's a Big 12 football player chasing him across a baseball diamond.

Inappropriate aggression is hardly limited to the base paths. Hitters are also governed by the Code, with specific sections covering both type of swing and when it's employed.

Take a game between the Twins and the Red Sox in 2006, which Minnesota led 8–1 in the bottom of the eighth inning. With two outs and nobody on base, Torii Hunter drew three quick balls to start his at-bat against Red Sox reliever Rudy Seanez. The last thing a pitcher wants to do with his team down by a wide margin late in the game is walk batters, which not only suggests unnecessary nibbling but extends a game that players want to end quickly. When a count gets to 3-0, as it did with Hunter, it's a near-certainty that the ensuing pitch will be a fastball down the middle.

The unwritten rulebook does not equivocate at this moment, prohibiting hitters in such situations not just from swinging hard, but from swinging at all. Hunter did both, and his cut drew appropriate notice on the Minnesota bench. "After he swung I said to him, 'Torii, you know, with a seven-run lead like that, we've got to be taking 3-0,' " said Twins manager Ron Gardenhire. "He honestly had not even thought about it."

"I wasn't thinking," admitted Hunter. "I just wanted to do something. I knew a fastball was coming, and if I hit a double or whatever, we could get something going. I was just playing the game. I got caught up in it." The incident serves to illustrate the depth of the Code's influence. Hunter was generally aware of the unwritten rules, and except for rare instances of absentmindedness abided by them—while simultaneously disdaining much about their very existence. "Man on second, base hit, and you're winning by eight runs, you hold him up at third," he said. "You play soft, and I hate that part of the game. I hate that you don't keep playing the way you're supposed to, but you have these unwritten rules that you don't run the score up on guys. Well, okay, what if they come back? The runs we didn't score, now we look bad. We don't think about that. At the same time, those rules have been around a long time, and if you don't fly by them, you'll probably take a ball to the head, or near it.

"You don't want to embarrass anybody, but what's embarrassment when you're trying to compete? There's no such thing as embarrassment. You're out there to try to win, no matter what the score looks like. Whether it's 4–3 or 14–3, you're trying to win. I've seen guys come back from 14–3 and win the game 15–14. If I go out there and try not to embarrass you and you come back and win, I look like the dummy."

It's a powerful system that forces an All-Star to override his competitive instincts for a code in which he does not believe. If one wants to avoid retribution, one must embrace the unwritten rules; barring that, Hunter learned, an act of contrition can suffice.

After the game, Gardenhire took the outfielder to the visitors' clubhouse to speak to Red Sox manager Terry Francona, trying to wipe away the potential for hard feelings. To abide by the unwritten rule that bars opposing players from the locker room, the meeting took place in a rear laundry room in the bowels of the Metrodome. There Hunter informed both managers that he had swung out of inattention, not disrespect.

"We wanted to make sure [Francona] understood," said Gardenhire. "I went there to let him know that I know the game too. It's a manager's responsibility when a player swings 3-0 to make sure the player understands that. I wanted him to know we didn't give a sign for him to swing away, that Torii just made a mistake. I thought that it was good for Torii to explain it to him, so I took him over."

Francona brushed it off as no big deal, saying that his mind had been wrapped around devising ways for the Red Sox to come back in the final frame and that he hadn't even noticed. He did, however, express his appreciation for the visit. And the rationale worked. It appeased the members of the Red Sox who had noticed—there were several—and no beanballs were thrown the following day.

"You see those types of things and you know it's being taken care of internally," said Red Sox pitching coach Al Nipper. "You say, Hey, it's an honest mistake, it wasn't something intentional, where the guy's trying to show you up. We all make mistakes in this game. Ron Gardenhire is a class manager, and that was a true coaching moment for him. . . . I guarantee you, that was a moment he probably didn't relish to have to do with a veteran, but he had to do it."

There are some in the game who feel the same way about swinging at the first pitch in an at-bat while holding a big lead. Some hard-liners even insist that swinging at a 2-0 pitch with such a lead is too much. "You want to get greedy as a hitter, but you don't want to embarrass anybody," said Doug Mientkiewicz, who is just such a Code warrior. "Taking big swings and falling over the plate is along the lines of disrespecting somebody else."

"You don't cherry-pick on the other team," said Sparky Anderson. "You don't take cripples. Three-oh, he's struggling, he's got to lay the ball in there. Don't do it to the man. He's got a family, too."

In 2006, the Washington Nationals limped into San Francisco with a MASH unit where their catching corps should have been. Starting catcher Brian Schneider suffered a debilitating lower-back strain in Los Angeles a day earlier, and backup Matt LeCroy had been released eleven days previous. That left only one player on the roster with catching experience—Robert Fick, primarily a first baseman who had caught in 132 games over eight previous big-league seasons.

In the fourth inning, however, it all came apart. Fick, on first after singling, tore rib cartilage diving back to the bag on a pickoff throw. Had there been another catching option for Nationals manager Frank Robinson, Fick would have come out of the game immediately. As it was, Fick's injury prevented him from swinging a bat, but he was still able to squat and catch, so he stayed in.

The single had been part of a five-run rally that gave Washington a 6–1 lead. But after catching the bottom of the fourth, Fick was in such serious pain that Schneider volunteered to come off the bench, bad back and all, to take over. He made it as far as the on-deck circle, where he was preparing to bat in Fick's spot with two outs in the fifth. Within moments, however, Nationals hitter Damian Jackson lined a foul ball directly into Schneider's right wrist, giving him injuries in two places and sending him back to the dugout. There was no other option—Fick *had* to bat for himself. Which leads to a question: What does a hitter do when he can't swing a bat?

The answer: He bunts. It was Fick's only alternative, short of watching every pitch he saw. There were two problems, however. One was that Fick pushed his first bunt attempt foul, leaving him standing at the plate and awaiting the next pitch from San Francisco starter Noah Lowry. The other was that neither Fick nor anyone else in the Nationals dugout told the Giants what was going on. All Lowry saw was a player bunting after a five-run rally that broke the game open. He drilled Fick with his next pitch.

"I thought it was unbelievable, ridiculous," said Lowry. "Sometimes during a game emotions take over. The emotions were already there, and to add that icing on the cake. . . . There comes a point where you have to draw the line and say, 'Hey, have respect for me, have respect for the game.' "

It wasn't until afterward that the left-hander found out about Fick's ribs (the injury was enough to send the would-be catcher to the disabled list the next day) and the various maladies of Washington's other catchers, and he felt terrible. Had there been some communication—Fick telling Giants catcher Todd Greene about his predicament, and Greene relaying that information to Lowry, perhaps—might it have made a difference?

"Yeah, of course," said the pitcher. "Knowing he was hurt would have been a completely different story. . . . When I heard about why he was doing it I felt like a jerk. But, not knowing, you just play the game the way you know how to play it."

The only way a major-leaguer can steal 130 bases in a season is if some of them come at inappropriate times. Rickey Henderson, the only guy to have achieved that total, wasn't much concerned with the opinions of his opponents, and occasionally paid the price when angry pitchers went gunning for retribution. Henderson, of course, had a built-in defense mechanism—no pitcher wants to put on base a guy with an unrivaled ability to score from first without a ball ever leaving the infield. Henderson's Hall of Fame–caliber myopia was also well known—what Rickey did on a ballfield had nothing to do with anyone but Rickey. How could a guy who played only for himself possibly show someone up? With those things in mind, many pitchers opted to leave him alone.

"Let me tell you about Rickey," said Lopes, who teamed with Henderson in Oakland for two and a half seasons and professes to maintain an abiding affection for him despite the incident in Milwaukee. "How can I say this? You kind of let certain things slide because it's Rickey being Rickey. Did he really know he was showing you up? Was he trying to, or was he just oblivious to the whole situation, saying, 'What's everybody mad at me for?' "

"He was Rickey," said Bruce Jenkins, who covered the A's for the *San Francisco Chronicle* in 1982, when Henderson set the stolen-base record. "He was just way too cocky. But he was also innocent. He had no malice at all."

No matter how innocent Henderson may have been, or what kind of danger he represented on the base paths, he did manage to elicit responses from a few pitchers, whose retaliatory strikes took a toll in an unusual way. "One thing about Rickey that nobody seemed to consider was that he threw left-handed but he batted right-handed, so when he got drilled his elbow would get swollen," said A's teammate Dave Henderson. "Everybody would get on his weak throwing arm. But you forget that when we get drilled it's our glove hand. When Rickey got drilled it was his throwing arm. Everybody used to get on him about missing the cutoff man and having a weak arm, but that's because it was always so swollen. When your elbow's pregnant, it's hard to throw." Indeed, when Henderson first got to the big leagues, the book on him was that he had a fantastic arm; over the years, however, it became a liability, part of the price he paid for being Rickey.

Of course, before Rickey was Rickey, Lou Brock was Lou Brock, and when the Cardinals outfielder stole a then-record 118 bases in 1974, he too took occasional liberties. Brock figured, said teammate Bob Gibson, that if a big lead is good, a bigger lead is better. "When Brock would keep stealing after we had built a three- or four-run lead, guys on the bench would say, 'Goddamn it, Brock, you can't do that!' " Gibson recalled. "He'd say, 'Fuck you. I'm gonna do it.' . . . His attitude was to beat the other team as badly as possible, and that was my kind of baseball."

2

Running into the Catcher

In a collision at the plate in 1973, Al Gallagher, leading with his left shoulder, knocked Boston catcher Carlton Fisk backward, failing to dislodge the ball but managing to seriously piss off the Red Sox star, who gave him an ominous stare as he made his way back to the dugout. Gallagher had to avoid a Luis Tiant fastball in his next at-bat, an obvious message, at which point Fisk started in verbally from behind the plate. Gallagher took kindly to neither gesture, and the benches quickly emptied.

The play wasn't especially noteworthy—similar things happen nearly every day around baseball—but it serves as a good example for the rules governing such collisions. To wit: After the game, Fisk, known for his adherence to the unwritten rules, seemed almost remorseful about his actions. "Gallagher had every right to the baseline," he said. "I guess I just got tired of eating my lunch at home plate every day."

Which just about says it all: Catchers don't much enjoy being run over, but it is part of their job description—most of the time. If a catcher is prepared for an impact, virtually anything goes. If the runner catches him before he can set up, however, the catcher is exceptionally vulnerable, which is why the Code offers protection in that situation, approving collisions only when necessary. (Of course, just as runners are discouraged from hitting a catcher who doesn't yet possess the baseball, so too is it known that a catcher has no business standing in the baseline before the ball arrives. This gray area must often be navigated in an eyeblink as a situation unfolds.)

Among the most famous plays in this category was Pete Rose's flying takeout of Cleveland catcher Ray Fosse in the 1970 All-Star Game in Cincinnati. In the twelfth inning, as Rose tried to score from second on a base hit, the throw from outfielder Amos Otis came in up the line toward third, forcing Fosse to move toward Rose to field it.

Rose, who usually slid feetfirst into the plate, opted instead for the showmanship points of a dive. As Fosse moved up the line, however, Rose belatedly realized that such a tactic would take him directly into the catcher's shin guards and a certain out. Staggering, he righted himself, then plowed ahead and straight through Fosse, who hadn't yet caught the ball. The hit was so forceful that Rose missed the next three games.

It was a hard play and a clean hit, but it was also an exhibition game with nothing on the line but pride. Which is why, when Fosse was diagnosed with a separated shoulder that ultimately affected the rest of his career (he missed no time but hit only two home runs the rest of the season, after hitting sixteen previously, and never again hit more than twelve), the question was raised: Was it worth it?

"Look, I'm the winning run in the All-Star Game in my hometown," said Rose. "I just want to get to that plate as quickly as I can. Besides, nobody told me they changed it to girls' softball between third and home."

To compound matters, Fosse was bowled over twice more in the season's second half on virtually identical plays in which he was moving up the line to field errant throws. "They were young players, rookies," he said of the runners involved. "I don't know if they thought, 'Pete Rose can do it in an All-Star Game, so I can do it too.' On one of the teams I looked over into the dugout and there were a couple of players I knew. They kind of gave me that look that says, 'I can't understand why he did that.' It was as much about what happened afterward as what happened at the All-Star Game itself."

Catchers, of course, are far from defenseless, and the Code offers them copious opportunity for retaliation. Fosse's retort to one of those players involved grinding the ball into his face on a later play at the plate. "I can still see his eyes," he said. "He was saying, 'Oh my God, it's payback time.' " When the runner was called out, he simply picked himself up and returned to his dugout without a word.

"I might take a spike in the shoulder, but I've got my shin guard in his neck," said Fred Kendall, who caught in the big leagues for a dozen seasons and whose son, Jason, became an All-Star catcher in his own right. "There are ways to counter it, if that's the way he's going to play. . . . If I take the baseball and put it in the web of my glove—the web, not the pocket—and I tag you, it's just like taking a hammer and whacking you in the teeth; if I take my mask off and I throw it right where you're going to slide; if I place my shin guards the right way, it's like sliding into a brick wall."

Catcher Ron Brand put it more succinctly. "If you get the ball in time," he said, "nobody can hurt you."

3

Tag Appropriately

The tactics of aggressive infielders go relatively unnoticed on a baseball diamond, plied under cover while thousands of unsuspecting fans look elsewhere: a catcher's shin guards crunching down on a player's leg, an infielder's knee atop the fingers of a diving baserunner, even a relay throw at eye level to force a runner to bail out of the way. The only people completely aware of the nastiness are the guys who bear the brunt of the attacks, who know all too well that infielders are happy to turn the tables whenever possible.

A fierce tag is one of the primary methods a fielder can utilize to be intentionally aggressive. It doesn't necessarily stop baserunners from attempting to take extra bases, but it's certain to make them aware that the opposition's paying attention. "I'd tag guys hard on the head, on the hands," said shortstop Chris Speier. "If you're going to steal this base, you're going to pay for it."

"If you've got a clear shot to slap him in the face, do it," said another middle infielder. "The next time, he's going to take you out into left field, and he won't even apologize." Negro Leagues shortstop Willie Wells is said to have gone so far as to shove rocks into the fingers of his glove to lend extra heft to his tags.

The players best able to batter an opponent in such a manner are first basemen, who over the course of a single at-bat can field multiple pickoff throws and lay down a succession of punishing tags. Few baserunners complain about the practice, but all are aware of which players to watch out for.

"Willie Stargell would slap you so nicely," said Dusty Baker. "He'd smile, then drop that hammer on your head, on your ribs. . . . It makes you shorten your lead. The ball would be right in the web of the glove, and it was the ball that hit you on the bone. It would be up against the smallest, skinniest part of the glove, and—*pow!*—oh boy, that would hurt. Pops would slap you silly over there, and what could you do?"

"Randall Simon and Carlos Delgado just beat you up," said noted base-stealer Dave Roberts in 2007. "That's just what they do. It's why I try not to stay at first base too long, to get out along my way."

Many of these men are actually known as nice guys who are well liked around the game. Bill White didn't let a friendly disposition keep him from pounding the heads of runners who dived back to first base. Willie McCovey delivered among the hardest blows in the business (although, like Stargell, he did it with a smile), inspiring Lou Brock to claim that leading off against the Giants was the worst experience one could have. (Will Clark labeled McCovey's tag "the Sledgehammer.") There's a reason that so few players complained about it, however: These fielders are all protected by the Code, which says it's just the price runners pay for doing business.

4

Intimidation

The pitcher has to find out if the hitter is timid, and if he is timid, he has to remind the hitter he's timid.

—Don Drysdale

When Phil Garner was a young infielder with the Oakland Athletics, he made a mistake that would inform his decisions on plate strategy for the rest of his career. Facing Nolan Ryan in a 1976 game, Garner flailed at six fastballs in his first two plate appearances, many on the outside corner. Such was his futility that he was inspired toward action that in retrospect he sees as inexplicable: He tried to extend his reach by crowding the plate.

"I leaned out to just peck the ball," he said. "In a flash, in that thousandth of a second, I saw his fastball, thrown as hard as he could throw it, coming right behind my ear. My whole life passed before me. I tried to dig a hole beneath the batter's box, because I was scared to death."

It was all the edge Ryan needed. The pitcher got two quick strikes, and, said Garner, "as he was winding up to throw his next pitch, I was already walking to the dugout. It was strike three for me, and I was just happy to be out of there."

The power of intimidation cannot be overstated in sports. If, as Yogi Berra famously said, 90 percent of the game is half mental, then dominating the mental half will produce impressive results. The most accomplished professionals will attest—as Yogi was probably trying to—that physical tools don't mean a thing without proper focus. And part of that focus involves imperviousness to tactics of intimidation.

The most humbling intimidator on a baseball diamond is simple, overwhelming success. If, going into a game, a player or team feels that the battle is already lost, then it probably is. As the 1998 Yankees were rolling up 114 wins, for example, every team they faced looked on with admiration and a healthy dose of trepidation. For teams without that level of ability, the easiest advantage to gain is through a bullying presence. Skill, after all, is finite; fear is not. "If a guy's just wearing you out, you might knock him down," said longtime Oakland A's pitcher Steve McCatty. "You don't want somebody feeling comfortable up there. It's common sense."

Take someone like Hugh Casey, who was never able to become a full-time starter over his nine-year big-league career in the 1930s and '40s, but was nonetheless one of the most feared pitchers in the game, a reputation owed mostly to his willingness to throw at the head of any opponent at any time. Baseball annals are filled with legendary knockdown stories featuring as their primary characters Casey's fastball and some unwitting dupe who took it upon himself to crowd the plate.

"He was mean," said his teammate Dodgers pitcher Rex Barney. "He would set you up and then he would knock you down. And he'd look you right in the eye when he did it, too. And yes, he'd actually throw at guys in the on-deck circle. I saw him do it in Brooklyn." (In 1946, Casey did, in fact, throw a pitch at Marty Marion of the St. Louis Cardinals, who was standing near the batter's box, timing Casey's warm-ups—a violation of another unwritten rule.) Casey even went so far as to throw three straight pitches at the head of plate umpire George Magerkurth in 1941, after Magerkurth had called a dubious balk on him to force in a run.

None of this endeared the pitcher to anyone other than his teammates, but it was terrific for his reputation. Casey led the league in hit batsmen in his first full season, and drilled six more the next year, in addition to his steady array of knockdowns and brushbacks. The message went out immediately, and he rode that intimidating reputation to the end. The reality, however, says something different. The eighteen victims over his first two seasons constituted more than 60 percent of his career total; Casey never again plunked more than two men in a year. Hitters were afraid of him, and that's all that mattered.

Twenty-five years later, hitters were also afraid of Dock Ellis, who in at least one regard was more fearsome than Casey: Whereas it took the old Brooklyn star two full seasons to cement his reputation, Ellis earned his stripes over the course of a single game. The right-hander possessed a clear understanding of the power of intimidation, having seen it in action as his Pittsburgh Pirates teams terrorized the rest of the National League, bullying their way to three division titles and one World Series between 1970 and 1972. In '73, though, things began to change—the Pirates inexplicably lost their bravado and many more games than expected, finishing below .500 and in third place in the National League East. When they opened 1974 by lurching into last place with a 6–12 record, Ellis took it upon himself to spur a roster-wide attitude adjustment.

He chose as his victims the Cincinnati Reds, themselves coming off two straight division titles and on their way to ninety-eight wins. If Pittsburgh's new timidity tipped the balance of swagger in the National League against them, the prime beneficiary was Cincinnati. Ellis wanted to reverse that trend.

"[Other teams used to] say, 'Here come the big bad Pirates. They're going to kick our ass.' Like they give up," said Ellis, who later gained notoriety when it became known that the no-hitter he threw in 1970 was augmented by LSD. "That's what our team was starting to do. When Cincinnati showed up in spring training, I saw all the ballplayers doing the same thing. They were running over, talking, laughing and hee-haw this and that. Cincinnati will bullshit with us and kick our ass and laugh at us. They're the only team that talk about us like a dog."

When Ellis took the mound against Cincinnati on May 1, 1974, he had only one strategy in mind: to drill every batter that stepped in against him. The first was Pete Rose, who ducked out of the way when a first-pitch fastball sailed toward his head, then jumped forward to avoid the second pitch, which flew behind him. The third pitch, aimed at his rib cage, found its mark. Man on first, nobody out.

The second batter, Joe Morgan, caught Ellis's first pitch with his kidney. First and second, nobody out. Third up: Dan Driessen. Ellis's opening shot sailed high and inside for a ball. The second pitch found the middle of Driessen's back.

The bases were now loaded, but the pitcher was hardly deterred. Cincinnati's cleanup hitter, Tony Perez, took stock of the carnage and realized his only possible salvation was to stay light on his feet. He proceeded to dance around four straight offerings—including a near wild pitch that flew behind him and over his head—to draw a walk and force in the game's first run. When Ellis went 2-0 to Johnny Bench, Pirates manager Danny Murtaugh couldn't take any more and removed the pitcher from the game.

"[Ellis's] point was not to hit batters," wrote Donald Hall in *Dock Ellis in the Country of Baseball*. "His point was to kick Cincinnati ass." His point was also to inspire his teammates, to instill a measure of toughness in a languor-prone Pittsburgh squad. It might be coincidence, but after that game—which the Reds won, 5–3—the Pirates went 82-62 and won the National League East for the fourth time in five years.

The most incredible thing about Ellis's feat isn't the fact that he avoided ejection, fine, and suspension—it's that he wasn't even the first player to attempt such a strategy. Nearly forty years earlier, in 1937, St. Louis Cardinals star Dizzy Dean unleashed similar tactics. Unlike the threat Ellis perceived from Pittsburgh, Dean reacted to something much more tangible: getting thrashed by the New York Giants. It started in the sixth inning of a game in which New York's Burgess Whitehead was on second, with Dick Bartell at the plate. Dean induced Bartell to pop up to shortstop Leo Durocher, but umpire George Barr, under instructions from National League commissioner Ford Frick to more closely enforce the balk rule, decided that Dean failed to come to a complete stop before delivering the pitch. He waved Whitehead to third and returned Bartell to the batter's box, whereupon the hitter smoked the next pitch for a line drive that was dropped by right fielder Pepper Martin, allowing Whitehead to score. Another error and a subsequent single gave the Giants a 4–1 lead, and Dean completely unraveled.

The Hall of Famer proceeded to throw at everyone in the lineup save Whitehead, with whom he had previously played in St. Louis, and Giants pitcher Carl Hubbell, who had the power to return the favor. Wrote John Drebinger in *The New York Times:* "The Giants went up and down at the plate like duckpins." Durocher said that one of Dean's offerings even struck New York player-manager Bill Terry twice, hitting him in the back, then bouncing up and hitting him in the neck. The assault finally ended when Giants outfielder Jimmy Ripple laid down a ninth-inning bunt, then threw a punch at Dean when the pitcher moved to cover the base, sparking an enormous on-field brawl so ferocious that police intervention was required. Incredibly, Dean was never thrown out of the game.

Dean's performance stuck with Durocher when he took over as manager of the Brooklyn Dodgers in 1939, as he sought ways to counter Cincinnati's superior firepower. The Reds won the pennant during Durocher's first season with Brooklyn, and in '40, despite his team's scorching 27-12 start, Cincinnati nonetheless held a one-game lead when the clubs met on June 8. So Durocher changed tactics.

After two Dodgers pitchers surrendered eight runs over the first three innings, Durocher decided to stick with right-hander Carl Doyle, even though he'd given up three runs in his single frame of work. Durocher didn't want Doyle in the game to keep things close, however; over the next two innings the right-hander gave up twelve runs on twelve hits, walked three, and threw two wild pitches. The manager's intent was to have his pitcher send a message, which he did by hitting four Reds batters—tying a modern record—all while offering "frequent 'duster' pitches," according to *The New York Times*. As with Ellis's strategy, the evidence is purely theoretical, but Durocher's plan worked—the following season, Brooklyn won its first pennant in more than twenty years.

With first base open during a game in 1961, Dodgers manager Walter Alston ordered Don Drysdale to issue a free pass to Frank Robinson. The Cincinnati outfielder was on his way to winning the NL MVP Award; in Drysdale's mind that made him the perfect candidate to be knocked down. Robinson was a ten-year vet, and though Drysdale knew his opponent was probably the toughest player in the league and beyond intimidation, the big pitcher loved a challenge. Rather than sail four balls wide of the strike zone, Drysdale took action.

The first pitch rocketed directly at Robinson's head, dropping the slugger to the dirt. In response, Robinson got up, spat fire, and moved closer to the plate. The following pitch again knocked him down. Again he moved closer. Next two pitches, same thing. "I was mad inside at Drysdale, but I refused to show it because I knew that's what he was trying to do, upset me," said Robinson. "By upsetting me he knew I couldn't play at my best, so I just refused to let it bother me." Still, there wasn't much he could do against the pitcher. Drysdale hit Robinson four times over the course of his career (the only player he tagged more was Ernie Banks) and knocked him down on countless other occasions, which helped hold the

Hall of Fame slugger with the .294 lifetime average to a paltry .213 mark over seventy-nine lifetime at-bats against the right-hander.

The approach was typical Drysdale. Dodgers teammate Ron Fairly tells the story of Alston going to the mound with instructions for Drysdale to give a free pass to Pirates slugger Donn Clendenon, and barely making it back to the dugout before the pitcher planted a fastball in the batter's rib cage. "When the inning ended, Alston says to him, 'I thought I told you to walk him,' " said Fairly. "Drysdale says, 'No, you said to put him on. I can get him there in one pitch—I don't need to throw four. Besides, it might help the next time he comes up.' Sure enough, the next time he came up Don threw him three little sliders away, and Clendenon just kind of waved at them and struck out."

The fact that Fairly was mistaken—Drysdale never hit Clendenon with a pitch in the seven seasons during which the two competed—hardly makes the story worse. This is the way Fairly remembers Drysdale, and even if the story actually took place against a different hitter or different team—even if it never took place at all—this tale, told with love and admiration, is a result of Drysdale's legacy.

All this intimidation serves a purpose. After all, a ball needn't make contact with a player to drive fear into his suddenly palpitating heart. It's the near misses that inspire philosophical soliloquies from uncontemplative men about the meaning (and shortness) of life. Catcher Randy Knorr put it in baseball terms: "They say the anticipation of death is worse than actually dying. Well, the anticipation of getting hit is a lot worse than actually being hit. You can't play your game. You think you're going to get drilled, so you aren't focused on hitting. You're focused on avoiding."

There are two options for pitchers who want to instill fear without having to hit a batter: the brushback and the knockdown.

The brushback is more common, if only because it's more utilitarian. Assuming an absence of acrimony between hitter and pitcher, any clear-headed batter should take an intentionally thrown brushback pitch to carry a single meaning: Move off the plate.

A more interactive pitching tactic is the knockdown, intended less to move a batter from one side of the box to the other than to get him off his feet. It's a powerful message—a "brushback pitch with attitude," according to Drysdale's peer in intimidation, Bob Gibson.

Take Roger Clemens, who in Game 4 of the 2000 ALCS sent consecutive first-inning pitches at the head of Seattle shortstop Alex Rodriguez, making use of Drysdale's maxim that the second knockdown was more important than the first, because it showed that the first wasn't a mistake. Clemens ended up with a complete-game one-hitter, with Rodriguez going 0-for-3 with two strikeouts. A year later, Clemens again faced the Mariners in the playoffs, again in Game 4, whereupon he threw a fastball at Bret Boone's chin. The second baseman went hitless against the Rocket, who reprised his previous performance by giving up only a single hit (this time over five innings) as the Yankees tallied another victory. Said Clemens: "I want to jiggle their eyeballs."

A good knockdown can take a hitter not just out of an at-bat, but out of an entire game, or even a series. Sometimes the World Series. In the 1980 Fall Classic between Philadelphia and Kansas City, the underdog Phillies, after unexpectedly winning the first two games, quickly began to falter. The Royals took Game 3, then knocked Philadelphia's Game 4 starter, Larry Christenson, out of the box before he could record his second out of the game. By the time reliever Dickie Noles replaced Christenson, Kansas City had four runs in and a runner at second, still with only one out in the first. The Royals were on the precipice of a massive momentum swing, and Noles's goal was simply to minimize the damage.

He succeeded in shutting down the rally, but gave up a second-inning homer to cleanup hitter Willie Mays Aikens, the slugger's second of the game. This is where Noles's issues began—not with the home run itself, but with the fact that Aikens lingered in the batter's box to admire his blast.

In just his second big-league season, Noles already possessed a reputation as one of the game's prominent hotheads, built largely upon his willingness to knock opponents down at any opportunity—and opportunity was about to come knocking again.

The next hitter, Hal McRae, hustled his way into second with a double, then pumped his fist—which served only to stir the pitcher further. When Noles noticed McRae standing atop the glove of second baseman Manny Trillo, who had dived to make a belated tag, he began to seriously fume.

After retiring Amos Otis for the third out of the inning, the pitcher stormed into the Philadelphia dugout. Bypassing manager Dallas Green and the team's position players, he made a beeline for the water jug at the far end of the bench, where fellow pitchers Bob Walk, Marty Bystrom, and Tug McGraw were sitting. "Who the heck do these guys think they are, doing all this crap, standing at home plate and watching their home runs?" he spat, talking to no one in particular. "Somebody has to put this down."

McGraw looked up slowly, then said the one thing the young right-hander most wanted to hear. "Don't tell me about it," said the veteran reliever. "You have to *show* me, brother."

Bystrom asked, "What are you waiting on?"

"It's not a bad idea," added Walk. "Do it."

That was all Noles needed. Aikens's actions demanded response; the hitter would go down in his next at-bat. Noles worked through a scoreless third inning, counting down, Royal by Royal, until the fourth spot in the lineup came around again. Aikens eventually stepped to the plate as the third batter of the fourth inning, but before he could, the guy before him in the order changed Noles's plan entirely.

That was George Brett, who had tripled in Kansas City's four-run first and was 6-for-11 with a home run to that point in the series—without question the Royals' MVP. When he couldn't catch up to Noles's first-pitch fastball, however, he stepped out of the batter's box to get his bear-ings. As Noles watched in disbelief, Brett lingered for a moment away from the plate before slowly making his way back in. The pitcher's next offering, also a fastball, was fouled off. Now it was 0-2. Again Brett stepped out, and again he took longer to return than Noles would have liked. This time, he gazed at his bat for a moment with an expression that the pitcher read as "How could I miss two straight fastballs?" That the slugger was coming off a season in which he hit .390 hardly mattered; Noles stared daggers toward home plate. At that moment, his target shifted from Aikens to Brett.

Under ordinary circumstances, baseball's code dictates that a guy like Brett—a five-time All-Star about to win an MVP Award—could take as long as he pleased against Noles, just twenty-three and still in his first full big-league campaign. Furthermore, the Code says unequivocally that, unless a pitcher is a superstar himself, he does not intentionally knock down one of the five best third basemen of all time.

This, however, was the World Series, and this was Dickie Noles, who at that moment had concerns more important than the unwritten rules. Besides, targeting Brett made sense on multiple levels. "George was their best hitter," said Phillies shortstop Larry Bowa. "If Dickie was sending a message, you send it to their best hitter, you know?"

That message, according to Noles: " 'I'm coming at you guys and I ain't playing around.' . . . I was trying to take his head off."

Noles's 0–2 pitch did very nearly that, riding in directly at Brett's jaw. The third baseman avoided it only with an acrobatic tumble that left him splayed flat on the ground, facing the mound and dazed. "If I didn't get out of the way," he said, "it would have hit me in the head." A hush descended on what had been a raucous Royals Stadium. Noles took several steps toward the plate, an invitation for Brett or his teammates to react.

What he got was Royals manager Jim Frey, streaking onto the field "like a little bantam rooster," according to Philadelphia's Del Unser, before Brett had a chance to regain either his feet or his senses. Frey screamed at plate umpire Don Denkinger, "Stop it right now! Don't tell me he's not head-hunting there! Don't tell me he's not taking a shot at the head! Stop it right now—he's going to hurt somebody!"

Frey had been primed for this moment by one of his coaches, Bill Connors, who had worked with Noles in the minor leagues and knew all about his tendencies. The manager's protest was a powerful combination of passion and volume; that it didn't gain more traction was largely due to a single impediment: Pete Rose. While most of Philadelphia's players were as stunned by Brett's treatment as their counterparts on the Royals, Rose didn't waste a moment, racing from his position at first base to place himself between Noles and Frey. Whatever void in credibility had been created by the pitcher's inexperience was instantly filled by Rose's superstar status. "He wasn't throwing at him," Rose definitively told the manager. "Yes, he was!" shouted Frey. "No, he wasn't," replied Rose. "If he was, he'd have hit him." Rose spun to stare directly at Brett, the slightest hint of a grin tracing his face. He then turned toward the Kansas City dugout, his glare lingering, almost daring the Royals to respond. The message was clear, said Noles: "Rose was telling everybody on the field, 'I'm behind this kid. *We* did this, not just Dickie.' "

With that, Rose patted the pitcher on the rump, said, "You just pitch your own ballgame," and trotted back to first.

Said Noles, looking back: "I don't think the Royals handled that part very well."

Kansas City's handling of it started with Brett, who flailed at a slider on his hands for strike three. It continued with Aikens, who ended the inning by striking out on the same curveball he'd hit out of the park an inning earlier. McRae, the Royals' leadoff hitter the following inning, also fanned, the third Royals hitter in a row to do so.

"I don't think you can say that [Noles' pitch] was the one thing that turned around the Series," said Green, "but it was a big piece of the puzzle. We were struggling, and it brought us back into focus." It did just the opposite for Kansas City. Virtually every member of the Royals has denied it since the moment it happened, but the upending of George Brett absolutely erased whatever momentum they had been building. The Royals, who by all rights should have been riding a wave of energy after holding on to win the game, mustered just four more runs over the Series' remaining twenty-two innings. Brett went 3-for-11 from that point on, and Aikens was held to a single hit. The Phillies won in six.

Noles, while appreciating the significance of his action in retrospect, later came to recognize the importance of the Code regarding brushbacks, knockdowns, and hit batters—specifically the part about never throwing at an opponent's head. "I don't brag about it," he said. "The mentality I had when I was twenty-three years of age later changed. . . . I was trying to take his head off, and I'm not proud of that." One thing that didn't change for Noles was his feeling about how he'd have reacted had he been a member of the Royals when Brett went down. "If I'm on that team, I can't wait for number 20 [Brett's third-base counterpart on the Phillies, Mike Schmidt] to come up, because I'm going to plunk him—not in his rear end, but in his ribs. You took a shot at my guy's head; I'm putting one in your guy's back or his ribs. If it hurts, good. If it knocks him out of the game, better."

Sound extreme? No less an authority than Brett himself agrees. "As far as I was concerned, that was very legit, what Noles did," said the Hall of Famer. "He knocked me off the plate, and that was part of the game of baseball. . . . No hard feelings, no nothing. I just wish one of our pitchers would have done the same thing to Mike Schmidt. That's how the game is played. That's how the game *wasn't* played that day."

Fearlessness is a boon for pitchers, but it can backfire on them too. Even the most aggressive pitcher can take things too far, and when he does it can be all too easy for him to psych himself out instead of his opponents. Few examples are starker than the one provided by the game's master intimidator, Nolan Ryan.

It began on April 30, 1974, when Boston's Doug Griffin attempted to lay down a bunt against the cantankerous flamethrower. Ryan's feelings about this strategy were hardly a secret, so when a hundred-mile-an-hour message pitch found its way toward the right-handed batter's box it shouldn't have come as much of a surprise. The pitcher insists that he wasn't trying to hit Griffin with the pitch, just place a fastball where it would be difficult to bunt. Instead, the ball tailed in and struck the wide-eyed hitter behind his left ear. Griffin was unconscious before he hit the ground.

"That's the first time the thought crossed my mind that I was capable of possibly killing somebody," Ryan said. Griffin suffered a concussion and temporary hearing loss, and though it's impossible to say with certainty, it's likely that the injuries—which necessitated two full months of recovery—led to the premature end of his career three years later, at age thirty.

It may have been the first time Ryan considered the concept of unintentional manslaughter, but it wasn't the last. Starting that day, for the first and only stretch of his career, the pitcher grew apprehensive. No longer the intimidator, he became the intimidated—fearful not of another player but of the potential damage his fastballs could inflict. As a result, the frequency and ferocity of his inside pitches diminished, and the advantage he had so carefully cultivated began to disappear. Ryan described the process of dealing with the aftermath of Griffin's beanball as "trauma."

This was the same man who, when he faced Boston's Dwight Evans— making his first plate appearance since being knocked unconscious by a pitch from Rangers reliever Mike Paul—started the outfielder off with a fastball *behind him.* Asked later if Ryan was trying to intimidate him, Evans said simply, "Intimidate and kill are different."

It's difficult to believe Ryan capable of passivity, but even he admits that, for the stretch in question, despite pitching effectively, he lost his edge. What he needed to get it back was a direct confrontation with his fears. He got that chance about six weeks after Griffin returned to Boston's lineup, when the Red Sox traveled to Anaheim. If Griffin thought the ensuing showdown was traumatic, he should have talked to Ryan, who found himself with a nearly unprecedented case of nerves. The right-hander pitched Griffin tentatively, consistently keeping his pitches on the outside part of the plate through the infielder's first two at-bats. Any residual fear Griffin held over Ryan's inside heat was beside the point, because he wasn't getting any.

Griffin appreciated the diet of outside fastballs, slapping two ground-ball singles in his first three at-bats. It was after the second hit that Ryan began to understand that he was effectively beating himself. "I had to block out what had happened from my mind," he said. "I had no choice but to block it out or I'd become a defensive pitcher instead of an aggressive one." The next time Griffin came to the plate he was greeted by a series of inside fastballs, and could only tap a ground ball to shortstop Bobby Valentine.

Ryan summed it up when he said, "Baseball is a business, and you have to do what's necessary to win." Don Drysdale's assessment of that type of situation was even more succinct: "Show me a guy who doesn't want to pitch inside," he said, "and I'll show you a loser."

5

On Being Intimidated

The catcher warns the rookie batsman, "Look out for this fellow. He's got a mean bean ball, and he hasn't any influence over it.".... Then the catcher signs for the pitcher to throw one at the young batter's head. If he pulls away, an unpardonable sin in baseball, the dose is repeated.

—Christy Mathewson, *Pitching in a Pinch*, 1912

When it comes to dealing with schoolyard bullies, the inevitable lesson we teach our kids is to stand up for themselves, because bullies don't possess the fortitude to fight back. It's a basic tutorial on the concept of fear, illustrating how quickly the intimidator can become the intimidated. Whether or not it's true on a playground, the concept holds some merit on a baseball diamond.

In 1984, the Giants found themselves in an ongoing feud with St. Louis pitcher Joaquin Andujar, who frequently tried to establish his menacing mound presence through early-innings use of brushback and knockdown pitches. That appeared to be his strategy on July 17, when he hit San Francisco's second batter of the game, Manny Trillo. In retrospect, it wasn't his best decision.

"Manny was a teammate of mine on three teams and a very good friend, and a guy you should not hit when I was the pitcher," said Mike Krukow, on the mound for the Giants that day. "And when Andujar got him I said, 'Okay, boys, wear your batting gloves on the bench because we're going to fight when this asshole steps up to the plate.' "

When Andujar came up, two innings later, Krukow didn't hesitate, putting everything he had into a fastball aimed directly at his nemesis . . . and missed. The ball ran inside and backed Andujar up, but didn't come close to damaging its intended target. This only made Krukow angrier. The pitcher snapped the return throw from catcher Bob Brenly, stalked across the mound, and glared at the hitter. Again he fired his best fastball at Andujar . . . and again he missed. At that point, home plate umpire Billy Williams interceded, levying a hundred-dollar fine and telling Krukow, "I gave you two, and that's enough."

The pitcher knew he was beaten. He hadn't been able to hit Andujar when he had the chance, and now he was out of chances. So he seized his only remaining opportunity, dropped his glove and rushed the plate in a rare instance of the reverse mound-charge. Krukow was able to throw a quick punch at his counterpart before the two were separated.

Inexplicably, once the fight was broken up, neither pitcher was ejected. "Now, how about that?" said Krukow, still amazed, decades after the fact. "Billy Williams says to me, 'Now, that's it, I'm going to leave you in the game. You're not going to throw at him anymore?' I said, 'No, no. I'm all right. Everything's cool. I got him.' "

The umpire allowed Krukow to return to the mound, still in the middle of Andujar's at-bat. At that point, said Krukow, the first thought that flashed through his mind was "Son of a bitch—I have another chance to get him!" It didn't take long, however, for the right-hander to realize the ultimate futility of the situation; in addition to Williams's warning was Krukow's own fear of missing Andujar a third straight time. Instead, he bore down and struck his antagonist out.

Although Krukow did no immediate damage at the plate, his tactics certainly had an effect. When Andujar got back to the mound, his 13-7 record and 2.88 ERA were rendered meaningless; the would-be intimidator quickly unraveled, giving up four runs to the Giants in his next inning of work, and seven runs overall in just over four frames. It was his worst start of the season, almost certainly a result of the confrontation a half-inning earlier. "We exposed his macho," said Krukow. "It was great."

If Andujar is to be given any sort of a pass, it's that his ability to absorb intimidation should be judged primarily from the mound, not the plate. Should a position player let similar intimidation tactics affect him—even something as slight as a cringe at an inside fastball—the opposition will notice, and word travels fast.

"Most of the time, you figure out a player's reputation early—guys you could throw at, guys you could knock down," said fourteen-year big-leaguer Dave Henderson. "Guys who if you knock them down it makes them better players, and guys who if you knock them down you can make them cower."

"The idea is to see how you react to being knocked down," said long-time Dodger Ron Fairly. "And if it doesn't bother you, they'll turn around and say, 'Well, if it doesn't bother him, we're not going to do that. We've got to figure out a different way to get him out.'"

Examples abound of batters who reacted poorly to tactics of intimidation. After six-time All-Star Joe Medwick was hit in the head by Cardinals pitcher Bob Bowman in 1940, he never recovered from his ensuing plate-shyness. Though still able to play at a high level for the next nine seasons, Medwick never again reached the astounding numbers he put up previously, which led to the 1937 NL MVP and five consecutive top-eleven finishes in the award's balloting. And Medwick was hardly alone. Hall of Famer Frank Chance had a tendency to freeze on pitches aimed at his head, and suffered so many beanings that he went deaf in one ear and reportedly suffered from a lisp and double vision. A half-century later, Don Zimmer had such a reputation for freezing in the batter's box whenever a fastball sailed high and tight—the probable result of two ferocious beanings early in his career—that he actually had an inverse effect on pitchers, many of whom feared throwing inside for fear they might do serious damage when he failed to get out of the way. Don Drysdale went so far as to identify Zimmer as the only batter he steadfastly refused to throw at intentionally.

"I kind of enjoy the competition with a guy who's not afraid to throw the ball inside and make his pitches," said seven-time All-Star Tim Raines. "Roger Clemens threw at me a couple times, but I still swung the bat well against him, and he decided not to do it anymore. It's all about intimidation. If you let guys intimidate you, they'll continue to do it."

When Ted Williams was a twenty-year-old rookie with the Red Sox in 1939, Browns manager Fred Haney, who knew Williams from their days in the Pacific Coast League, had his pitchers test him immediately. The teams met in St. Louis, and the first pitch Williams saw knocked him to the ground. It didn't have the effect for which Haney had hoped, however: Williams knocked the next offering off the wall in right-center field for a double. In his next at-bat, Williams was again thrown at and again hit the dirt. Again he responded, blasting a home run to right field soon thereafter. It wasn't long before word circulated around the league that such tactics only made the slugger better, and pitchers quickly abandoned the strategy.

Thirty years later, Drysdale's continuous knockdowns of Willie Mays became legendary, partly because of their relentless nature and partly because Mays never let it affect him. He hit .324 with eleven home runs and twenty-seven RBIs against Drysdale, and was never bothered, he said, "because my head ain't gonna be here when the ball is."

By the 1970s, however, baseball was a different game, played by men with different attitudes. Brushbacks and knockdowns were no longer taken for granted as part of a pitcher's repertoire, and as such became things to which batters reacted with anger. Take an incident in which Jim Colborn tried to intimidate Jim Rice—himself one of the most intimidating sluggers of his time. "He threw a pitch close to Jim's chin, and Jim trotted out to the mound to have some words with him," wrote Bill Lee in *The Wrong Stuff*. "I thought Colborn was going to commit suicide. Rice told him, 'If you come that close to me with one more pitch, I'm going to tear your head off.' When the other pitchers around the league heard about this, the brushback pitches became fewer in number. A pitcher doesn't like to give up the inside of the plate, but he also values his life and limbs."

Hitters have their own methods for countering intimidation offered up by pitchers. Frank Robinson would move closer to the plate in response to a brushback pitch, but Robinson was far tougher than the average major-leaguer. A more common intimidation deterrent is for a hit batsman to avoid rubbing the spot where the baseball drilled him.

"You learn that early—don't rub it," said Dave Roberts, an outfielder for the Indians, Dodgers, Red Sox, Padres, and Giants. "Whether it's giving the pitcher satisfaction or showing weakness or whatever, it's just something you don't do."

"If you were down at first base rubbing it, I promise, your teammates would let you know something about it," said Will Clark. (Exceptions are made for someone who comes from the Hal McRae school, and rubs the spot to apply a coat of tobacco that he's just spit into the palm of his hand. "That," said McRae, "was part of the intimidation factor too.")

Pete Rose made a point of not just refusing to rub, but sprinting to first base immediately after being hit, doing everything he could to show that the pitcher had been unable to hurt him. (When Dock Ellis tried to hit every batter in the Reds lineup in 1974, he seriously considered skipping Rose, because he knew the lengths to which Rose went to prove he hadn't been wounded. He drilled him anyway. True to form, Rose responded by picking up the baseball, tossing it gently back to the mound, and sprinting to first.)

Thurman Munson took things a step further in 1975, when, after being hit by a fastball from White Sox pitcher Goose Gossage, he sent a note to the Chicago clubhouse. "I took your best shot right on the elbow, you big donkey, and I'm still playing," he wrote, signing it, "The White Gorilla."

How far will a player go? Sandy Koufax once fractured Lou Brock's shoulder with a pitch, knocking him out of action for three days and wrecking him physically for a month. "You could hear the thud all over the stadium," said Don Drysdale, watching from the Los Angeles bench. "Brock went down like a deer who'd been shot." The outfielder was pulled from the game as soon as he staggered to first base, but never once did he massage the injury.

It's basically a hitter's answer to any pitcher with the temerity to drill him: *I'm tougher than you.* Intimidation flows in two directions, after all, and the ability to withstand somebody's best shot without so much as a grimace can itself be intimidating. "It's a statement," said McRae: " 'I'm not hurt. You *can't* hurt me.' "

6

Slide into Bases Properly

In the 1970s, Don Baylor was the most feared baserunner in the American League, a guy who roared into second base with unmatched intensity, ready to level any middle infielder who had designs on turning him into the lead out of a double play. Players put up with it, though, for two reasons: Baylor was both clean and consistent. Although middle infielders didn't like it, they knew exactly what to expect when Baylor was at first, and were therefore rarely angry when they ended up upended. ("Shortstops and second basemen did not want to be around when Donny Baylor was coming into second base," said Mike Hegan, "but most of them dealt with it pretty well when they were.") This isn't necessarily true for the guys who came in hard only on occasion, a tactic that keeps infielders from being able to accurately anticipate any given play. Phil Garner once felt this way about Cubs first baseman Bill Buckner.

"I was playing second base in Pittsburgh and we were running for the pennant," he said. "Buckner absolutely smoked me on a double play—damn near broke both my legs." Garner wasn't ticked off at the play itself, which was clean and not unlike the treatment he regularly received from players like Baylor and Hal McRae (who was so consistently ferocious on the base paths that the 1978 rule disallowing the hindrance of a fielder who has just made a play is known informally as the "Hal McRae Rule"). Garner was angry because he'd never seen it before from Buckner. "This sumbitch slides thirty feet short for 160 ballgames, and now, in the 161st he's going to slide in hard?" said Garner. "Fuck that. Play the game hard

55

in Game 1 just like you did that day." Buckner hadn't violated any of base-ball's *written* rules—his play wasn't dirty, just devious—but in Garner's mind he'd clearly violated the Code. The next time Garner had the chance to turn Buckner into the lead out of a double play, he aimed his relay throw directly between the baserunner's eyes. Buckner threw up a hand in self-defense; he deflected the ball but broke a finger in the process. Message sent.

Or take Carlos Delgado, who, while on base as a member of the Toronto Blue Jays in 2004, took out Red Sox first baseman Doug Mientkiewicz with a forearm shiver. One problem with the play, at least to Mientkiewicz, was that he wasn't playing first base at the time but had volunteered to man second after Boston experienced an unforeseen shortage of players at the position. The infielder had, at that point, played all of one inning there in his seven-year major-league career and was by no means comfortable.

Also, in Mientkiewicz's opinion, such takeouts weren't a regular part of Delgado's repertoire. "I'd seen him veer off on double plays for five years and not even slide into second," he said. "Yet he sees somebody playing second who's never played there before and he takes full advantage of it. If Aaron Rowand had knocked me on my ass I don't think I'd have been that mad, because Aaron goes full tilt from the word 'go.' . . . If I were to always see Carlos taking guys out at shortstop, I never would have said a word."

When Mientkiewicz got up screaming, the pair had to be separated. Red Sox pitcher Derek Lowe drilled the Toronto All-Star during his next at-bat, and Delgado was forced to avoid several other pitches during the course of the three-game series. ("Curt Schilling missed him once and came to me and apologized," said Mientkiewicz.)

At least the play was clean. That's not always the case, and few things cause tempers to skyrocket on a ballfield like a dirty takeout.

"There are unwritten rules about how to slide at second base," said Krukow, now a broadcaster for the Giants. "It's sort of taken on a new definition. Before, you basically couldn't go in standing up to take a guy out. Then there were cheap barrel rolls over the bag—if they were high barrel rolls they were unacceptable, but low barrel rolls were acceptable. When A-Rod took out Jeff Kent and sprained Kent's right knee in 1998, he [low] barrel-rolled him. On TV that night, Kuip [Krukow's broadcast partner, Duane Kuiper, a twelve-year major-league second baseman] and I said, That's a legit play. After the game, Kent was pissed about it. He said that was a horseshit slide. No, it's not. Basically, a low barrel roll—anything within arm's distance of the bag—is acceptable. A high barrel roll or going in high is unacceptable. It's unwritten." (Acceptable or not, the following night, Giants pitcher Orel Hershiser drilled Rodriguez in the shoulder.)

Craig Biggio found out the hard way about the changing attitudes toward barrel rolls after he went into Cardinals second baseman Tommy Herr with such a slide. "He just looked at me as I ran off the field," Biggio said. "Next time I went up to hit, I got drilled in the middle of the back. Then I did it to Ron Oester in Cincinnati. He just looked at me, and the next time up I got drilled in the middle of the back. Right then and there I said, 'I guess you don't roll-block anymore.' Painful way, message sent, you live and learn."

In the realm of clean plays, the capper for infielders is the unnecessary takeout slide, like the one that comes after the relay throw has been released—meaning there's nothing to gain through the action. The most extreme example of this happened in 1985, when Oakland baserunner Dave Kingman plowed into Yankees shortstop Dale Berra. Not only did Berra have no relay to deliver, but the game had ended before Kingman left his feet. With a tie score in the bottom of the ninth inning, the A's had the bases loaded, Kingman the runner at first. When Oakland outfielder Steve Henderson drew a base on balls to force home the winning run, Kingman simply spun and started trotting toward the home clubhouse along the third-base line. As he neared the pitcher's mound, however, the slugger was startled to hear teammates—worried about a repeat of "Merkle's Boner" seventy-seven years earlier, in which the Giants lost a decisive game when baserunner Fred Merkle failed to advance fully on what would have been the game-winning hit—screaming for him to turn around and touch second. (Third-base coach Clete Boyer said that he was "about to tackle" Kingman before he left the field.)

In reality, baseball rules stipulate only that the runner on third and the batter must touch their respective bases in such a situation (Merkle had been ruled out for failing to touch second base on a hit, not a walk), but there was enough confusion on the field that New York catcher Ron Hassey fired the ball to Berra in hopes that the runner might be called out and the game extended. At that point, Kingman didn't hesitate, spinning toward second and roaring in with a vicious slide, even though the game had officially ended. Umpire Rick Reed went so far as to call the runner safe. "I don't know what I was doing," said Kingman. "I just short-circuited." (New York manager Billy Martin protested that Kingman had run outside the baseline, but crew-chief umpire Rich Garcia clarified that the complaint would have been valid only had Kingman been trying to avoid a tag.)

From that point on, said A's manager Jackie Moore, "I think we'll make sure all our players know to touch the next base."

7

Don't Show Players Up

It was a simple question. From the batter's box at Candlestick Park, Willie Mays looked at Yankees pitcher Whitey Ford and, pointing toward Mickey Mantle in center field, asked, "What's that crazy bastard clapping about?"

What that crazy bastard was clapping about only tangentially concerned Mays, but the Giants superstar didn't know that at the time. It was the 1961 All-Star Game, and Ford had just struck Mays out, looking, to end the first inning. The question was posed when Ford passed by Mays as the American League defense returned to the dugout—most notably among them Mantle, hopping and applauding every step of the way, as if his team had just won the World Series. There was a good story behind it, but that didn't much matter in the moment. Willie Mays was being shown up in front of a national baseball audience.

Under ordinary circumstances there is no acceptable reason for a player to embarrass one of his colleagues on the field. It's the concept at the core of the unwritten rules, helping dictate when it is and isn't appropriate to steal a base, how one should act in the batter's box after hitting a home run, and what a player should or shouldn't say to the media. Nobody likes to be shown up, and baseball's Code identifies the notion in virtually all its permutations. Mantle's display should never have happened, and Mays knew it.

Mantle had been joyous for a number of reasons. There was the strikeout itself, which was impressive because to that point Mays had hit Ford like he was playing slow-pitch softball—6-for-6 lifetime, with two

59

homers, a triple, and an astounding 2.167 slugging percentage, all in All-Star competition. Also, Ford and Mantle had spent the previous night painting the town in San Francisco in their own inimitable way, and Ford, still feeling the effects of overindulgence, was hoping simply to survive the confrontation. Realizing that he had no idea how to approach a Mays at-bat, the left-hander opened with a curveball; Mays responded by pummeling the pitch well over four hundred feet, just foul. Ford, bleary and already half beaten, didn't see a downside to more of the same, and went back to the curve. This time Mays hit it nearly five hundred feet, but again foul. It became clear to the pitcher that he couldn't win this battle straight up—so he dipped into his bag of tricks.

Though Ford has admitted to doctoring baseballs in later years, at that point in his career he wasn't well practiced in the art. Still, he was ahead in the count, it was an exhibition game, and Mays was entitled to at least one more pitch. Without much to lose, Ford spat on his throwing hand, then pretended to wipe it off on his shirt. When he released the ball, it slid rotation-free from between his fingers and sailed directly at Mays's head, before dropping, said Ford, "from his chin to his knees" through the strike zone. Mays could do nothing but gape and wait for umpire Stan Landes to shoot up his right hand and call strike three.

To this point in the story, nobody has been shown up at all. Ford may have violated baseball's actual rules by loading up a spitter, but cheating is fairly well tolerated within the Code. Mays's reaction to the extreme break of the pitch may have made him look bad, but that was hardly Ford's fault. But then came Mantle, jumping and clapping like a kid who'd just been handed tickets to the circus. It didn't much matter that the spectacle was directed not at Mays but at Giants owner Horace Stoneham, who immediately understood the motivation behind Mantle's antics.

Stoneham had gone out of his way to make Mantle and Ford feel at home upon their arrival in town a day earlier, using his connections at the exclusive Olympic Club to arrange a round of golf for the duo, and went so far as to enlist his son Peter as their chauffeur. Because the pair of Yankees had failed to bring golf equipment, their first stop was the pro shop, for shoes, gloves, sweaters, and rental clubs. The total came to four hundred dollars, but the club didn't accept cash. Instead, they charged everything to Stoneham, intending to pay him back at the ballpark the following day.

That night, however, the three met at a party at the chic Mark Hopkins Hotel. Ford attempted to settle his tab on the spot, but Stoneham's response wasn't quite what he anticipated: The owner told him to keep his money . . . for the moment. Stoneham then proposed a wager: If Ford retired Mays the first time they faced each other the following afternoon, he owed nothing. Should the center fielder hit safely, however, Ford and Mantle would owe Stoneham eight hundred dollars, double their original debt. Ordinarily, this sort of bet would be weighted heavily in favor of the pitcher, since even the best hitters connect only three times out of ten, but Ford was aware of his track record against Mays. Nonetheless, the lefty loved a challenge even more than he loved a drink, and quickly accepted Stoneham's terms.

Mantle, however, wasn't so cavalier, telling Ford frankly just how bad a deal it was. "I hated to lose a sucker bet," he said later, "and this was one of them."

That didn't keep Ford from sweet-talking him into accepting Stoneham's terms. In center field the next day, Mantle found himself significantly more concerned about the potential four-hundred-dollar hole in his pocket than he was about the baseball ramifications of the Ford-Mays showdown. So, when the Giants' star was called out on the decisive spitter, it was all Mantle could do to keep from pirouetting across the field. Said Ford, "Here it was only the end of the first inning in the All-Star Game, and he was going crazy all the way into the dugout."

"It didn't dawn on me right away how it must have looked to Willie and the crowd," said Mantle. "It looked as if I was all tickled about Mays striking out because of the big rivalry [over who was the game's pre-eminent center fielder], and in the dugout when Whitey mentioned my reaction I slapped my forehead and sputtered, 'Aw, no . . . I didn't . . . how could I . . . what a dumb thing.' "

That Mantle got away with it was largely due to the fact that Ford later explained the entire affair to Mays, much to May's amusement. In this regard, Mantle was luckier than most players, who usually learn of their indiscretions from well-placed fastballs, not from conversation. For example, stepping out of the batter's box once a pitcher comes set isn't something that inspires retribution in most pitchers, but it did for Goose Gossage—in a spring-training game, no less. And Randy Johnson drilled a player in a B-squad game for swinging too hard. New York Mets closer

Billy Wagner considered hitting a spring-scrimmage opponent from the University of Michigan who had the nerve to bunt on him. ("Play to win against Villanova," the pitcher said afterward.) Nolan Ryan felt similarly when major-leaguers laid down bunts against him, and Don Drysdale and Bob Gibson were likely to knock down any opponent who dug in. All these pitchers felt justified in meting out justice for infractions that the majority of their colleagues barely noticed.

Several code violations, however, are universally abhorred. At or near the top of any pitcher's peeves is the home-run pimp, a hitter who lingers in the batter's box as the ball soars over the wall. The first great player to fit this bill was Minnesota's Hall of Fame slugger Harmon Killebrew, by nature a quiet man who happened to take delight throughout the 1960s in watching his big flies leave the yard. "Killebrew was the first one I saw (do it)," said Frank Robinson. "He would stand there and watch them. But heck, he hit the ball so high, he *could* watch them." Reggie Jackson, widely credited with bringing the practice to prominence in the 1970s, credits Killebrew with providing inspiration.

Jackson, of course, added panache and self-absorption to the act, combined with a thirst for attention that Killebrew never knew. During Jackson's days with the Yankees, he went so far as to claim the final slot in batting practice because it afforded him the largest audience before which to perform. This became known as "Reggie Time," and the slugger saw fit to bestow it upon some lucky teammate if he was unable to take that slot on a particular day.

Barry Bonds eventually became the torchbearer for home-run pimping, not only watching but twirling in the batter's box as a matter of follow-through. David Halberstam wrote of Bonds's mid-career antics for ESPN.com: "The pause at this moment, as we have all come to learn, is very long, plenty of time for the invisible but zen-like moment of appreciation when Barry Bonds psychically high-fives Barry Bonds and reassures him once again that there's no one quite like him in baseball."

Admiring one's own longball isn't all that sets pitchers off. When Phillies rookie Jimmy Rollins flipped his bat after hitting a home run off St. Louis reliever Steve Kline in 2001, the Cardinals pitcher went ballistic, screaming as he followed Rollins around the bases. "I called him every name in the book, tried to get him to fight," said Kline. The pitcher stopped only upon reaching Philadelphia third baseman Scott Rolen, who was moving into the on-deck circle and alleviated the situation by assuring him that members of the Phillies would take care of it internally.

"That's fucking Little League shit," said Kline after the game. "If you're going to flip the bat, I'm going to flip your helmet next time. You're a rookie, you respect this game for a while. . . . There's a code. He should know better than that."

The primary purpose of batter's-box theatrics is to gain attention, but showboating at the plate can serve more than one agenda. There are those, for example, who feel that a well-timed piece of showmanship can serve as a highly appropriate retaliatory measure. Pitchers don't care for it, but it's certainly safer than being charged.

It's St. Louis's Albert Pujols responding to a homer he hit against Pirates pitcher Oliver Perez by flipping his bat high in the air, a retort to Perez waving his arms enthusiastically at his home crowd after retiring Pujols earlier in the game. It's Colorado's Matt Holliday spending extra time contemplating a home run because Giants pitcher Matt Cain had hit him in his previous at-bat. Even a master showboater like Jackson occasionally used his pimping abilities for payback, once responding to a drilling from Cleveland pitcher John Denny by homering off him, watching the ball even longer than usual, pumping his fist at the pitcher, then making his way around the bases at a glacial pace. He topped it all by tipping his cap to the crowd, then after crossing the plate, punctuated the display by charging Denny, which incited a near-riot at Yankee Stadium.

And that's just regular-season antics. Giants slugger Jeffrey Leonard turned it up a notch against St. Louis during the 1987 NLCS when he unleashed what he called his "one flap down" home-run trot against the Cardinals. The curious gait, in which Leonard's left arm dangled limply while he dipped his inside shoulder into the turn at each base, was employed after Giants players noticed their family members stuck in poor seats for the first playoff game in St. Louis. "We all got angry," said Leonard. "So I said to myself, If I hit a home run I'm just going to clown this fool out there." Leonard hit four homers over the course of the series, affording him multiple opportunities to clown plenty of fools. Each time, his arm hung low to his side, infuriating Cardinals players and fans, who had no idea there was more to the gesture than sheer showmanship.

No less subtle was the payback Dave Henderson delivered to Mariners manager Dick Williams. Henderson had spent his entire professional career in the Seattle organization until being traded to Boston in 1986 in a deal orchestrated by Williams. Two years later, Henderson—by then a member of the Oakland A's—hit an opening-day home run against Seattle and saw it as an opportunity to make a statement.

"You know how you fade a little bit on a home run?" Henderson asked, referring to the batter's act of leisurely drifting out of the baseline in the early stages of his home-run trot. "Well, I faded all the way to the dugout. I was so far over I could kick gloves off the top step. I faded so far that I almost went into the camera well before I realized I was going past the base, so I had to take a sharp turn and go straight back toward first. Now, *that's* hot-dogging."

Watching an opponent showboat is enough to send many players into fits of apoplexy, but as far as indignity goes, few things cut more thoroughly than public statements of disrespect made by members of the opposition. Even something as simple as a guarantee of victory—a player's ultimate declaration of belief in himself and his teammates—is taken as a slap by those he indirectly promises will lose. When someone comes out with something truly inflammatory, it can prove so provocative to his opponents that it may swing a game, or even a season.

Take the 1988 National League Championship Series between the Dodgers and Mets. In Game 1, Los Angeles pitcher Orel Hershiser, on his way to winning the Cy Young Award, had shut New York down over eight and a third innings before handing a 2–1 lead to reliever Jay Howell just two outs shy of victory. Hershiser faced thirty-one batters before he gave up a run; Howell faced three, and gave up two. Improbably, the Mets emerged with a 3–2 victory.

Mets ace David Cone, 20-3 and third in the Cy Young Award voting, was slated to start Game 2. First, however, he had a column to write for the New York *Daily News*. Technically the column—which Cone was contracted to produce throughout the playoffs—was ghostwritten by *News* columnist Bob Klapisch under the pitcher's byline, with Cone offering input after every game. It was a standard arrangement; another Mets pitcher, Ron Darling, had a similar deal with the *New York Post*.

If the pen is mightier than the sword, however, Cone may have inadvertently fallen on his own plume. After New York's stirring comeback, Klapisch found Cone in the giddy Mets locker room, where the two discussed many aspects of the evening—the performance of New York's starting pitcher, Dwight Gooden; Cone's excitement about pitching the following night; the game-winning rally.

Then Klapisch asked Cone what he thought happened to Howell in the ninth. Cone was, in his own words, still "in my bench-jockeying mode," and responded that Howell kept going back to his best pitch, the curveball, again and again, failing to mix up his repertoire to a degree that would throw Mets hitters off balance. The strategy, Cone said, reminded him of when he was a high school pitcher, throwing curve after curve after curve.

The sentence that made it to print read slightly differently: "Seeing Howell and his curveball reminded us of a high school pitcher." Cone has never denied uttering those words, but has long stressed that the context was skewed. One lesson he learned when the paper came out the next day was that context doesn't count for a hell of a lot in the face of opponents spitting fire over your sentiments. "All of a sudden," said Cone, "it was me calling Jay Howell a high school pitcher."

Just as suddenly, the Dodgers had new life. Manager Tommy Lasorda brought a copy of the *Daily News*—not so easy to find on the streets of Los Angeles—into the clubhouse and ran it through a copy machine. Before the game, he rallied the team around him and exploded. "When we got to the clubhouse that day, the article was posted all over the place—we couldn't miss it," said Dodgers catcher Mike Scioscia. "We had our pregame meeting, and Tommy used it for all it was worth. He kept saying that [Cone] was calling all of us a bunch of high-schoolers, not just Jay Howell. He kept saying that they thought we were a bunch of high school kids, on and on. He was pretty emotional, of course, as only Tommy can be. . . . Tommy loved to use whatever he could to motivate his teams, and that was an opportunity he jumped on. He was all fired up, and so were we when we took the field."

As soon as Cone heard about the article, he jumped into action, seeking out Howell, Hershiser, and Lasorda to explain his side of things. It didn't do much good. "They listened," said the pitcher, "but they were pretty cool about it." When Cone took the mound, the Dodgers bench, fired up by Lasorda's speech, started riding him hard, offering up, said the pitcher, "bench-jockey insults that were as bad as I have ever heard." It was vicious, it was loud, and it was relentless. "Everybody, right down to the trainer, was screaming at me," said Cone, whose father, Ed, was sitting next to the Dodgers dugout and heard every word.

It worked. Cone, whose 2.22 ERA during the regular season was second in the National League, lasted just two innings, giving up five runs before being removed for a pinch-hitter in the third. It was the shortest outing he had ever made as a big-league starter. "It was the first time my legs ever got heavy," he said. "I was so nervous that I was physically affected by it. My legs felt like tree trunks trying to walk out to the mound." That day, Cone learned one of the great lessons in baseball or any sport: Don't rile your opponents, especially through the media.

Cone's "high school" comment was easy for the Dodgers to pounce upon, but some statements are so innocuous that it's hard to fathom that they could offend anybody. Still, they sometimes do. In the victorious visitors' clubhouse after the Indians won the 2007 American League Division Series at Yankee Stadium, for example, Cleveland's Ryan Garko told the press that celebratory champagne tasted just as good on the road as it did at home. A week later, however, when the Indians raced out to a three-games-to-one lead over the Red Sox in the ALCS, Boston players mistakenly—or perhaps intentionally—advanced the notion that Garko's statement was not in reference to the Indians' previous series, but to clinching the pennant at Fenway Park. With the quote posted on the inside of Boston's clubhouse door as inspiration before Game 6, the Red Sox went on to win en route to the world championship.

Nearly as innocent were the comments made by A's third baseman Eric Chavez before his team faced the Yankees in Game 5 of the 2000 ALDS. Responding to a press-conference question about his opponents, who had won the previous two titles, Chavez talked about how great the Yankees had been in recent years, what a terrific job they'd done, and how difficult it was to win as consistently as they had. He also added that they'd "won enough times," and that it would be okay for somebody else to play in the World Series for a change. Chavez was twenty-two years old, wide-eyed and hopeful. There was nothing malicious in his tone.

Unfortunately for the A's, the press conference at which Chavez was speaking was being broadcast live on the Oakland Coliseum scoreboard for early-arriving fans. Also watching were the Yankees, on the field for batting practice. "So he's dropping the past tense on us? Did you see that?" spat third baseman Scott Brosius from the batting cage. One New York player after another—Derek Jeter, Paul O'Neill, Bernie Williams—took Chavez's comments and blew them up further. The Yankees hardly needed additional motivation, but now they had it. Their first three hitters of the game reached base, four batters in they had the lead, and by the end of the frame it was 6–0. The A's were in a hole from which they could not climb out before they even had a chance to bat.

"You don't want to light a guy up," said longtime catcher Bill Freehan, repeating ages-old wisdom. "Just let a sleeping dog lie."

Managers are hardly exempt from the unwritten rules, in ways that stretch far beyond the purview of ordering retaliatory strikes. Perhaps most prominent is the mandate to protect one's players at all costs. This has nothing to do with strategic maneuvers like deciding who bats cleanup or pitches the eighth inning, but instead covers things like restraint from overt criticism and refusing to speak publicly about players' private issues. Prominent in this category is the greatest indignity of all: Except for pitchers or in case of injury or a double-switch, a manager shall never pull a player from the field in the middle of an inning.

That doesn't mean it doesn't happen. Frank Robinson was one of the toughest players in baseball history, a guy who during his Hall of Fame playing career exhibited virtually no mental weakness on a ballfield, the perfect example of an indestructible personality. As a manager, however, he was once broken down completely by this section of the Code. It happened in 2006, when the seventy-year-old Robinson was managing the Washington Nationals. Over the previous weeks he had watched helplessly as his catchers went down to injury, one by agonizing one. Starter Brian Schneider was disabled with a hamstring strain. Robert Fick, who was primarily an outfielder/first baseman anyway, missed the first six weeks of the season with elbow damage, and had come off the disabled list to be used only as a pinch-hitter, not to play in the field. (Two months later, he'd suffer that rib injury against the Giants and be drilled by Noah Lowry for bunting with a big lead.) The only other guy on the club with catching experience was Wiki Gonzalez, who by that point wasn't actually on the team—he was due to be outrighted to Triple-A New Orleans the following day and had already appeared in what would be his final game for Washington.

Desperate before a game against the Astros, Robinson turned to one of his favorite players, Matt LeCroy. Although LeCroy had come up as a catcher, he had primarily been a designated hitter to that point in his seven-year career and had spent all of one inning behind the plate the previous season. Additionally, LeCroy was battling bone spurs in his elbow. LeCroy was willing to catch, but he'd effectively be taking one for the team—and both he and Robinson knew it.

The Astros stole a base against the injured catcher in the second, and another in the fourth. By the sixth inning, they had homed in on his weakness and began a slow, painful process of exploitation, swiping four more bags in the frame. In the seventh, Morgan Ensberg stole Houston's seventh base of the night, advanced to third on LeCroy's second throwing error of the game, then scored on Preston Wilson's single, to close what had been a 7–1 Nationals lead to 7–5. At that point, Robinson couldn't take any more. In the middle of the inning he instructed Fick—who had started only twenty games as a catcher over the previous four seasons—to strap on some shin guards, and walked slowly toward the plate to replace LeCroy.

Robinson knew the Code, and, as repugnant as he found it, he felt he had no choice. He wasn't angry at LeCroy, but sorry for him. Sorry that he was exposed as being so vulnerable, sorry he couldn't get the job done, sorry circumstances dictated that he had to be out there in the first place. LeCroy certainly took it well, saying, "If my daddy was managing this team I'm sure he would have done the same thing," but when Robinson was asked about it after the game, one of the hardest men in baseball was unable to maintain his composure. As he talked, tears streamed down his cheeks.

"It's not LeCroy's fault," he said. "We know his shortcomings. They took advantage of him today. That's my responsibility. I put him in there. . . . That's on my shoulders." In protecting his player from one evil—the base-path assault of the Houston Astros—Robinson exposed him to another: potential ridicule from fans and players alike. The manager was forced to choose between two barely palatable options, and ultimately decided to put the good of the team ahead of the good of both LeCroy and, to gauge by his analysis of the situation, himself.

Robinson wasn't the first manager to pull a player midway through an inning, but his motives were certainly the most pure. When Billy Martin pulled Reggie Jackson from right field in the middle of the sixth inning of a game in 1977 for failing to hustle after a ball, his primary goal was to embarrass the superstar. "When a player shows the club up," spat the manager after the game, "I show him up."

Martin was more straightforward than most managers, but he wasn't alone in his motivation. In 1969, Mets left fielder Cleon Jones had given a similarly lackadaisical effort while chasing a double into the corner at Shea Stadium, and was subsequently pulled mid-inning by manager Gil Hodges. Unlike the Martin-Jackson saga, however (which nearly ended in fisticuffs in the dugout), there were a number of mitigating circumstances involved. To start, Jones was playing on a sore leg. Also, the field was soaked after days of persistent rain, and the outfielder had been chasing balls through the slog for hours—it was the second game of a double-header, and to that point in the day New York had been outscored by the Astros 24–3. The double in question was Houston's sixth hit of the inning (in addition to two walks); Jones followed up his leisurely effort at corralling the hit by lofting a lazy throw back to the infield. "Without an injury, on a dry field in a close game, I might have dived for the ball," he said, "but I'm only saying that because of what happened next."

What happened next was Hodges calling time and emerging slowly from the dugout, head down, ostensibly to visit Nolan Ryan on the pitcher's mound. Instead, he veered slightly, heading toward shortstop Bud Harrelson. Hands in pockets, Hodges finally looked up, altered his route again, and tramped out to left field. Putting his arm around Jones, he asked the player if he was hurt. Jones mentioned his hamstring. "If you're not running good," Jones recalled the manager saying to him, "why don't you just come out of the ballgame?" The two men walked together back to the dugout. It was as ferociously passive a display as can take place on a ballfield, and the immediate assumption was that Hodges wanted to make a statement both to his star outfielder (whose .346 batting average at the time ranked second in the league) and to the rest of the team.

Even though Hodges publicly pinned the move on Jones's injury, bullpen coach Joe Pignatano said that after the game Hodges could clearly be heard yelling at the player from behind his closed office door: "Look in that mirror and tell me if Cleon Jones is giving me 100 percent!" Jones's opinion was that Hodges's message was intended for the entire roster, to counter a lack of life on the bench amid a pair of blowout losses. If that's the case, it worked: After that day, the Mets—to that point 55–43 and five and a half games behind the Cubs—compiled a 45–19 record, en route to a World Series win over Baltimore.

There's one more possibility for Hodges's motivation in pulling Jones, though, and it had nothing to do with firing up his team: The manager was willing to embarrass his player in order to save face for himself. It's possible that Hodges, weighed down by the marathon drubbing, simply lost track of where on the diamond he was heading. "Gil once told me that he was just going to the mound to take out the pitcher," said one of the manager's close friends, National League executive Frank Slocum. "He told me he was walking with his head down and when he looked up, he realized he was almost at third base. He didn't want to turn back to the mound, so he kept walking."

That the man who would guide the Mets from 101 losses to a world championship in just two seasons got lost on his way to the pitcher's mound may seem like the least plausible explanation of the bunch, but Slocum's story is corroborated by perhaps the subject's greatest authority—Hodges's wife, Joan. "Gil wasn't the type of man who would make up stories. He would give it to you straight or he wouldn't give it to you at all," she said, talking about the questions she had for her husband after he returned home from the game. "He said to me, 'You want the gospel truth?' I said, 'Yeah, I'm your wife.' He said, 'I never realized it until I passed the pitcher's mound, and I couldn't turn back.' "

·   ·   ·

For the all the preening exhibited by the game's greatest hot dogs, some players put just as big a premium on *not* being noticed. These are the guys who put their heads down and race around the bases after hitting home runs, who walk briskly from mound to dugout after stifling a potential rally. Usually it works, but sometimes the desire for anonymity is so great that it actually calls attention to itself.

Pitcher Allie Reynolds, a six-time All-Star with the Yankees and Indians, was just such a player. He'd never had the chance to pimp a home run, having failed to hit one during the first six years of his career. On opening day, 1948, however, despite a .143 lifetime batting average, Reynolds somehow smacked an Early Wynn fastball into the left-field bleachers at Griffith Stadium. Reynolds ran with his head down, taking extra precaution to keep from offending the pitcher he had just victimized. His eyes were so low, in fact, that he never saw the ball leave the park, and figured his shot for a double. And when, approaching second, he looked up to see the Yankees' third-base coach with his arms raised in celebration, he mistook it for a "stop" sign. So he did.

The New York dugout started hollering at him to complete the circuit; Reynolds wasn't buying it. Senators infielders Al Kozar and Mark Christman informed him that he had hit a home run, to which Reynolds replied, "I've seen you guys talk people off bases before." Finally, Yankees manager Bucky Harris convinced Reynolds that his home run was legitimate, and the pitcher completed his circuit. "After they talked me off second I finally got to do my home run trot, even if it was only halfway," Reynolds said. "Everyone in the place got a big laugh out of it."

In the end, of course, Reynolds's self-effacement garnered more attention than he would have received had he stood in the box watching his homer like Reggie, pirouetted like Barry Bonds, and flipped his bat like Albert Pujols—or even just jumped and clapped like Mickey Mantle.

8

Responding to Records

Tigers pitcher Denny McLain always had a soft spot for Mickey Mantle, having idolized him as a boy growing up in Chicago. When they met at Tiger Stadium in September 1968 the two were at opposite ends of their careers, McLain peaking en route to thirty-one wins and both the Cy Young and MVP awards, while Mantle was nine days from retirement. The great slugger's previous home run, almost a month earlier, had him tied with Jimmy Foxx on the all-time list with 534.

Before the game, McLain decided to do his hero a favor. Recalled Tigers catcher Jim Price, "Denny told me, 'Let him hit one.'" Price relayed the good news when Mantle stepped into the batter's box, at which point the Yankees star extended his bat over the plate to indicate just the spot in which he'd like to see a pitch. McLain delivered, and Mantle connected for a homer. Said Price, "Denny stood out there on the mound and clapped." Mantle had his milestone, and McLain had his joy.

Properly dealing with records—either one's own or someone else's—has long been a part of the Code. It's why Yankees outfielder Tommy Henrich laid down a curiously timed ninth-inning bunt to avoid a possible double play, assuring Joe DiMaggio another chance to extend his hitting streak in 1941. (DiMaggio did.)

It's also why, when Yankees second baseman Bobby Richardson went into the final day of the 1959 season needing a hit in his first at-bat to push his average to .300, manager Casey Stengel informed him that since the Yankees didn't have a single .300 hitter on the roster he'd be immediately removed from the game should it happen, to avoid falling below the mark in ensuing at-bats. It's also why members of that day's opponent, the Baltimore Orioles, took up the cause: Brooks Robinson informed Richardson that he'd be playing deep in case the hitter found appeal in bunting; pitcher Billy O'Dell offered to groove pitches; and catcher Joe Ginsberg verbally called for pitches instead of dropping down signs. Umpire Ed Hurley even got in on the act, offering that, if Richardson could "just make it close," things would go his way. Said Richardson, "There couldn't have been a more complete fix on." (The fix might have been on, but it wasn't complete. Richardson doubled in his first at-bat, refused Stengel's entreaties to leave the game, went 2-for-3, and ended up at .301.)

It was also why Yankees general manager Ed Barrow called a rainout on a day in which there was no rain, simply because Lou Gehrig and his record streak of consecutive games were still at home, in bed with the flu. "Say, Ed," a reporter asked Barrow the next day, "you really didn't think it was going to rain, did you?" "Damn it, of course I did!" Barrow snapped. "Gehrig will be able to play today."

When Don Drysdale was on the precipice of breaking Carl Hubbell's National League record for consecutive scoreless innings in 1968, he loaded the bases against the Giants with nobody out in the ninth inning. When he hit the next batter, Dick Dietz, it forced in a run and killed his streak at forty-four innings, four outs short of Hubbell's mark. Plate umpire Harry Wendelstedt, however, ruled that Dietz made no effort to get out of the way of the pitch, and ordered him back to the plate with a full count, whereupon he flied out to shallow left field. Drysdale got out of the inning unscathed, in the process tying Doc White's 1904 record with his fifth straight shutout, and eventually ran his streak to fifty-eight and two-thirds innings.

If Drysdale needed assistance from an umpire while playing the Giants to set his mark, so too did the successor to his record. In 1988, Orel Hershiser compiled forty-two consecutive shutout innings in pursuit of Drysdale's standard before finally allowing a run on, of all things, a fielder's choice—against the Giants, of course. Umpire Paul Runge, however, belatedly called hitter Ernie Riles out at first, ruling that baserunner Brett Butler went out of his way to interfere with Dodgers shortstop Alfredo Griffin on the play at second, ending the inning and wiping the run off the board. ("That slide was just like every other time I slid," said an indignant Butler, who had indeed advanced directly into the bag.) Hershiser went on to run his scoreless-innings streak to fifty-nine. "It was a slow chopper, and there was no way they were going to get him at first no matter what I did, so what incentive did I have to try to take [Griffin] out?" said Butler. "A lot of times when records are in the balance like that, there's no explaining some of the things that happen. People react in different ways."

If the previous two examples are any indication, umpires are interested in seeing records broken. Opponents, however, are another matter. As DiMaggio built his fifty-six-game hitting streak in 1941, A's pitcher Johnny Babich vowed to end the festivities by retiring DiMaggio in his first at-bat, then walking him in every plate appearance thereafter. DiMaggio's teammates were furious, but it was the Clipper himself who administered the most appropriate response. In his first trip to the plate, DiMaggio lined a ball between Babich's legs and into center field for a single.

In 1961, Roger Maris was denied his final chance to tie Babe Ruth's home-run record within 154 games when Orioles manager Paul Richards called for closer Hoyt Wilhelm to come on in the last inning of a meaningless game in which the Orioles trailed, under threat of a fine if he threw the slugger anything but knuckleballs. Maris struck out.

For Babich and Richards, the only things on the line were pride and history. When a team has the opportunity to directly assist one of its own, however, tactics can get even weirder. In 1929, New York Giants outfielder Mel Ott and Philadelphia's Chuck Klein were tied with forty-two homers apiece as their teams met for a doubleheader on the last day of the Phillies' season. (The Giants had one game remaining, against Boston.) Klein took the home-run lead in the first game with his forty-third longball, after which Phillies pitchers responded by walking Ott in the first, fourth, sixth, eighth, and ninth innings of the nightcap—including once with the bases loaded—to keep his total static and effectively hand the crown to Klein. It might not have been sportsmanlike, but at least they had the interests of a teammate at heart.

The same couldn't be said for St. Louis manager Jack O'Connor, whose motivation wasn't in anyone's best interests, but to bring down a hated opponent whose team he wasn't even playing at the time. It happened during a doubleheader on the final day of the 1910 season between O'Connor's Browns and the Cleveland Naps. Cleveland star Napoleon Lajoie, despite his .372 batting average, still trailed Ty Cobb's .380 for the league lead, and had all but given up hope of catching him. At that point, Cobb, the three-time defending batting champion, was merely the least-liked player of his time; over the next eighteen seasons he would cement his reputation as the most reviled player ever. Lajoie, meanwhile, was so popular that the Cleveland franchise had renamed itself in his honor.

With his 107-loss Browns having nothing else for which to play, O'Connor opted to help dethrone Cobb by positioning rookie third base-man Red Corriden far behind the bag whenever Lajoie came to bat. The hitter's drives were so fierce, said O'Connor, that the strategy was for Cor-riden's safety.

Lajoie, oblivious to the tactic, hit a triple in his first at-bat. When he noticed the chasm between Corriden and the batter's box during his sec-ond trip to the plate, however, he took advantage and bunted for a base hit. O'Connor made sure that Corriden's positioning against Lajoie didn't change throughout the game; subsequently, neither did Lajoie's tactics. With Cobb sitting out his own game, three straight bunt hits in the opener for Lajoie, and another four in the nightcap, put the batting title squarely in the Cleveland star's sights. In Lajoie's final plate appearance of the sea-son, however, he tired of the routine and swung away, hitting a grounder to shortstop Bobby Wallace. That left him with eight hits in nine at-bats and a whisker short of Cobb, who beat him .3850687 to .3840947 to win the title and the luxury Chalmers automobile that went with it. The sub-sequent outcry led to O'Connor's dismissal; he never managed a big-league ball club again. (Seventy-one years later, the commissioner's office found that Cobb had been incorrectly credited with an extra 2-for-4 game that season and recalculated his season average to .383. Twenty-two years after his death, Lajoie was crowned the American League's batting cham-pion for 1910.)

Although it was less contentious, a similar tactic was attempted in 1953 to help Cleveland's Al Rosen win the American League's triple crown. Heading into the final day of the season, Rosen already held a slight edge in the home-run race and had the RBI title locked up. His most precarious category was batting average, in which he was tied for the league lead with Senators first baseman Mickey Vernon.

In Cleveland's game against Detroit, the Tigers took a page from the Jack O'Connor playbook and positioned their infield very deep—an invi-tation for the well-liked Rosen to bunt. Rosen, however, harboring an abiding sense of fair play, chose instead to swing away and went 3-for-5 with two doubles.

In the Senators' game against the Philadelphia Athletics, Vernon collected two hits in his first four at-bats. Shortly thereafter, Rosen's game in Cleveland ended, giving Vernon a razor-thin lead heading into his final plate appearance. Having been notified of Rosen's line, every player on the Washington bench understood the situation: A hit would cement the crown for Vernon, and an out would hand it to Rosen. The Senators decided to go with option three: Don't give Vernon the chance.

The slugger was scheduled to bat fourth in the ninth inning, and when Washington catcher Mickey Grasso doubled with one out, it seemed like a certainty that Vernon would again reach the plate. Grasso, however, managed to get picked off at second, a development observers attributed to the fact that he more or less wandered away from the base. Kite Thomas followed with a single, but when he tried to stretch it to a double without benefit of running hard, he was easily thrown out for the third out of the inning.

Whatever instincts Vernon may have had toward justice became irrelevant; he never made it to the plate and Rosen missed his triple crown by .0011 points.

Whatever problem one might have with the likes of Grasso, Thomas, or Jack O'Connor, at least they were aware that something great was going on. The same couldn't be said for rookie Angels reliever Tim Fortugno in 1992, after George Brett collected his three thousandth hit. It was hard to miss, actually, since the game was stopped for five minutes as Kansas City players mobbed the third baseman and Anaheim fans applauded. But literally moments after the game resumed, Brett, in the middle of a conversation with first baseman Gary Gaetti, was unceremoniously picked off first base. Fortugno, said Brett, "didn't let me finish my sentence."

"All of a sudden, I forgot I was on base . . . ," the third baseman said, laughing. "It was kind of a comical way to put an exclamation point on the whole thing."

Just as circumstances surrounding streaks or records compel entire sections of the Code, respect for single-game feats also has its place in the book. Primary in this category are the appropriate methods for dealing with no-hitters. In the press box, an unwritten rule for official scorers holds that the first hit of any game must be unequivocally clean; if it reasonably could have been ruled an error and no subsequent hits are tallied, outcry is certain.

On the field, things take another turn. The more a pitcher mows down the opposition, the more the opposition is expected to respect the feat. Cardinals outfielder George Hendrick did exactly this in 1984, when he stepped to the plate with two outs in the ninth inning against Reds ace Mario Soto, who had yet to allow a hit. Hendrick stood passively and watched the first two pitches of the at-bat split the plate for strikes. Rather than go for the kill, however, Soto inexplicably used a third-pitch fastball to buzz Hendrick's chin, knocking him to the ground. The slugger got up, slowly returned to the box, and knocked Soto's next offering over the fence in left field. "I don't know why he did that," Hendrick said afterward. "I was going to let the man have his no-hitter."

Players aren't always so generous. When Detroit pitcher Tommy Bridges was within an out of a perfect game against the Senators in 1932, Washington manager Walter Johnson—despite trailing 13–0—sent up curveball-hitting specialist Dave Harris as a pinch-hitter, to try to figure out the bender with which Bridges had baffled Washington all afternoon. Harris connected for a single, and Johnson absorbed criticism from around the league. Bridges himself abstained, however, saying, "I would rather earn it the competitive way than have it handed to me."

Whatever heat Johnson took had nothing on Padres catcher Ben Davis, who turned heads with his at-bat in a 2001 game against Arizona. Davis came up in the eighth inning as the twenty-third hitter to face Curt Schilling, entirely cognizant that his team was 0-for-22 to that point. Because swinging the bat against the big right-hander had not yet paid dividends, Davis switched gears and, noting the deep positioning of third baseman Craig Counsell, laid down a bunt. Although the execution was lacking—Davis popped the ball up, just over Schilling's head—the hit nonetheless fell between the mound and second baseman Jay Bell, who was also stationed deep. Davis safely reached base with his team's first hit.

The Arizona bench exploded at the audacity, calling the player gutless and intoning that he was afraid to take his hacks like a man. To judge the play by the unwritten rules, the Diamondbacks had a point. "The first hit of a no-hitter is not a bunt," said Kansas City Royals pitcher Danny Jackson fifteen years earlier, in 1986, after Angels rookie Devon White attempted to break up his own no-hitter with a failed eighth-inning bunt attempt. "I don't know how long he's been around," Jackson said about the outfielder, "but he's got to go down." Arizona manager Bob Brenly felt the same way about Ben Davis, calling the play "chickenshit" and saying that Davis "has a lot to learn about how the game is played."

"It wasn't the heat of the pennant race in September, or something like that," said Diamondbacks left fielder Luis Gonzalez. "They say every game counts, but when a guy's doing something masterful like that, if you get a hit you want to earn it in the right way." Third baseman Matt Williams said he wouldn't have done it. First baseman Mark Grace said that, although he didn't fault Davis, if it was him he wouldn't have had the balls. Schilling was "a little stunned" at the move; his experience taught him that players should earn their way on base in that type of situation.

There was, however, a mitigating factor. The score of the game was 2–0, and when Davis reached base it brought the tying run to the plate. The Padres clearly hadn't been getting it done against Schilling in any other regard, so from a strategic standpoint Davis's approach worked. "I don't know if you saw my swings against him . . . ," the catcher said. "I'm just trying to get on base any way I can right there, and I did."

"What if it's the seventh game of the World Series? Would they or anybody be upset?" asked Padres manager Bruce Bochy. "No, because that's a huge game and you're trying to win." Arizona, he said, wanted the Padres to "drop our weapons and raise our hands."

Even Schilling grasped both sides of the argument. Though stopping short of taking Davis's side, he expressed understanding for those who did. "Whether I agree with it being the right thing to do or not is not really relevant," he said. "It was a 2–0 game. . . . If it's 9–0, yeah, I think it's a horseshit thing to do. But it was a 2–0 game and the bottom line is, unwritten rules or not, you're paid to win games. That's the only reason you're playing in the big leagues."

One interesting aspect of the play was that even among the ranks of baseball's old guard—guys who lived for and played by the Code—there was hardly unanimity of opinion. Cases were made both for and against Davis, with precedents cited from every generation—like the bunt by

Milwaukee catcher Bill Schroeder that broke up a 1987 no-hitter by Royals left-hander Charlie Leibrandt in the sixth inning. Nineteen years after that, when Tampa Bay rookie Ben Zobrist bunted for his team's first hit in the sixth inning of a game against Seattle's Jerrod Washburn, the pitcher himself agreed that nothing improper had transpired. "If it was the eighth or ninth, maybe that would have rubbed me the wrong way," Washburn said, "but bunting is just part of the game, and he was just trying to make something happen."

The Schilling–Davis affair, however, was full of gray area. Some baseball people will accept a no-hitter-spoiling bunt if bunting is an established part of the hitter's offensive repertoire—but Ben Davis was hardly a bunter. In fact, said Brenly, "That was the only time Ben Davis ever tried to bunt for a base hit to my recollection. . . . For a backup catcher who had never bunted for a base hit before in his life to do it, I thought that was unnecessary to begin with, and disrespectful, to top it off."

The notion of disrespect stems from the fact that Davis clearly took advantage of Counsell's extra-deep positioning, as the infielder attempted to protect against hard-hit balls that might otherwise have shot by him. Counsell felt safe at that range because he thought there was little chance that a runner as slow as Davis would so blatantly violate the unwritten rules.

Part of the problem was that Davis's bunt wasn't even good enough to benefit from Counsell's positioning. "I was mad that it was such a bad bunt and was still a hit," said Schilling. "He bunted as bad a ball as you can bunt, to the most perfect spot in the infield to bunt it. . . . I never said it was a horseshit *play*. I thought it was a horseshit *bunt*."

Once the dust settled a bit, the last man standing at the center of the controversy wasn't Schilling or even Davis—it was Brenly, who, as the most outspoken critic of the play, was left in its aftermath to defend his initial anger. He has since softened his stance, even going so far as to admit that much of his posturing was simply a matter of standing up for his pitcher, to make sure that "Curt Schilling knew that I was looking out for his interests."

Still, years after the fact, he had a question for which he says he never received an adequate answer: "If it's such a good fuckin' play, why didn't he do it every time?"

9

Gamesmanship

Lonnie Smith was on first base. It was the eighth inning of the seventh game of the 1991 World Series, and for baseball's last teams standing, runs were difficult to come by. Each club's starting pitcher—John Smoltz for Atlanta and Jack Morris for Minnesota—had thrown seven frames of shutout ball, which is what made the prospects of Smith's leadoff, check-swing single so exciting. At age thirty-five, Smith could still run, and with the concrete-hard surface of the Minnesota Metrodome's outfield turf able to shoot balls into the gaps like slap shots on a hockey rink, he was likely to score if one of his teammates could come through with a well-placed hit. These were Lonnie Smith's final albatross-free moments, just before he became the victim of perhaps the most prominent fake-out in baseball history.

When the next batter, Terry Pendleton, got the extra-base hit the Braves so desperately sought, rocketing a double between Twins left fielder Dan Gladden and center fielder Kirby Puckett, there was no doubt in the ballpark that Smith would score. On the Braves bench they knew it. Smoltz, having been removed moments earlier and watching the game on a clubhouse TV, knew it. Millions of viewers around the country knew it. Twins second baseman Chuck Knoblauch, though, wasn't so sure.

Smith had taken off on a delayed steal when the pitch was released, which should have prompted him to look toward the plate to pick up the ball. Had Pendleton failed to swing, or swung and missed, Smith would have known to slide in anticipation of a play at second; once contact was made, he then could have decided what to do based on where the ball was hit. But Smith didn't look. Smith had no clue where the ball was.

This was an especially egregious mistake in a ballpark like Minnesota's, with a pillowy white dome interior that provided ample camouflage for fly balls. Smith was helpless, and made no effort to hide his confusion. He looked left. He looked right. He couldn't find the ball.

Enter Knoblauch. While Gladden raced toward the wall to track down the gapper, Knoblauch, a rookie second baseman, acted as if he were fielding a ground ball, then pantomimed a throw to shortstop Greg Gagne, who ran to "cover" second. The decoy (shortened in baseball terminology to "deke") wasn't enough to fool Smith entirely, but it did serve to delay him. He slowed as he rounded second, then came to a complete stop four steps past the base. He looked to the outfield to see what was going on, because he knew that with defensive whiz Kirby Puckett in center field, anything was possible. He took two more hops toward third. It wasn't until the ball hit the turf in front of the left-center-field wall that Smith was finally able to track it down, and having received no prior instruction from Braves third-base coach Jimy Williams, he belatedly trotted to third as Pendleton pulled into second. Against the odds, Smith hadn't scored.

Some paint Smith as the goat of the series for his baserunning gaffe. Others exonerate him, because Atlanta still had runners at second and third with nobody out, yet failed to bring a run home. (Morris retired Ron Gant on a grounder to first, and after intentionally walking David Justice, induced Sid Bream to ground into an inning-ending double play.) When the Twins plated a run in the tenth to take the game and the championship, Smith's baserunning miscue was up there with Morris's ten shutout innings as the day's primary topics of conversation.

Never mind that Smith hit three home runs in the series. Never mind that he already had three championship rings from other clubs, and clearly knew how to win. It was all about the fact that the fourteen-year veteran had been suckered by the rookie, and at tremendous cost. And though Smith still insists that Knoblauch didn't fool him—"If I did think Knoblauch had the ball, why didn't I slide?" he asked—it's difficult to argue against the fact that, at the very least, the deke cost Smith precious moments of hesitation.

In numerous ways, a deke isn't so different from many other pantomimed aspects of baseball. A pitcher who may not be able to locate his fastball has to pitch as if he can, at least until the other team catches on. A slugger with a recently injured shoulder will attack pitches with as close to his standard form as possible (if not his same effectiveness), hoping that the pitcher will fail to recognize a weakness upon which to prey. A diving outfielder will act as if he's caught a ball he actually trapped. If these people can fabricate their own reality on and around a baseball diamond, why not a guy with a glove on his hand?

To Hall of Fame third baseman George Kell, the deke was an integral part of the game, because any extra moment it bought could be enough to keep a runner like Lonnie Smith from advancing. "But I would never do it unless it was a key run—maybe could turn around the ballgame or something," he said. "You can't get away with it but a time or two, and then they know you're going to fake them."

"You know not to trust middle infielders—it's their job to deke," said former infielder Bip Roberts. "Your job as a runner is to pick up the baseball, not the fielders. You look into the hitting zone, and if the ball's hit, you find it. If you can't find it you look at the coach. If you look at the infielder it's bad baserunning."

The deke has been part of baseball history for as long as there's been baseball history. In 1892, with Cleveland's Jesse Burkett on second base, Boston catcher King Kelly watched a clean hit as if the fielder had no chance for a play at the plate. Seeing Kelly drop both mask and mitt, Burkett slowed, thinking he would score easily. When the throw arrived at the plate, however, Kelly caught it bare-handed and tagged out the befuddled runner.

Kansas City Royals shortstop Freddie Patek went so far as to bobble air in an effort to elicit slides. Patek's keystone partner, Cookie Rojas, helped out by moving in to make phantom pivots near the base.

"I don't think any baserunner should fall for a deke," said Rangers manager Ron Washington. "There are things I'm supposed to be doing when a ball is put in play, so how can you deke me? A ball is hit, and I'm supposed to know where that ball is at all times. And if I run blind and get deked out, whose fault is that? Is that the infielder who deked me out, or is that my fault for not knowing what's going on?"

Ask Johnny Jeter. In a 1972 game between the Giants and Padres, Jeter stole a base so easily that there was no throw. He dived headfirst into the base anyway, a clear sign that he hadn't looked in to follow the action. Seeing this, San Francisco shortstop Chris Speier pounced. "Hold up, hold up—foul ball," he said nonchalantly. Astonishingly, the ploy worked. Jeter started back to first base, Giants catcher Dave Rader fired the ball to second, and Jeter was tagged out. "Oh shit, was he pissed," said Speier, grinning at the thought more than three decades later.

Infielders' proximity to baserunners gives them a natural advantage when it comes to deking, but outfielders can get in on the act as well. Jim Rice made a habit of treating many balls hit over his head at Fenway Park as if they would end up clearing the Green Monster by a mile, gazing up with detachment as the hitter started into his home-run trot . . . before racing to the carom and firing the ball in to second. "You could make a great video of all the shocked faces of baserunners who were cut down at second because they fell for this trick," said outfielder Doug Glanville.

Ironically, one of the most noteworthy instances of an outfield deke involved Rice's Red Sox—with Boston cast as the victim. It happened in 1978, during the one-game playoff between the Red Sox and the Yankees to determine who went to the American League Championship Series. Boston, trailing 5–4 in the bottom of the ninth at Fenway Park, had a runner, Jerry Remy, on first base with one out. Things appeared promising when Rick Burleson hit a fly ball that Yankees right fielder Lou Piniella lost almost immediately in a patch of sunlight. But Piniella never hesitated, casually acting from the outset as if he were going to make the catch. Remy, who should have made it to third base without issue, was forced to stay near first until he saw that the ball wouldn't be caught, at which point he could advance no farther than second. When Rice followed with a deep fly ball that would have easily scored the tying run from third, the Red Sox sensed an incredible opportunity wasted. Boston's final batter, Carl Yastrzemski, popped out to end the game.

The common factor in the dekes by both Knoblauch and Piniella is that a postseason hinged on each. The grand stage of the playoffs, in fact, has inspired a number of such noteworthy plays—none more original than that of A's closer Rollie Fingers.

It happened during the eighth inning of Game 3 of the 1972 World Series against the Reds. Fingers, with his team trailing 1–0, had been called upon to get the A's out of a one-out, runners-at-the-corners jam. Oakland had scratched out only three hits against Reds pitcher Jack Billingham to that point, and its hopes of getting back into the game hinged on Fingers's ability to keep runs off the board. When the runner at first, Bobby Tolan, swiped second, it only seemed logical that Oakland manager Dick Williams would order an intentional walk to Johnny Bench to set up a double play.

Williams, however, was a gambler. Bench might have been a future Hall of Famer, but so was Fingers. The manager opted to let his pitcher pitch, intervening only once Bench worked the count to 3-2. Williams called time and approached the mound.

"Dick gets there and he starts gesturing all over the place," said Fingers. "He's pointing at the on-deck circle and then to first base. All the time he's telling us that [A's catcher Gene] Tenace is supposed to stand up when he gets behind the plate. I'm supposed to go into my stretch like we're going to intentionally walk Bench. And he wanted me to throw a slider for a strike. He wanted to make sure that in case we didn't fool Bench, he wanted it to be a breaking pitch that he'd be swinging at."

Fingers delivered: A perfect slider on the outside corner was taken for strike three. He then intentionally walked Tony Perez to load the bases, and retired third baseman Denis Menke to get out of the jam. "Bench told me later that that was the most embarrassing thing that ever happened to him in baseball," said Fingers.

Knoblauch, Piniella, and Fingers respectively represent dekes from infielders, outfielders, and pitchers. Less common but still valid are those from baserunners, an example of which was perpetrated by Oakland's Jay Payton in a 2006 game against the Devil Rays. On first base, Payton took notice when the hitter, Dan Johnson, lost track of the count and started trotting to first base after receiving only his third ball of the at-bat. Gauging the indifferent reaction of the defense, Payton took off toward second at an easy canter, fast enough to make it close if the defense caught on, but slow enough to avoid raising suspicion. When the umpire informed the teams that the hitter had not, in fact, walked, Johnson was forced to return to the plate. Payton, having advanced while the ball was in play, stole second in one of the truest senses of the term, deking an entire stadium in the process.

. . .

Fielders like the deke, and managers like the deke, and, okay, maybe baserunners aren't such fans, but can the play ever be considered a *bad* tactic?

"I think it's horseshit," said Ron Hassey, who played for six teams in fourteen years as a big-league catcher. "It's part of the game, but I think it's horseshit to get a guy down [into a slide] if you don't have the ball. . . . You can get somebody hurt when there's not even a play there."

Hassey's right. A number of players have been injured by ill-timed or unnecessary dekes, which leads to an unwritten rule about when it is and isn't appropriate to use the maneuver. For outfielders like Piniella and baserunners like Payton, there are no limits—nothing they do could put an opponent in physical peril. But infielders throwing down phantom tags at the last possible moment can cause awkward slides, and the potential for damage is very real. "If a guy is stealing, you don't pretend the throw is coming," said second baseman Craig Grebeck. "If he's coming in standing up and you all of a sudden look like the catcher is throwing the ball, a late slide can tear up an ankle or a knee."

That's exactly what happened to Gene Clines in 1973. Clines, a fourth-year outfielder with the Pirates, was on first base in a game against San Diego; with a full count on the hitter, he took off for second. The pitch was taken for ball four, but instead of simply strolling to second, Clines—who never peeked homeward to assess the situation—proceeded full speed ahead. Padres shortstop Derrell Thomas waited until Clines was nearly atop the base, then inexplicably threw his glove down as if a late throw were about to arrive. Clines, flustered, went into a hurried slide and badly injured his ankle. "That play right there cost me a lot of time," he said, still angry at the thought more than three decades later. "I never fully recovered for the rest of that year." Clines, batting .291 going into the game, missed three weeks, and hit just .227 in the two months thereafter.

Dusty Baker, playing for the Dodgers on a bad knee in 1981, was deked by former teammate and good friend Darrell Evans on a similar play at Candlestick Park. Baker had gone from first to third on a base hit against the Giants, and Evans, manning third base, put down a late phantom tag. "Darrell is deking me when the throw wasn't even there—it was to second base and cut off," said Baker. "I tried to slide late and I stumbled and almost hurt my knee again. I said, 'D, we were teammates—what are you trying to do to me?' He just said, 'I don't know.' "

Los Angeles pitcher Tom Niedenfuer responded by drilling Evans later in the game at Baker's request. "He spent the next three days with his elbow in a sling," Baker said. "Later, he asked me, 'Dusty, did you guys drill me on purpose?' Of course I told him no."

A deke is essentially baseball pantomime, a player catching a ball that isn't really there, then tagging a befuddled opponent. Its inverse is the hidden-ball trick, in which a fielder applies a tag with a ball the runner thinks is somewhere else. The play usually involves the first or third baseman receiving the ball from an outfielder after a hit, then acting like he's given it to the pitcher, often through a fake handoff near the mound. When the baserunner takes his lead, the fielder has simply to tag him; as long as the pitcher isn't atop the mound when this happens, it's perfectly legal.

"A lot of people thought it was kind of a chickenshit play," said Steve Lyons, "but my feeling always was, Pay attention." Lyons's favorite situation in which to utilize the strategy was on tight double plays, when all eyes were on the first-base umpire to see whether he'd call the runner safe or out. Because many first basemen naturally hop off the bag toward the pitcher, said Lyons, "all you have to do is take three more steps, give [the pitcher] a little nod, hang on to the ball, turn around, and come back to first base. Guys get off the base too early all the time."

Third baseman Matt Williams was one of his era's foremost practitioners of the trick, going so far as to induce runners off the base. With the Giants in 1994, Williams pretended to give the ball to pitcher Dave Burba, then returned to his position and asked the runner, Dodgers rookie Rafael Bournigal, if he "could clean the bag off." The runner graciously stepped aside, which Williams immediately made him regret. "The intent was not to embarrass anybody or to pick on anybody," he said after pulling the trick against Royals rookie Jed Hansen three years later. "But you want to win, and we needed to win that game."

At least he got that much out of it. Lyons said that in the minor leagues he once pulled off the play at first base on consecutive days, against the same baserunner, Carlos Martinez. "He was probably pissed off, but the embarrassment when you actually get caught overrules everything," he said. "You get caught, you're embarrassed, you start walking back to the dugout. He was big enough to pinch my head off if he wanted to."

Lyons once hid the ball so well that baserunner Scott Fletcher wasn't the only one completely snookered—so was the umpire, who called the runner safe on the play. "I got in a pretty good argument over that one," said Lyons. "I said, 'Do you think I'm stupid enough to pull the hidden-ball trick, have everybody in the entire ballpark not know that I have the ball, fool every player on both my team and their team, fool the guy who's on first base, and then tag him *before* he's off the bag? Do you think I'm that dumb?' And what I didn't realize until that point was that I didn't really give the umpire a shot to know I had the ball. In fact, I fooled *everybody*. It's a little unfair to have him make the right call on that play if he doesn't know I have the ball, so after that I tried to make sure that they did. It's pretty hard to try to hide the ball from everybody in the world and still show it to the umpire and say, Hey, I've got it here, keep your eyes open—but that's what I tried to do."

Philadelphia infielder Steve Jeltz presented an even harder-luck case in 1986. He had the ball, showed it to the nearest infield umpire, and picked the runner, Curt Ford of the St. Louis Cardinals, cleanly off second base. The only problem was that Phillies catcher John Russell, unaware of what was going on across the diamond, requested time out, which plate ump John McSherry granted just as the shortstop was racing to apply the tag. Because the ball was no longer in play by the time Jeltz reached Ford, the runner was allowed to return to second.

If only Lonnie Smith had been so lucky.

10

Mound Conference Etiquette

Jim Barr was an outspoken pitcher who over the course of a dozen seasons developed what can be charitably described as a philosophy of independent thought when dealing with managers. Another way to put it is that he wasn't shy about expressing disagreement with his skipper, something that's discouraged in most pitcher-manager relationships and is expressly verboten when done in public. Should it happen on the mound during a game, even the most levelheaded manager will get ticked off. If that manager happens to be Frank Robinson—who was known for harboring little appreciation for independent thought from his players—look out.

With his Giants holding a 7–5 lead against the Mets at Shea Stadium in 1983, Barr, in his fourth inning of relief work, walked Dave Kingman to give New York two baserunners with two outs. The walk had been semi-intentional, Barr having decided he'd be just as comfortable facing the next hitter, Brian Giles (of Manhattan, Kansas, not his All-Star namesake), whose .238 season average included zero home runs. When the right-hander's first pitch to Giles sailed wide, however, out came Robinson, who quickly signaled for closer Greg Minton. Barr wasn't pleased.

"One ball doesn't bother me, because I don't walk very many guys," said the pitcher, describing the scene. "All of a sudden, out of the corner of my eye, I see Frank coming out, and as soon as I see him signal to the bullpen it was 'You gotta be kidding me.' . . . I wasn't wild; I could throw strikes when I wanted to." Frustrated, Barr didn't wait for his manager to reach the mound before flipping him the ball—a clear act of insolence in the hard-edged presence of Robinson, who made it clear to his pitchers that they were to hand him the ball as they departed.

Barr planned on storming to the dugout, but was interrupted when Robinson caught the baseball, grabbed the pitcher by the arm as he tried to pass, spun him around, and dragged him back up the hill to await Minton's arrival. Robinson had been the league's most fiery player, and his managerial furnace burned nearly as hot.

As the duo waited for Minton to arrive, Robinson told Barr exactly what he thought of his stunt, poking a finger into the right-hander's chest to emphasize his point. Barr was no stranger to confrontation with his managers, having once called Giants skipper Wes Westrum "gutless" for removing him for a pinch-hitter. As a member of the California Angels in 1979, he almost came to blows with broadcaster Don Drysdale over criticism the ex-pitcher had leveled his way. On the mound at Shea, it was hard to miss the battle brewing, and the New York fans looked on in delight. All four members of the Giants infield raced in and surrounded the pair in an attempt to calm things down.

Barr didn't help matters when he decided that if he wasn't allowed to leave until Robinson gave him permission, he wouldn't leave at all. This meant that when Minton arrived at the mound he found two people, Robinson and Barr, standing between himself and the catcher, which made it somewhat difficult to warm up. "It seemed like five minutes," said Barr, "even though it was probably only ninety seconds." Robinson finally led Barr back to the dugout, at which point both pitcher and manager had to be restrained from going after each other.

Barr was hardly the first pitcher to treat a visit from his manager like he was about to be served court papers. Hall of Famer Early Wynn was reportedly once so upset to see White Sox manager Al Lopez coming to the mound that, rather than handing over the ball, he fired it into his manager's stomach. The action was apparently enough for Lopez to reassess his previous estimation of the diminishing velocity of Wynn's fastball, and the manager left him in the game. In a similar move, St. Louis Cardinals manager Eddie Dyer left the dugout for a mound visit in 1946, but was quickly warned by pitcher Blix Donnelly that he'd be hit between the eyes with the baseball if he got any closer. More intelligent than brave, Dyer ceded the battle (Donnelly stayed in the game) but won the war shortly thereafter, when the pitcher was sold to Philadelphia.

The greater the pressure, of course, the better the mound discussions. Mix in the anxiety of the postseason, and players can find it difficult to hold back. Nerves can get frayed in October even when things are going well, and when they aren't—like when a manager has to remove his starting pitcher in the second inning of a World Series game—it can be disastrous.

This was the case in Game 4 of the 1977 Fall Classic, when Dodgers manager Tommy Lasorda took the long walk to remove his starter, Doug Rau, who had given up two doubles and a single in the second frame, allowing one run while failing to record an out. Yankees were at second and third, and no matter how Lasorda might have reacted to a similar situation during the regular season, his team was down two games to one, and he couldn't afford to let this one get out of hand. The conversation is truly memorable, though, because Lasorda was wearing a microphone for the TV broadcast. Also, as Lasorda admitted to one of his coaches in the dugout, his goal was to stall for time and allow reliever Rick Rhoden additional warm-up tosses. Before he ever left the bench Lasorda had made the decision to remove Rau, but the pitcher, not privy to his manager's thinking, lobbied to remain in the game—which was exactly what Lasorda didn't want to hear.

RAU: I feel good, Tommy.

LASORDA: I don't give a shit you feel good. There's four mother-fucking hits up there. [There were actually only three.]

RAU: They were all fuckin' hit the opposite way. . . .

LASORDA: I don't give a fuck.

RAU: Tommy, we got a left-handed hitter. I can strike this mother-fucker out.

LASORDA: I don't give a shit, Dougie.

RAU: I want to get out of this myself.

LASORDA: I may be wrong, but that's my goddamn job.

RAU: I ain't fuckin' hurtin'.

LASORDA: I'll make the fuckin' decisions here, okay?

RAU: [Tommy John] gave up three runs on the fuckin' board yesterday.

LASORDA: I don't give a fuck! Don't give me any shit, goddamn it! I make the fuckin' decisions. Keep your fucking mouth shut—I told you.

Second baseman Davey Lopes, interjecting on behalf of the sport's image: "Hey, hey, hey. This looks bad up here. Just back off the mound. You want to talk about it, talk about it inside."

LASORDA: We'll talk about it in my fucking office.

RAU: If I felt bad, then I wouldn't say nothing.

LOPES: I'm just saying, talk about it inside. This is not the place to be talking about it, okay? That's all I'm trying to say. I'm just trying to avoid a fucking scene out here, that's all.

LASORDA: That's right. It's fucking great for you to be out here talking to me like that.

RAU: If I didn't feel good, I wouldn't say nothing.

LASORDA: I don't give a shit, Doug. I'm the fucking manager of the fucking team. I gotta make the fucking decisions. And I'll make them to the fucking best of my ability. They may be the fucking wrong decisions, but I'll make it. Don't worry about it. I'll make the fucking decisions. I gave you the chance to walk out here. I can't fuck around—we're down two games to one. If it was yesterday, it's a different fucking story.

RAU: We got a left-handed hitter coming up, why—

LASORDA: I don't give a shit! You got three left-handed hitters and they all got hits on you. Rivers, Jackson, and that fucking other guy. That guy who just hit the ball was a left-hander, wasn't he? [Chris Chambliss, who had doubled, was indeed left-handed.]

RAU: I jammed him. I pitched it on the inside part of the plate. . . .

91

LASORDA: I don't give a shit whether you jammed him or not—he didn't get out. I can't let you out there in a fucking game like this— I've got a fucking job to do. What's the matter with you?

It's rare insight into the language of diplomacy from baseball's putative ambassador. Lasorda made his fucking decision, and though Rhoden let both runners score, he held the Yankees from there. It didn't do much good, however, because the Dodgers lost the game 4–2, and the series in six.

To get around those kinds of conversations, Hall of Fame manager Sparky Anderson implemented a rule with his pitchers. "I don't want to hear you," he said. "Just give me the ball. I have no desire to hear a pitcher's feelings, because if something goes wrong I'm the one who's gonna get fired, not the pitcher."

The manager's also the one who's going to get booed, as demonstrated in a story told by Rangers skipper Bobby Valentine: "Okay, so I'm the manager of Nolan Ryan," he said. "Nolan and I get along fine. I have asked him to do only one thing for me. I said, 'Nolan, every time you pitch at our stadium, it's filled with people who have come just to see you. Now, a lot of those times, I'm going to have to be the guy who has to come out and get you. This is not going to be a popular decision. When I come out and get you, can you just stay on the mound for a minute? Give the ball to the relief pitcher and wait. I'll say what I have to say and we'll walk off the mound together to a great standing ovation. Okay?' He never does it. I go out to get him. He gives the ball to the relief pitcher. He walks. Yaaaaaaaaaaaaaaay. I talk. I walk. Booooooooooooo. Valentine, you no-good blankety-blank."

Robinson, Lasorda, and Valentine all knew what they wanted when they left the dugout. Should a manager head to the mound without such certainty, however, he's invariably looking for a clue to his pitcher's ability to continue in the game. This brings up another unwritten rule about mound etiquette: When a manager asks how a pitcher feels, the pitcher lies.

No matter how much respect a pitcher holds for his manager, he's rarely happy to see him heading to the mound. Even if the pitcher is clearly spent, his shoulder, elbow, or hip shooting pain with every pitch, he'll insist to his last breath that he can still get the job done. "They're starting pitchers," said Tony La Russa. "They *need* to be heroes."

"If you don't say the right thing it's perceived as a lack of heart," said pitcher David Cone, who admitted to deceiving manager Joe Torre about his condition during a mound conference in the sixth inning of Game 3 of the 1996 World Series. (Cone insisted he was fine, stayed in the game, and, despite increasing fatigue, willed his way out of a jam.) "All guys worth their salt do it," he said. "That's why it's hard for a manager to go out there. They know that in the heat of battle it's hard to get straight answers from a pitcher."

"When [Cone] lied to me, he had to make it the truth," said Torre. "He just had to find a way to get it done, and that's what separates those guys. That's what matters."

It's the same section of the Code that prevents players from missing games for all but the most serious injuries. Anything less than an unflinching desire to compete—or at least the appearance of such—is perceived as weakness of character. It's a fine line walked by athletes, and especially star players; even though staying in a game at limited capacity might hurt one's team, asking out when it counts is tantamount to surrender. Few in baseball want to see perceived cowardice in action from their teammates, even if it's ultimately for the collective good.

As for Jim Barr and Frank Robinson, the pair made up quickly after their Shea Stadium spat, but that didn't much change the pitcher's outlook on what had happened. In fact, it was a full decade before Barr finally understood his manager's position—and it took Barr's appointment as pitching coach at Sacramento State University for it to happen. Suddenly Barr was the one examining situations, noticing when guys start to leave pitches high in the strike zone, playing lefty-righty percentages, and knowing what's available in the bullpen. He soon made it a practice to deliver a speech at the beginning of every season outlining one of his most intractable rules, which bore echoes of Sparky Anderson: When Barr visits the mound for a pitching change, he wants only for the departing player to give him the ball and walk quietly away, no questions asked.

"Now that I'm a coach I understand exactly where Frank was coming from," he said. "I tell my pitchers: 'Guys, I know you want to stay in there, but from personal experience . . . just hand me the ball and say goodbye.'"

PART TWO

RETALIATION

11

Retaliation

In 1986, Mike Scott pitched like a Hall of Famer, winning the NL Cy Young Award and throwing a no-hitter in his second-to-last start of the season to clinch the NL West title for Houston. He opened the playoffs against the Mets nearly as strong, allowing only two hits through seven shutout innings in Game 1 of the NLCS, his split-fingered fastball dropping like an anvil as it rocketed toward the strike zone. By the time Lenny Dykstra came to the plate in the eighth, eleven Mets had already gone down on strikes, and New York was just five outs away from falling into an early hole in the series.

That the Mets still had hope was thanks to the spectacular performance of their own pitcher, Dwight Gooden, who had held the Astros to a single run. So, when Danny Heep, pinch-hitting for Gooden, delivered a one-out single in the eighth inning to give his team just its fifth baserunner of the game, it was a minor cause for celebration on the New York bench.

Next up was Dykstra, nicknamed "Nails" for his crash-and-burn style of play. Just twenty-three, he lived for this sort of competition and was the only player in the Mets' starting lineup whom Scott had been unable to strike out. In the eighth he made contact again, topping a ball to the right side of the infield that Astros second baseman Bill Doran was able to knock down with a dive. When Doran's wide throw was bobbled by first baseman Glenn Davis, however, Dykstra was safe, and New York had two baserunners—its best rally of the game.

That's what Dykstra did right. Here's what he did wrong: When he crossed the bag and spun to see the umpire signal safe, he let loose his emotions, turning toward the Houston dugout, pumping his fist, and unleashing a primal bellow.

Whether or not Scott noticed is unimportant to this story, because Dykstra's actions caught the attention of the one guy on Houston's bench he'd have been best off leaving alone. Had Nails considered it, he'd probably have agreed that it was in his best interests to avoid riling up Nolan Ryan.

Ryan was scheduled to start Game 2 for the Astros, and looked on quietly from the bench as Dykstra's histrionics played out. Without removing his gaze from the area near first base, Ryan tapped the leg of pitcher Larry Anderson, sitting just to his left. "That boy," he said, in his slow Texas drawl, "just asked for a bow tie."

It was a euphemism that, except by Ryan himself, likely hadn't been used in the major leagues for thirty years. Ryan had picked it up as a young pitcher in the 1970s from none other than Satchel Paige, in his lone encounter with the former Negro Leagues star. Paige, then about seventy, had gone to meet the fireballer who was setting all the strikeout records, and gave Ryan a piece of advice that stuck with him for the rest of his career: "One of the best pitches is the bow-tie pitch."

Ryan had no idea what Paige was talking about. A bow-tie pitch, explained the ancient ballplayer, was "when you throw it right here"—he then mimed a horizontal line across his Adam's apple, as if slashing his own throat—"where they wear their bow tie."

Ryan took Paige's wisdom to heart, and began utilizing it with regularity. The bow tie is a purpose pitch, an intimidator, and it meshed nicely with Ryan's demeanor. "The bow tie was part of Ryan's mound presence," said Craig Biggio, who caught Ryan as a rookie with the Astros in 1988. "If he didn't like the way somebody played the game, they got hit. They got on the ground."

"[Dykstra] was really clapping there, and it was showy," said Astros pitcher Jim Deshaies, who watched the moment unfold alongside Ryan on the bench. "That didn't fly very far with Nolan."

Ryan didn't have to wait long to make his feelings known. It was his job to follow up Scott's five-hit shutout in Game 1, and the second batter he faced was none other than Dykstra, who compounded his troubles by lay-ing down a bunt. The entire league knew how Ryan felt about players bunting on him, mostly because the pitcher himself informed them of the fact with a regular pre-game ritual in which he tamped down the grass around home plate with his toe while staring daggers into the opposing dugout. His message: No bunting on me, fellas. And there rarely was.

Dykstra was thrown out, and when he came to the plate with two out in the fifth inning, the pitcher forced him to the dirt with a second-pitch fastball that sailed inside at neck level. It was a Ryan-model bow tie, custom-fitted and personally delivered. "You've seen the cartoon where Charlie Brown goes to kick the football and Lucy pulls it out and his feet go flying up in the air?" asked Anderson. "That's what Lenny looked like."

Dykstra didn't stay down long, leaping up and glaring at the mound. As intimidating as Ryan could be, Dykstra wasn't one to be bullied. Two pitches later, he drilled another fastball into left field for a base hit, and the Mets went on to score three runs in the inning, eventually winning 5–1. After the game, Dykstra wondered if there was intent behind Ryan's knockdown, but it probably should have been clear to him. The pitcher recognized behavior that needed correcting, and used fastballs to make his points.

In that much, at least, Ryan was ordinary; fastballs are the weapon of choice for most angry pitchers. It might seem that such heavy-handed tactics would only foster more conflict, but it's actually just the opposite. Because most baseball people understand the Code's eye-for-an-eye men-tality, getting even is not just tolerated, it's usually expected. Should a team or player fail to retaliate when the opposition oversteps its bound-aries, a loss of respect may result, in the other dugout and around the league.

"It's a delicate subject, of course. To the uninitiated or uninformed, it might appear to be childish or an emotional thing, but it's not," said Dick Bosman, who spent eleven years as an American League pitcher and nine more as the pitching coach in Baltimore and Texas. "An example: When you have a guy on the other team who, out of frustration, drills the next guy after someone on your team hits a home run—and I'm talking about the home-run hitter not standing there and doing six pirouettes like some of the players today, but he just hits the home run and runs around the bases—that pitcher's angry because he screwed it up and made a bad pitch and the ball went into the stands. That constitutes a situation in which you have to make sure you protect your teammates. In my mind, the first guy in the next inning gets it. . . . Now, what happens then? That guy goes back to the dugout and tells the pitcher who originally drilled our guy, 'You better knock that stuff off, because you're going to get some of us hurt.' That's how that's taken care of."

A profound majority of baseball's policing emanates from the pitcher's mound, and covers numerous Code violations: shows of disrespect, like stealing a base while holding a big lead; or acts of showboating, such as watching a home run; or pumping a fist after beating out an infield single in the 1986 NLCS. It can come in reaction to an opposing player's success, or some long-held grudge that was never resolved in its own time. The retaliation is not always understood by the victim or even the pitcher's own teammates, but if it's genuine, there's always a reason for it.

"You have to do it, because if you don't do it then maybe the next day somebody will take a liberty that they shouldn't," said longtime Royals pitcher Paul Splittorff. "It's protecting us."

It's rare for a hitter to request retaliation on his own behalf, largely because most pitchers don't need to be told. They judge the appropriate response by any number of things, none more immediate than the reaction of their offended teammate. During a game in 2006, for example, A's pitcher Joe Blanton hit Blue Jays third baseman Troy Glaus to lead off the second inning. (It appeared to be unintentional, although Glaus had hit two home runs in the previous meeting between the teams ten weeks earlier.) As it happened, Oakland's designated hitter, Frank Thomas, led off the following inning for the A's, and the first pitch from Toronto starter Ted Lilly hit him in the back—clear retaliation—and drew warnings for both benches from umpire Jeff Nelson.

As one of the best players in the American League for a decade, Thomas was no stranger to being the unwitting subject of similar retaliatory measures. He didn't so much as look at Lilly after getting hit, just trotted to first base as if he had drawn a walk.

"That's happened to me thirty, forty times," he said later. "Nowadays it's what you expect. [Glaus] is their big guy, their big slugger, and we got him. He was the first one up in the inning, and I was the first one up the next inning. I knew I was going to wear it. You just take it and move on down to first. That's baseball."

Thomas's attitude informed the reaction on the A's bench. Because the slugger was calm about the matter, so too were his teammates; had he reacted differently, the situation could have been far more volatile. "We all saw what happened, but Frank took it calmly, so we took it calmly," said Oakland third-base coach Ron Washington. "If Frank had taken it with an uproar, we'd have taken it with an uproar. We have to wait for the reaction of the guy who it happened to. If Frank had charged him, there would have been a fight. If Frank had raised some hell going down to first base, we'd have raised some hell. But Frank took it calmly and went on down there, the umpire checked everything, and we played baseball."

Of course, such ironclad protection does have its downside. One member of the A's posited that Lilly's retaliatory strike against Thomas threw the pitcher off his rhythm, which appears to be true: Six of the next eleven batters reached base, including a Jay Payton home run. "When he hit Big Frank, he wasn't so sure that Big Frank wasn't coming out to get him," said the Athletic. "He thinks he helped his team by hitting Big Frank, but I'll tell you what—his heart was pumping a mile a minute until he realized that Frank was just going to take first base. And after that, Lilly couldn't find the strike zone. He was all over the place."

If a pitcher has any doubt about what he should or shouldn't do on a teammate's behalf, it doesn't hurt to check in. After Barry Bonds was hit by a Randy Johnson fastball in 2004, for example, Giants pitcher Jerome Williams—scheduled to start the following day's game—looked down the bench to see if the superstar wanted a response. "I shook my head either yes or no, and he said no," said Williams. "I'm showing him respect by asking if he wants me to do something because he got hit. Do you want me to shake them up or hit somebody? Because I'm going to protect you if you say yes." The concept is so ingrained that when Royals pitchers failed to retaliate after Mike Sweeney and Jermaine Dye were hit by pitches in 2001, Kansas City general manager Allard Baird apologized to the players directly: "I can promise you as long as I'm general manager that will never happen again." Alternatively, pitchers who protect teammates earn immediate and abiding respect. Every member of the Los Angeles Dodgers appreciated Don Drysdale's two-for-one policy, in which he made it known that he'd drill two opponents for every Dodger who got hit.

Sometimes the two-for-ones are aimed at the same player, because getting him once just doesn't seem like enough. After Rangers catcher Ivan Rodriguez was hit on the elbow by Cleveland's Jack Morris in April 1994, he took out his frustration by barreling high, hard, and late into shortstop Omar Vizquel on a subsequent play at second, spraining Vizquel's knee so severely that the shortstop spent the next fifty-one days on the disabled list. Rodriguez was just twenty-two years old at the time but already in his fourth big-league season, and Indians players felt that he should have known better. Rodriguez maintained that he was merely trying to break up a double play, but Cleveland shortstop Alvaro Espinoza, Vizquel's replacement, called it "dirty baseball." "It was really kind of a cheap shot," said Vizquel later. "Why should he take it out on me? Go out there and see Jack."

The following day, Indians manager Mike Hargrove told the press that he had no problem with good, hard baseball, but, he added, "that slide wasn't good, hard baseball. From the looks of it he went down there with every intention of hurting someone, and he succeeded. That's the sad part of the whole deal." From that moment on it became clear that Rodriguez was a marked man. Texas manager Kevin Kennedy, ever the pragmatist, chose to sit his catcher for the final two games of the series to keep him from the business end of an ill-intentioned pitch. This saved Rodriguez in the short term, but only delayed the inevitable because the two teams had nine games remaining against each other that season, the next of which was scheduled for five days later, in Cleveland. Retribution didn't take long to follow.

In the seventh inning of the first game of the series, Rodriguez was anything but surprised when Indians starter Charles Nagy hit him on the hip. Not only did the Texas catcher fail to complain, he went so far as to pick up the ball, flip it to Nagy, and trot quietly to first. In his mind, his account was settled, and according to many who observe the Code, it should have been. Cleveland reliever Jose Mesa, however, wasn't yet satisfied.

It took Mesa two months, until July 5, to get his own shot at Rodriguez, at which point he drilled the catcher on the left elbow. Members of the

Rangers organization were both surprised and upset. "I thought this was finished in Cleveland," spat Kennedy after the game. "Ivan took it like a man that time. We won't forget this." They sort of did, though. Rodriguez ceased to be a target for the Indians, both teams moved on, and the animosity between the clubs fizzled, just like the Code dictates it should.

Pitchers who opt for retaliation walk the line between making their intentions obvious enough for the hitter to recognize and vague enough to pass muster with umpires. Should a purpose pitch be too well disguised, the hitter might think it unintentional and thus miss its point; if it's too blatant, the pitcher risks ejection.

There are tells, however. Just as hitters can pick up a curveball by its spin, many players feel that a pitcher's motion helps them discern the intent behind a hit-by-pitch. "When guys are throwing regular pitches, they throw toward the center of the plate," said seventeen-year veteran Oscar Gamble. "But when they're throwing at you, their arm comes straight toward you." Randy Knorr judged intent by the focus of a pitcher's gaze at his point of release: Staring right at the batter was a clear indication of purpose. "Body language," said Andy Van Slyke, "will tell you more than anything else."

The best way for a hitter to really know whether or not he's been hit intentionally is to understand whether the game situation even calls for retaliation. Not only will he better identify the moments in which a pitcher has something in mind other than throwing strikes, he'll be prepared to react accordingly. Because, if the situation calls for retaliation, that means it's not personal. And if it's not personal, it becomes just another thing that happens during the course of a baseball game.

"Whether [your teammates] are right or wrong, you want to keep their respect," said pitcher Jason Schmidt. "But there are some times when you're, like, 'You know what? You have to wise up—this is not the situation. He wasn't trying to do that.' "

Take Reggie Sanders, who charged the mound in 1994 after being hit by Pedro Martinez. That the pitcher was trying to protect a 2–0 lead in the eighth inning was one clue it might have been unintentional; that it was an 0-2 count was another. That Martinez was in the middle of throwing a perfect game should have put to rest any lingering doubts. Without a shred of hyperbole, Sanders was the most obviously *un*intentionally hit batsman in the history of the game.

Still, it wasn't enough to keep him in the batter's box. Martinez had been brushing back Cincinnati batters, including Sanders, all afternoon. After one such pitch in the fifth inning, Sanders gave the pitcher a long, angry glare, which Martinez returned in kind. After he plunked Sanders three innings later, Martinez even went so far as to raise his arms in frustration before realizing that it would be a good idea to defend himself.

When hitters do pick up on a pitcher's obvious retaliation, it's beneficial for them to know into which of three general categories the original infraction falls (discounting personal vendettas that have nothing to do with game situations): them or one of their teammates breaking an unwritten rule, being on a team that's having a great day at the plate, or having exceptional personal success against a pitcher or team.

The first of those categories is self-evident, especially considering the topic of this book. Many players know when they have violated a tenet of the Code, even if they realize it only after the fact. Should they somehow overlook their infraction, they have a bench full of teammates to inform them—if not in the moment, then later, in search of an explanation for why pitchers are subsequently attempting to drill them.

A pitcher aiming at a hitter simply because his team is pounding the ball, however, is driven almost entirely by aggravation: Pitcher gets battered, pitcher gets irritated, pitcher takes it out on whoever's at the plate. "Venting frustration" is how Giants pitcher Mike McCormick put it. This is generally frowned upon, but there is a gray area that includes a pitcher's possible attempt to disrupt the other team's rhythm and force hitters to concentrate on something other than pitch location and break.

The tactic has long had a place in baseball strategy, but was especially prevalent between the 1920s and '80s. Slap hitters during this time were often resentful of their power-hitting teammates, not just because, as Ralph Kiner once said, "home-run hitters drive Cadillacs." The less intimidating guys in a team's lineup were the ones who ultimately paid the price for the sluggers' success, getting thrown at frequently after a teammate's homer. Second baseman Jerry Coleman was a vocal critic of this tactic after following the likes of Mickey Mantle and Yogi Berra in the Yankees lineup. "I never liked that crap—the guy in front of me hits a home run and I get knocked down," he said. "I didn't do anything to you, for crying out loud. Go after *him*."

This understanding, though, helps mitigate the situation for some hitters. "In 1974, I was playing for the Yankees, and I hit behind Graig Nettles the whole month of April," said first baseman Mike Hegan. "And Graig hit eleven home runs. And I was on my back eleven times. That's just the kind of thing that happened. I got up, dusted myself off, and got ready to swing at the next pitch. It's just what you do."

When a player gets drilled because he himself owns a pitcher, however, it's a bit different. Too much success practically screams for a don't-get-comfortable message pitch, especially if the hitter's been having his way with balls on the outer edge of the plate. An inside pitch not only puts him on guard, it backs him up and reduces his reach; should one of those inside pitches happen to hit the guy, so be it. For most players, this is acceptable. Take the 1972 game in which Andy Messersmith hit Don Baylor; in six previous plate appearances against Messersmith, the rookie had four hits, including a double, a home run, and a walk. The pitcher responded by plunking him in the back without so much as looking in for a sign from the catcher. As Baylor staggered toward first base, he looked quizzically toward the mound. "Well," said Messersmith, "don't you think it's about time?"

A decade earlier, in September 1962, Cardinals outfielder Curt Flood's bunt single and double made him six-for-his-last-twelve against Don Drysdale, inspiring the pitcher to re-evaluate their relationship. In the fourth inning of a game in which Drysdale had already allowed four runs, Flood stepped to the plate with the bases loaded and one out. Drysdale's leash was short, but it didn't matter; the right-hander buried a pitch into the startled hitter's ribs. It drove in a run but served two purposes: It kept the outfielder from swinging his red-hot bat, and, more important, it put Flood in his place, at least as far as his future positioning in the batter's box was concerned. When the outfielder complained to teammate Bob Gibson about the pitcher's tactics, he didn't get the sympathetic ear for which he had hoped. "I told him, 'If you had eight hits in a row off me, I'd hit you too,' " said Gibson. "And I laughed."

.   .   .

On September 3, 1974, Cleveland's Oscar Gamble lit up the Tigers like he was taking batting practice, clubbing three home runs off two pitchers while going five-for-nine over the course of a doubleheader. When the teams met less than a week later for the opener of their next series, Gamble, the game's second batter, reasserted himself immediately, swatting a two-run blast that put Tigers starter Lerrin LaGrow into an early hole. As was Gamble's way, he watched each of his home runs for several moments longer than was appreciated on the opposing bench. He knew the Tigers wouldn't take it well, but, as was also his way, he didn't care. The man in possession of the biggest hair in the history of the game was in the business of making sure people watched him.

When Gamble led off the third inning with a single, igniting a four-run rally that chased LaGrow, he should have known what was in store. With two outs in the bottom of the sixth and the Indians leading 7–0, Gamble came to the plate and was promptly drilled by Tigers reliever Vern Ruhle. "Oscar's a little guy, and it hurt him, boy," said pitcher Dick Bosman, that day's starter for the Indians. "And nobody said anything."

At this point, Bosman was torn—stand up for his teammate, or protect his shutout? Gamble's success had clearly made him a target, but excessive showmanship was also a factor. And if that was the case, was it Bosman's duty to stand up for someone who essentially brought the punishment on himself?

"I've had teammates that weren't exactly the greatest teammates, and they want you to do something [when they get hit]," said pitcher Jim Barr. "And you want to jump back and say, 'Why? You deserved it!' " You want to say that, but if you're in the major leagues, you don't. As catcher Jamie Quirk said, "Teammate bond is stronger than logic."

For Bosman, the internal dialogue didn't last long. "Oscar was Oscar, and I didn't think Oscar was going to change," he said. "You have to protect your teammates." Lending difficulty to the decision was Bosman's compunction to exact immediate retribution, which put him squarely between the horns of a different dilemma. The next batter was Detroit icon Al Kaline, thirty-nine years old, in his final season and just fourteen hits away from three thousand. There was less than a month left in the schedule; an ill-placed fastball could conceivably end Kaline's career just shy of the defining milestone. "I'm out there thinking, Where am I going to drill him?" said Bosman. "I don't want to break his hand or anything like that. If I hit him in the ribs, that might put him out."

The pitcher opted for the middle road, dialing down his response and merely brushing the slugger back before eventually striking him out. The message was nonetheless clear, and no less important: Don't mess with my guys.

Hard feelings can fester in the space between players who get hit and pitchers who fail to protect them. When Dodgers pitcher Jeff Weaver and Giants outfielder Michael Tucker got into a shouting match in 2004, some on the Giants bench felt retaliation was in order. Tucker had bunted down the first-base line, and Weaver, fielding the feed from first baseman Robin Ventura, stood in the baseline and gave Tucker a hard tag to the face as he approached.

Pitching that day for the Giants was Jerome Williams, the same guy who later that season looked down the bench after Barry Bonds was drilled by Randy Johnson to find out what his response should be. That he knew to do so was thanks to a lesson he learned from the Tucker-Weaver incident.

After Weaver's unnecessarily hard tag, Williams was approached on the bench by Bonds. "I'll never forget what Barry said," Williams recalled. "He said, 'Dodgers players do not disrespect Giants players, no matter what. So you take care of business.' " Williams, however, was only twenty-two and confused, and Bonds's message carried with it a degree of ambiguity. "I didn't know what taking care of business was, because I had a good game going on," said the pitcher, who had allowed just five hits to that point. "So I'm thinking, Okay, take care of business—get people out. What he meant was to take care of what happened. If you want to take care of it, take care of it now. Don't wait. I didn't know."

Shortly after Bonds's decree, Giants pitching coach Dave Righetti approached from across the dugout with a similar message—in both point and vagueness—telling Williams to do what he had to. Again he thought, Okay, go out there and pitch—which was likely not what either Bonds or Righetti had in mind.

The first Dodgers batter of the following inning was Adrian Beltre, who slapped a single on a 2-1 pitch. Williams looked toward the dugout and saw Righetti holding his head in frustration. "That's when I realized it," said the right-hander. "I was, like, 'Dang, I was supposed to hit him.' "

In the locker room after the game, Bonds chewed Williams out for not protecting his teammate and failing to show the Dodgers that neither he nor his ball club was scared. The pitcher had no idea how to respond. "I was young. It was my second year, and I didn't know these things," he said. "Now when that kind of thing happens I know that I have to take care of it right then and there. Then, boom, it'll be done and over with."

Sometimes it doesn't matter how well a batter or a team hits a particular pitcher, or whether any level of hot-dogging or insolence has taken place; sometimes a pitcher wants to hit a guy for strictly personal reasons. In the early 1970s, for example, Gaylord Perry felt this way about Lou Piniella— and Piniella hadn't even done anything to him.

Earlier in the season, Piniella, playing for Kansas City, responded to a brushback from Perry's brother Jim, a pitcher with Detroit, by charging the mound for the first and only time in his career. He later called it one of the biggest mistakes he ever made on a baseball diamond.

That's because not long thereafter the Royals visited Cleveland, where Gaylord Perry was eagerly awaiting their arrival. When Piniella stepped in against him, he shouldn't have been surprised to see a fastball headed directly at him. "Gaylord put one, I mean he put one under his chin," said Indians outfielder Oscar Gamble. "You know how you have to throw your bat and throw your arms and get out of the way and the ball is choking you? This ball choked Lou. He went down. Then he looked out to the mound and said, 'Damn, I didn't know he had a brother.' "

Consider it a lesson learned. "If I have any advice," said Piniella, "it's don't charge the mound of a brother who has a pitcher for a brother."

Making things personal can become problematic not just for the victim, but for the retaliator as well. If settling a personal score has any chance of affecting a game's outcome, or if a pitcher's hotheaded action results in one of his teammates' being thrown at, there are bound to be angry responses in the locker room. "When a pitcher takes it on himself to hit somebody and the rest of the team doesn't know, he's pretty much on his own," said catcher Randy Knorr. "There's a sign I would put down for that—the middle finger."

Methods exist to avoid suspicion in these cases, so pitchers can pursue their agendas while raising minimal hackles across the diamond. Standard methodology says to throw at least one ball, if not two or three, far outside the strike zone—high, wide, or both—which offers the appearance of wildness. "It's a mistake a lot of guys make," said pitcher Al Nipper. "A guy comes up and with his first pitch he drills [the batter], and then he's out of the game. You can't do that. You can't send a flare up. You have to camouflage it, because that hitter knows when he's been shot."

The personal reasons pitchers have for throwing at opponents are myriad. Bert Blyleven hit Baltimore's Phil Bradley in 1990 because of Bradley's hard-line stance in labor negotiations that, in Blyleven's opinion, prolonged settlement of the thirty-two-day lockout that delayed the start of the season. "It infuriated [Blyleven] because he was older and concerned about pension time," said a source in the Orioles organization, who added, "Fans and media people never understood what the intent was there. But the few players who knew about this did."

Sometimes responses can take weeks (Gaylord Perry versus Lou Piniella), or even longer. A story is told by someone with high-level, inside knowledge of the game, about a collegiate pitcher who was tasked by his coach with showing a prized, hot-hitting recruit around campus. The pitcher went all-out, taking him to the hottest spots, ferrying him to parties, and introducing him around. The recruit's reaction, however, wasn't equitable: He spent most of the evening off by himself, pantomiming his swing; the rest of the time he spent being rude to nearly everyone he met. In the end, he decided to attend a different school altogether.

Fast-forward several years. Both pitcher and position player are in the major leagues, and end up facing each other. And whenever the situation allows for it (which, frankly, isn't that often), the pitcher drills the hitter. When the situation doesn't allow for it, he merely brushes him back.

The names in the story have been deleted by request, but other incidents don't require anonymity. Take Stan Thomas, who set a Seattle Mariners team record on July 10, 1977, when he uncorked four wild pitches in the first two innings against Minnesota. All four—three in the first inning, one in the second, which allowed a runner to score—were aimed at the head of Minnesota's Mike Cubbage, in response to a five-year-old tiff over a woman the pair knew when they were minor-league teammates. As was fitting for a pitcher who would make only three more appearances as a major-leaguer, all four pitches missed their mark, the right-hander was knocked out of the game before he could record an out in the second, and the Twins romped, 15–0. "Thomas got his priorities mixed up today," said Cubbage afterward. "He's supposed to be trying to win a game instead of throwing at me."

Cubbage should have been glad that it wasn't Don Drysdale's girl-friend with whom he got involved. In the National League clubhouse prior to the 1968 All-Star Game, Dodgers catcher Tom Haller saw Houston's Rusty Staub rummaging through Drysdale's shaving kit, ostensibly to find evidence of the long-whispered rumor that Drysdale doctored the ball. Fifteen days later, Drysdale faced the Astros in Los Angeles. Trailing 1–0 with two outs and nobody on in the eighth inning, Drysdale—tipped off by his teammate—wasted little time in drilling Staub. "That's for looking through my goddamn shaving kit," he yelled as the hitter stumbled toward first. Staub might not have been the world's best sleuth, but he was smart enough not to say a word in response.

Modern managers infrequently issue direct orders for intimidation tactics, settling instead for complimenting the pitcher who delivers on his own accord. Hitting somebody with a baseball can be a heavy burden to bear, and although most managers appreciate the gesture when it's called for and handled appropriately, they don't want the accompanying responsibility. "I never absolutely directed anybody to hit someone," said Jerry Coleman, who managed the Padres in 1980. "I also didn't direct them *not* to hit somebody."

In the good old days, managers were more hands-on. Casey Stengel would "come to the mound and say, 'Mr. Craig, I think that fellow up at the plate there now needs to step back a little bit—he's kind of crowdin' you, and you should do something appropriate,' " said former pitcher and longtime Giants manager Roger Craig. "It was just a suggestion that you should be aware of what was going on. You always got the point. He was giving the Casey Stengel hint. Brush 'em back a bit."

Stengel's was a soft touch; other managers were more direct: "I will order it," said Frank Robinson in 1975, "and it better be thrown." Leo Durocher added to his mystique by putting hundred-dollar bills in Whit Wyatt's locker when the pitcher threw at opponents' heads. Gene Mauch would yell, "Spin his helmet!" to his pitchers from the dugout.

Occasionally it's not even the manager who orders it. During spring training with the St. Louis Cardinals in 1978, pitcher George Frazier made his first-ever appearance in a big-league uniform. After recording two quick outs against the Red Sox, he got ahead of the third batter he faced, Carlton Fisk, 0-2. Because the right-hander was on a roll, he found it curious when catcher Ted Simmons gave him the "flip" sign—flicking his thumb upward across his index finger—calling, for a reason Frazier couldn't fathom, for Fisk to go down. The rookie, terrified at the thought of crossing an icon like Simmons, hit Fisk between the numbers. Boston's All-Star threw down both bat and helmet and glared at Frazier all the way to first base. After the inning, Frazier approached Simmons to find out what Fisk had done to merit such retaliation. "Nothing," Simmons told the rookie. "I just wanted to see if you'd do it."

One manager noteworthy for his love of ordering retaliatory pitches was Billy Martin, who went from being one of the game's most intense, ready-to-fight players to being one of its most intense, ready-to-fight managers. "Billy would call down to the bullpen and say, 'Get Stan Thomas up,' " said Charlie Silvera, Martin's longtime coach, who fielded the manager's calls to the bullpen. (There was a reason Martin liked Thomas for the job—this was the same guy who, while with Seattle two seasons later, threw four pitches at the head of Mike Cubbage.) "He'd say, 'Tell Stanley to throw at him until he hits him.' Well, I'd get off the phone and alert the bullpen, 'Get ready, boys, we're going again.' They'd take out their false teeth and take off their glasses and spit out their tobacco and get ready for the big sprint to home plate."

As long as Thomas—or any other of Martin's pitchers—hit his mark, everything went smoothly with the manager. Should one of them fail—or, worse, refuse—there was perhaps no more vindictive man in baseball. Goose Gossage once did that very thing, and says that it strained his relationship with his manager for the duration of the time they spent together. It happened during spring training in 1978, shortly after Gossage joined Martin's Yankees from the Pittsburgh Pirates. The pitcher was shagging balls in the outfield when Martin ambled over. Gossage guesses the ensuing conversation was some sort of test; if it was, he failed miserably. According to Gossage, the dialogue went like this:

MARTIN: Goose, when you get in the game today, I want you to hit Billy Sample in the head.

GOSSAGE: What?

MARTIN: I want you to drill Billy Sample in his fucking head.

The pitcher deliberated for a moment before denying his manager's request, telling Martin that he had no bad feelings for Sample and wasn't about to fight somebody else's battle. Martin's response was to berate the pitcher, both on the field and in the clubhouse. This may well have contributed to Gossage's horrible start with the team, in which he took losses in three of his first four appearances. (He did manage to rebound, winning that year's American League Rolaids Relief Award.)

Though few managers were as fiery or as direct as Martin, the game has a long history of angry reactions when retaliation—whether ordered or not—failed to be carried out. When White Sox star Frank Thomas was hit by a pitch in 1998, it didn't matter to his manager, Jerry Manuel, that it happened in the first inning of a game early in spring training, and that the offending pitcher, Willie Blair, was clearly still working out off-season kinks. Chicago pitcher James Baldwin failed to respond in kind, so Manuel—in his first season at the helm of a big-league team—wasted no time in calling a clubhouse meeting. "The message was, we will not tolerate the guys who are the heart and soul of the team getting hit," he said, describing the moment. "Those are things they have to understand about me. That's part of the 'fearless' package and the 'respect' package. We're not looking to start anything, but we're definitely not looking to back off anything either."

Manuel's successor with the White Sox, Ozzie Guillen, felt similarly, occasionally to the point of controversy. In 2006, he quickly identified Texas's Hank Blalock as a target for retaliation after Rangers pitcher Vicente Padilla twice hit Chicago catcher A. J. Pierzynski during a game. That was the plan, anyway. Filling the space between conception and execution, however, was Guillen's choice of executioner: rookie Sean Tracey.

The right-hander had appeared in all of two big-league games to that point and was understandably nervous. Even under optimal circumstances he didn't have terrific control, having led the Carolina League in wild pitches two years earlier, while hitting twenty-three batters. When Tracey was suddenly inserted into a game at Arlington Stadium with orders to drill the twentieth major-league hitter he'd ever faced, it was hardly because he was the best man for the job. To Guillen, Tracey was simply an expendable commodity, a reliever whose potential ejection wouldn't much hurt the team, especially trailing 5–0, as the Sox were at the time.

If the manager knew his baseball history, he might have realized that precedent had already been set in this regard. In 1942, Boston Braves manager Casey Stengel, wanting to get even with the Brooklyn Dodgers for stealing his signs, ordered his own rookie pitcher—greener even than Tracey, appearing in just his second big-league game—to hit Dodgers shortstop Pee Wee Reese. Faced with an assassin's assignment, the nervous lefty tried three times to hit Reese, and three times he missed. The following day, a fuming Stengel shipped him back to the minors, an action he would later call his biggest mistake as a manager. It would be four more years before Warren Spahn returned to the big leagues, by which point he was better prepared to handle the rigors that came with his promotion.

The same probably won't be said about Sean Tracey. When the right-hander's first pitch to Blalock ran high and tight but missed the mark, Tracey did what he'd been taught in the minors, sending his next pitch to the outside corner in order to avoid suspicion. Blalock tipped it foul. When Tracey's third effort was also fouled back, for strike two, the pitcher altered his strategy and decided to go after the out, not the batter.

According to his manager, it was the wrong decision. After Blalock grounded out on the fifth pitch of the at-bat, Guillen stormed to the mound and angrily yanked Tracey from the game. He didn't let up after they returned to the dugout, berating the twenty-five-year-old in front of both his teammates and a television audience. With nowhere to hide, Tracey sat on the bench and pulled his jersey up over his head, doing his best to disappear in plain sight. Two days later, without making another appearance, he was returned to the minor leagues, and during the off-season was released.

In his previous game, Tracey had hit a batter without trying to, said

Tim Raines, Chicago's bench coach, "so we figured it'd be easy for him to hit a guy if he was trying. . . . But it's much harder than it looks. I think it's harder knowing you're going to hit a guy. And if the target knows you're trying to hit him, he's going to be loose in the box. It's not something you're taught. You can't practice hitting a guy."

Ultimately, Tracey shouldered the responsibility for his actions, saying he "learned from it," but the lesson was lost on his more tenured team-mate, Jon Garland, a seven-year veteran en route to his second consecutive eighteen-win season. Before Padilla's next start against the White Sox, Guillen launched a pre-emptive verbal sortie, positing to members of the media that if the Rangers right-hander hit any Chicago player, retribution would be fast and decisive. His exact words: "If Padilla hits somebody, believe me, we're going to do something about it. That's a guarantee. I don't know what's going to happen, but something's going to happen. Make sure [the Rangers] know it, too." Padilla did, in fact, hit Chicago shortstop Alex Cintron in the third inning, at which point it didn't take much predictive power to see that a member of the Texas lineup would soon be going down. The smart money was on the following inning's leadoff hitter, second baseman Ian Kinsler.

The smart money was correct, but the payoff left something to be desired. Garland's first pitch sailed behind Kinsler, a mark clearly missed. Plate umpire Randy Marsh, well versed in the history between the clubs, opted against issuing a warning, effectively granting Garland a second chance. The pitcher didn't exactly seize the opportunity, putting his next pitch in nearly the same place as the first. At this point, Marsh had no choice—warnings were issued and hostilities were, willingly or not, ceased. Guillen rushed to the mound for a vigorous discussion about the merits of teammate protection. Kinsler ultimately walked, and after the inning Guillen reprised his dugout undressing of Sean Tracey, spewing invective while Garland listened and the White Sox batted. "I make it clear, I won't wait for two months or until I see you in spring training or until I see you next year," Guillen told reporters the following day. "When you get it done, you get something done right away. If it didn't happen that day, we get over it and move on."

As Raines said, however, it's not as easy as it looks. A designated driller carries the expectations of twenty-four guys, plus coaches, plus fans. If he tends to internalize things the task can become difficult, with the necessary steps to intentionally hitting someone growing surprisingly involved.

One such pitcher was notoriously streaky left-hander Shawn Estes of the New York Mets, who, at the center of the baseball universe in June 2002, proved Raines's theory. Estes was in the spotlight as the man expected to avenge teammate Mike Piazza, who for nearly two years had been subject to the aggressive and occasionally bizarre intimidation tactics of Roger Clemens.

It started before Estes had even joined the team, during a Yankees-Mets game in July 2000. Clemens, traded to the Yankees a season earlier after winning back-to-back Cy Youngs with Toronto, had been laboring through an utterly mediocre campaign, during which he racked up a career-worst 4.60 ERA. New York management tied the pitcher's problems to the fact that he had drifted from the inside intimidation that so closely marked his past success. "He wasn't pushing people off the plate," said Yankees manager Joe Torre. "They were getting too comfortable hitting off him."

That applied to the Mets in general (Clemens was 1-4 with a 9.10 ERA against them) and Piazza in particular (the catcher was hitting an astounding .583 off the Rocket, with three home runs and nine RBIs in a dozen at-bats). Perhaps this motivated the pitcher. In the second inning, Clemens unleashed an inside fastball with such velocity that Piazza barely had time to flinch before it ricocheted off the "NY" on his batting helmet. The hitter fell like a chunk of granite, lying motionless in the dirt for several long moments as Clemens stood about thirty feet away, hands on knees. Piazza was eventually taken to the hospital and diagnosed with a concussion; he missed two games—one in the regular season and the other the All-Star Game, three days later. The tension created by the moment was enough for the All-Star representatives from both New York teams, who had planned to share a charter flight to Atlanta for the festivities, to scuttle their arrangement and make individual travel plans.

That Mets pitcher Glendon Rusch hit the next Yankees batter, Tino Martinez, in the backside was of little consequence to Mets fans, who wanted nothing less than an eye-for-an-eye measure of frontier justice. The Yankees, though, never afforded them that opportunity. Clemens didn't come to bat in games at Yankee Stadium, and the next time the teams met at Shea was for Games 3, 4, and 5 of the World Series—but Clemens, having started Game 2 at his home yard, never took the field. ("Did I juggle the rotation to keep him from pitching at Shea? Yeah, I probably did," admitted Torre. "I'm not going to deny that. I didn't need another soap opera.")

He got one, anyway. Even though Clemens wouldn't bat, that Game 2 matchup with Piazza was at the forefront of public anticipation, and the pitcher didn't disappoint—albeit in a way that defied comprehension. Piazza, the third batter of the first inning, split his bat while fouling off an inside fastball. The hit itself was inconsequential—the ball squibbed harmlessly foul outside the first-base line—but the bat's barrel helicoptered toward the mound, landing at Clemens's feet. The catcher trotted absentmindedly toward first, bat handle still in his fist, as he watched the ball roll farther and farther from fair territory. Then things got historically interesting.

Clemens bent, cleanly fielded the barrel, and threw it—jagged edge and all—toward Piazza. It landed several feet from the stunned Met.

Clemens seemed to realize immediately what he had done. Piazza, in disbelief, started walking toward Clemens and shouted, "What's your problem?" It was the pitcher's reaction at that point—the Rocket seemed as shocked as anybody—that Piazza used to opt against settling matters with his fists. "[Clemens] was obviously jacked up," said the catcher. "In essence, I think he kind of cracked." The pitcher's excuse: He thought it was the ball. (Needless to say, this reasoning was a hit with the media.)

Mets manager Bobby Valentine called it "an overemotional, rather immature act on a big stage." Although the only real harm done to the Mets was the two-hitter Clemens threw over eight innings, the incident left the team's fans clamoring for nothing less than Clemens's head on a stick.

After the game, the pitcher ended up an emotional wreck in his manager's office, sitting alongside Torre, pitching coach Mel Stottlemyre, and owner George Steinbrenner, after Stottlemyre found him sobbing unremittingly in the clubhouse. It was clear to those in the room that, despite the pitcher's brave face and outstanding performance, the moment had taken a toll. "Rocket's always very high-strung and emotional . . . ," said teammate David Cone. "Certainly, he was wound up. He was scrambling a little bit."

The Yankees won the series in five games, and Clemens was fined fifty thousand dollars for his actions. Like the rest of the country, Estes—then in the employ of the San Francisco Giants—watched the moment unfold on TV, unaware that he would ever become part of the story line. Estes had never even shared a field with Clemens, let alone built up any animosity toward him. But when the Yankees' next turn at Shea, in June 2001, again passed without Clemens's taking the mound, the showdown was delayed until the following season—less than three months after Estes threw his first pitch for the Mets, and a year and a half after Clemens thought a bat was a ball.

On June 15, 2002, Clemens finally took the mound in the Mets' ballpark. Estes didn't even realize that the fateful day would coincide with his turn in the rotation until reporters informed him of it, and even then he said he was aware of only "bits and pieces" of the story. That his teammates didn't exactly rush to fill him in wasn't too surprising—only seven of them were left from the 2000 World Series roster, and they pretty much kept to themselves. Pitcher Al Leiter—who Estes says would have been much better suited to this particular role of enforcer, partly because of his take-no-prisoners approach, but mostly because he had been with the club through the duration of the affair—remained silent. Valentine never said a word. Even Piazza steered clear of the subject. Estes was, in every sense, said a veteran Mets player, fighting "someone else's battle."

Complicating matters further in the pitcher's mind was his long-held belief that not only wasn't this his fight, but that it had been Piazza's—and Piazza made the choice to avoid it that day two Octobers before, after a baseball bat had been thrown in his direction. "Based just on what was said in the media, I couldn't understand how Mike didn't do anything," said Estes in 2006. "That was my feeling while I was watching that game—how does he not go after Roger on the mound right now? I would think that most guys would at that point. . . . I've played with Mike [in both New York and San Diego]. . . . I know his emotions going into that game. [Talking to him about it after the fact,] I know he wasn't real happy about getting hit in the head. . . . I cannot understand how he didn't retaliate."

That, however, wasn't the message the pitcher was getting from outside the clubhouse. Had the media ever made a bigger deal of a single at-bat? When Estes took the mound against the Yankees on June 15, he felt that the fans cared far less about the outcome of the game than they did about seeing Clemens lying flat on his back. The left-hander stewed.

Said Valentine: "I thought the whole thing was so overblown, so imma-ture, and so not right for baseball, but it was right for the media circus, so we played into that. It was more to appease the fact that Shawn was the guy who was going to have the ball and he was going to be [judged]."

Perhaps it was with that in mind that Valentine chose to wait until an hour before game time to tell his pitcher what he wanted to happen and how it was to go down. There would be signs from dugout to catcher and from catcher to pitcher, indicating when Clemens was to get it. Estes was expected first to listen, then to execute.

When Clemens finally stepped to the plate, it was as a man who in nine-teen years as a major-leaguer had never been hit by a pitch (but who had hit 132 batters of his own during that time). Bringing a year and a half of anticipation to a head, Estes received Valentine's relayed sign, stared at the hitter, took aim . . . and missed. He missed by so much, in fact, that Clemens barely flinched, didn't so much as move his feet as the eighty-seven-miles-per-hour fastball sailed behind him without so much as scraping his uniform. Estes pounded his glove, which sent reporters into a tizzy of speculation. Was he angry that he hadn't thrown a strike? That he hadn't hit the batter? Was the ball placed where he wanted it so as to save face while by some measure fulfilling his duty as designated sniper? Or was it all just part of a spectacle with Estes at its center, a psych game for both the Yankees and the American public? "I didn't execute my pitch," Estes cryptically told the assembled media after the game, care-fully omitting whether he was talking about the strike zone or Clemens's thigh. "You can draw your own conclusions on that."

Some said that it was a clear message and an appropriate response. Clemens, however, was so unperturbed that he appeared to smirk before tipping his cap, literally, to the left-hander after the pitch. Perhaps Estes was shrewd in delivering his point without getting thrown out of the game; he went on to hit a home run off a Clemens splitter in the fifth and shut out the Yankees on five hits over seven innings en route to an 8–0 vic-tory. Still, he didn't hit the guy. Yankees catcher Jorge Posada admitted to laughing when he saw it. That's not exactly striking fear into the opposition. Plate umpire Wally Bell issued a warning after Estes's attempt, precluding any notion of a follow-up.

"As a pitcher, your preparation and your mechanics all prepare you to throw the ball to a spot, usually to the catcher's glove, and that's where your focus is," said Estes. "Well, it's tough to take your focus off that and try to hit a moving object, because you know he's going to try to move. . . . It's not as easy as it looks. You only get one shot. I've played ten years, so there have been a few situations where I felt that I had to hit somebody, and I've been able to do it because they had no clue it was going to happen. . . . In this particular situation, I think because of the pressure involved, I knew I couldn't miss Roger. Let's not mess around, let's get it over with."

Was it unfair to put a pitcher in the middle of a volatile situation that he had no part in creating? Estes was struggling in his first season in New York; he wouldn't even make it through the year, getting traded to Cincinnati a month later. On this day he needed a good showing much more than he needed to avenge one of his teammates. Unfair is a matter of opinion, just as it's a matter of opinion whether Estes's final solution to the problem ultimately proved sufficient.

After the game, Clemens had no comment. The Rocket had, in at least some sense of the term, gotten his, and for the first time in almost two years the feud seemed to be over. Clemens didn't start at Shea Stadium in 2003, and by '04 was a member of the Houston Astros. (He didn't make another start at Shea until April 2005; at that point, Piazza was the only Met remaining from the 2000 World Series club, and the date passed without incident.)

But there would be one more chapter of this retaliation story before it ran its course. In the 2004 All-Star Game in Houston, the National League's starting battery was Clemens and Piazza; despite sharing the home clubhouse, the pair was noteworthy for their avoidance of each other. Not only did a public reconciliation fail to materialize, but the two shared not so much as a handshake, and Clemens spent much of his pregame time on the field warming up in the bullpen with someone other than Piazza.

Then the fireworks started. Clemens lasted just one inning in his home ballpark, giving up six runs on a single, double, triple, and two home runs.

Through it all, Piazza never once visited the mound to calm him. Afterward, the theorists started in: Had Piazza attained a measure of revenge by tipping the hitters to what was coming? The chance to embarrass Clemens in front of his hometown fans had to be appealing. But Piazza's not talking. Neither are the American League hitters. The plate umpire, Ed Montague, swears that he didn't hear a thing. And as far as Roger Clemens is concerned, the less he knows the better. Maybe Estes's miss didn't matter as much as people thought.

If retaliation has been established alongside eight-dollar ballpark beer as one of baseball's necessary evils, there are differing viewpoints on the best way to go about it. After all, said longtime manager Mike Hargrove, "Throwing at somebody is serious. The ball hurts when it hits you. You don't just do it on a whim."

It's generally a two–step process involving whom to get and how to get him, and there's little unanimity of opinion about the first part. A small sampling:

- "Eye for an eye," said slugger Frank Thomas. "If your number-three guy gets hit, then you hit their number-three guy. That's what I was taught. If they hit your superstar, you don't hit their leadoff hitter."

- "You hit my shortstop, I'll hit your shortstop," said Doug Mientkiewicz.

- "If someone threw at Willie Mays and the catcher or pitcher was up the next inning, they were just as likely to get the message as anyone else," said Jim Davenport, who played alongside Mays on the Giants for thirteen years, talking about both the man who threw the pitch and the man who gave the signal for it from behind the plate. "But if Milwaukee threw at Mays, it was probably going to be Henry Aaron who got the special delivery."

- "Different pitchers, different managers, different teams have different theories," said infielder Craig Grebeck. "A lot of teams like to get it done the next inning. What they want to do is get two quick outs so it doesn't affect the game—that way they can hit a guy with two outs and no one on. What they don't want to do is hit the leadoff guy in a close ballgame and all of a sudden they lose the game because the team gets riled up."

- "A lot of teams in the big leagues would throw at the next hitter who came up," said Hall of Famer Billy Williams. "Some teams would wait until the guy that could hurt you, the guy who drove in a hundred or hit thirty home runs, came up and would wait to get him. Other teams would wait until the pitcher was up, and they'd get him. Different ball clubs followed different versions of the rules."

- "If Jon Lieber hits Craig Biggio, they're going to hit Jon Lieber because he's the one who did it," said Mark Grace. "I personally believe in that. If the pitcher does something [bad], he should take the lump."

No matter what language a team chooses to speak, it's pretty well guaranteed to be understood by the opposition. One game, in fact, demonstrated most of the above tenets and more in just two hours and twenty minutes. It started in the fourth inning of a game between the Yankees and Blue Jays on April 21, 2000, when Toronto first baseman Carlos Delgado, batting cleanup, hit a fourth-inning home run off Ramiro Mendoza. Mendoza responded by drilling the next batter, Brad Fullmer. (It may well have been unintentional; Mendoza's control was clearly slipping—he also hit Marty Cordova later in the frame. As is the way with baseball retaliation, however, intent often doesn't matter.)

In the bottom of the fourth, Toronto's Chris Carpenter hit Yankees first baseman Tino Martinez, who, like Fullmer, was batting fifth in the lineup.

In the top of the fifth, Delgado—Martinez's counterpart at first base—was hit by Yankees reliever Todd Erdos.

In the bottom of the sixth, Carpenter drilled Derek Jeter, New York's superstar answer to Delgado.

In the next day's papers, the principals all issued standard denials of intent, and since no pitcher threw a ball anywhere near a batter's head, everybody seemed content with the way things worked out. Which brings into play an even more important factor than whom to get or when: how.

Aside from a few rogue moundsmen, there's relative consensus on this subject. Even if a hitter understands that he's about to be drilled, is fully on board with baseball's frontier justice, and is prepared to do nothing more than proceed to first base without issue after the fact, everything changes should the baseball arrive at or above shoulder level.

The beanball is the ultimate weapon in a pitcher's arsenal, and some of its most fervent practitioners have been among the least-liked men in the game. Yankees right-hander Carl Mays is the only major-league pitcher to kill a batter with a pitch—Cleveland shortstop Ray Chapman, whom he hit in the head in 1920, before helmets were worn. It's never been suggested that the result was intentional, but Mays had already established his status as a head-hunter, a guy who in the previous three seasons led the American League in hit batsmen once and twice finished second. Among the better pitchers of his generation, Mays is now known primarily for his part in one of the game's darkest moments. It's a constant reminder of what's possible on the wrong side of an errant fastball.

"I have a rule," said outfielder Dave Henderson. "You can drill me all you want. But if you throw at my face, it gets personal. I kill you first, then your grandpa, your grandma—I just go on down the list. It gets personal. Batters should get mad. The guys who get hit on the elbow and all that, I have no sympathy for them. Big deal, you got hit. I got hit in the head twice in my career; the other stuff didn't count."

It certainly does for owners, though, who are unwilling to chance the loss of a multimillion-dollar investment just because a pitcher's angry about said investment taking too long to get into the batter's box. As such, modern umpires have taken to systematically warning not just the deliverers of head-high fastballs, but any pitcher who comes too far inside too often. This was reinforced by a 2001 memorandum from MLB that read "Umpires should be mindful that, given the skill level of most major league pitchers, a pitch that is thrown at the head of a hitter more likely than not was thrown there intentionally," and which issued umpires the authority to eject a pitcher for such action, even without a prior warning.

The benefits of this policy are undeniable, because it minimized what seemed in the 1990s to be near-daily incidents of hitters charging the mound, as well as frequent occurrences of overt intimidation. Still, many within the game feel that the repercussions from such enforcement are hardly worth the advantages. For one thing, a generation of hitters has acquired a sense of entitlement about its immunity from inside pitches. For another, pitchers are more frightened than ever to work inside, which when they do only increases the indignation of batters not used to seeing that type of pitch.

"I realize that if you hit somebody in the head they could get hurt," said Jack McDowell, no stranger to pitching inside during the course of his career. "But show me the last guy who was hit by a pitch in the face and was hurt." Well, there's Dickie Thon. "Okay. And before that?" Tony Conigliaro? Mickey Cochrane? "And that's in the history of the game. It doesn't happen. It wasn't a problem where guys were getting hurt and the thing is out of control and we need to deal with it."

And there's the rub. Thon, whose drilling in 1984 left an indelible mark on the game for the next decade, stands as a testament to how baseball has evolved to the point where players no longer learn how to avoid the inside pitch. When the league office more stringently started legislating umpires' warnings, it inadvertently began to insulate players from the dangers they faced at the wrong end of a fastball. Because pitchers no longer threw inside as often or with the same intent, hitters stopped being so mindful of the practice.

The pitch that hit Thon ran inside, but instead of turning away, as was second nature to players a generation earlier, Thon drew in his hands, backed up, and spun his torso toward the mound. The ball sailed into the twenty-five-year-old's forehead after glancing off the ear flap of his batting helmet, shattering bones around his eye and ending his season after just five games. The year prior, Thon's twenty homers and seventy-nine RBIs won him a National League Silver Slugger Award and spurred Astros general manager Al Rosen to proclaim him a "future Hall of Famer." And though Thon came back from his injury to play nine more seasons with five teams, he was rarely anything more than an average hitter thereafter.

Phil Garner was Houston's second baseman at the time of Thon's beaning, and saw up close the devastating result when a hitter fails to properly handle a high inside pitch. As manager of the Astros two decades later, Garner noticed scant change in the way players reacted to similar situations.

"Hitters have gotten accustomed to not seeing pitches thrown up and in, and now they don't know how to get out of the way," he said in 2006. "You see it all the time. My guys [on the Astros] are bad at it. They take pitches like this [clinches fists into chest and leans backward] and they get hit on the hands. If they'd gotten used to getting out of the way of the ball, they'd do this [rotates torso so his back is to the mound], and they'll protect themselves. But they don't do it in the minor leagues, they don't do it up here. You don't get pitches thrown up and in here, so players don't learn how to get out of the way."

Many people cite the body armor that started to gain widespread use in the late 1990s as a contributing factor, but the problem started long before that. Some hard-line old-timers such as Les Moss, who had a thirteen-year career as a catcher in the 1940s and '50s, felt that the introduction of the batting helmet was what first started softening ballplayers. "It was better when we didn't have helmets," he said in 1988. "Guys were going down all the time, and I'm not talking about beanballs at the head, but just around the hands or the chest. Without that helmet you had to be ready to get out of the way. . . . Nowadays hitters go up there with those helmets and defy the pitchers to throw inside. It's like they don't think the pitcher is allowed to pitch inside of the corner, and when he does they freeze. They're just not prepared to hit the deck."

Take Houston's Jeff Bagwell. The four-time All-Star had his hand broken by pitches in 1993, 1994, and 1995 (Garner was not managing the team then), but instead of altering his stance or improving his pitch-avoidance technique, he took to wearing a protective covering to prevent any other such injuries.

Another downside of the warning system—in which an umpire sensing trouble issues a cease-and-desist order to both dugouts, with immediate ejection for both player and manager should any violation occur—is that it negates the time-tested practice of checks and balances. Once a warning is issued, retaliation is essentially legislated out of the game. This increases the risk of lingering bad feelings without an appropriate way to channel them. Some managers even go so far as to instruct their pitchers to take the first shot in a bad-blood situation quickly, which basically gives their team a free pass before warnings are issued and the business of tit-for-tat is shut down for the night.

"It was a lot better [under the old rules]," said longtime Braves manager Bobby Cox. "It was over with and done. Guys knew to expect it, and it was done right. We still do it, but you've really got to pick your spots."

On September 9, 1991, Cincinnati reliever Norm Charlton ignored a Code staple. It wasn't that he intentionally hit Dodgers catcher Mike Scioscia (which he did), or that he acted on suspicions that Scioscia, while as a baserunner at second, had been relaying signs to Los Angeles hitters (which he had been). Where Charlton went wrong was admitting his deed in front of the media. "I threw at him," the next day's *Cincinnati Post* quoted the pitcher as saying. "I hit him on the arm, but I didn't mean to hit him on the arm. He'll be lucky if I don't rip his head off the next time."

The unwritten rule broken by Charlton mandates that players, especially pitchers, refrain from confessing to anything improper in any forum beyond closed clubhouse doors. Charlton's comments took things a step further, in that he threatened the possibility of throwing at Scioscia's head. The reaction from National League president Bill White was predictable: Charlton was fined heavily and suspended for a week. The hanging judge had little choice—the defendant had already confessed to his crime.

The reaction from the Los Angeles clubhouse set an unusual tone. The Dodgers tore into Charlton with a voraciousness rarely recorded in the press. Had the pitcher omitted the line about ripping off Scioscia's head, it's likely that nobody in Chavez Ravine would even have noticed his comments, let alone addressed them. Instead, the Dodgers verbally unloaded, with manager Tommy Lasorda calling for Charlton's suspension and saying, "What he said was a disgrace to baseball. Who does he think he is, saying something like that? He talks about taking a guy's head off? He could have killed Scioscia. He could have taken out his eye. Just what kind of person is this guy?"

Dodgers pitcher Kevin Gross called Charlton's remarks "stupid," "dumb," and "idiotic." Even Charlton's own manager, Lou Piniella, distanced himself, saying the left-hander made a "foolish statement." "If I were a pitcher and I hit somebody for whatever reason, I think I'd have about eight reasons why I *wasn't* throwing at somebody," he said. "Being truthful is one thing. Being smart is another."

In baseball, being smart counts for a lot. When a pitcher confesses to hitting a batter intentionally, even if he goes about it more tactfully than Charlton, it's an admission that, at best, strikes an odd note with the viewing public. People inside baseball understand appropriate doses of retaliation, but the practice represents a level of brutality that simply doesn't translate in most people's lives.

This is the reason that such admissions leave the commissioner's office little choice but to levy punishment. It's why Frank Robinson—one of the most thrown-at players of his generation and in possession of a deep understanding of baseball's retaliatory code—was so heavy-handed when he served as Major League Baseball's director of discipline, long after his playing career had ended. It's why Jose Mesa was suspended for four games in response to hitting Omar Vizquel after saying he would do precisely that, even though he wasn't even thrown out of the game in which it happened. It's why normally outspoken White Sox manager Ozzie Guillen responded with nothing more than a knowing smile when asked whether he'd ordered one of his pitchers to throw at his former outfielder Carlos Lee during a 2006 spring-training game. It's why, after Dock Ellis famously and intentionally hit three batters in a row to open that game in 1974, Pirates catcher Manny Sanguillen proclaimed to the media that he had never seen anybody so wild, despite having been briefed by Ellis about his plan prior to the game. It's why, when Mickey Lolich of the Tigers and Dave Boswell of the Twins exchanged beanballs in a 1969 contest, each said afterward that his ball had "slipped."

Perhaps the best way to deal with this type of situation is to take the Andy Pettitte approach. The Yankees star didn't just dislike throwing at people—he was known to abhor the practice. (While winning twenty-one games and throwing more than two hundred innings for New York in 2003, Pettitte hit just one batter.) But in 2001, Pettitte's teammate Bernie Williams was hit in the head by White Sox pitcher Kip Wells, and for a few scary moments it appeared that serious damage had been done. Even though most people on the New York bench didn't feel the beaning was intentional, and Williams was ultimately okay, there was little doubt that retaliation was in order. Because it was Pettitte on the mound, it was Pettitte who inherited the duty. In the bottom half of the inning, he placed the Code over personal ethics and plunked Sox slugger Maglio Ordonez on the hip, eliciting hardly a peep of protest.

But it was Pettitte's reaction after the game that was truly emblematic of the *omertà* ethic. When the left-hander was asked if his pitch to Ordonez was intentional, he didn't offer up even the standard platitude that the pitch got away from him. Instead, eyes affixed firmly on his shoes, he said quietly, "I don't want to talk about that." Much can be read into the statement, but it's hardly prosecutable. By not saying anything, Pettitte avoided the necessity of either telling the truth or lying.

Pitchers are not the only ones to whom this lesson applies. Just ask Mike Scioscia, who at the beginning of this section was hit intentionally by Norm Charlton. Did he deserve what he got? Was he really stealing signs from the Reds? "On the record?" asked Scioscia. "No."

Because winning trumps retaliation in every imaginable circumstance, situations often arise in which retribution is tabled despite its merit, simply because the score is close and allowing an extra baserunner is too risky. This can delay the process for the duration of a game, a series, or even a season—which doesn't mean that it won't eventually happen.

"You put it in your memory bank, and you will get the guy, sooner or later," said one pitcher who spent sixteen years as a major-leaguer. "The situation will arise, and it's not going to go away. You remember. You remember what happened, and that time will come."

That time came for the Royals in 1998, in a game against the Angels that was marred by five beanballs, two all-out brawls, and twelve ejections. The initial fight started when Phil Nevin, playing his first (and only) season with Anaheim, was hit in the neck by a pitch from Jim Pittsley—the second time he'd been hit in the span of two innings. Nevin's teammates charged the field on his behalf, which spurred a back-and-forth bout of retaliatory strikes that became headline fodder across the country. After the game, Nevin adopted an air of confusion, telling reporters, "I don't have any bad blood with those guys."

But that wasn't actually the case. As soon as the game ended, the Angels congregated in their clubhouse and tried to figure out what had just happened. It was only then, away from the media, that Nevin came clean to his teammates: "I was with Detroit last year and [the Royals] thought I took out [Mike] Sweeney at home plate too hard one time. So that was for last year, when I was on another team."

Nevin had, in fact, flattened Sweeney the previous August, scoring from second on a base hit by Melvin Nieves. The collision was hard enough for Nevin to come away with a bruised shoulder and for Sweeney to emerge with seriously scarred feelings. "When I was about 15 feet from home plate, I saw his eyes widen," Nevin said at the time. "I knew the ball was coming and I had no choice but to go in the way I did." A year later, the incident would come back to involve his new teammates in the most vicious game most of them would ever see, and until it was over they had no idea why.

That the Royals were willing to wait a full season for revenge hardly set precedent. Take the time in 1973 when A's outfielder Billy North let go of his bat as he swung at an offering from Kansas City rookie Doug Bird, sending it sailing toward shortstop Freddie Patek. North jogged out to retrieve his lumber, but stopped at the mound on the way to ask the startled pitcher, "Do you remember me?" Bird replied that he did not. "I remember you," said North. "From Quincy." Then, to the surprise of everybody, he started swinging. "We were all stunned," said A's second baseman Phil Garner, watching from the dugout. "Everybody was stunned."

"We were on the bench saying, 'What the hell's going on?' " said A's catcher Ray Fosse. "They started fighting, so we as teammates ran out, and so did the Royals. When it was all over, we all asked, 'What the hell just happened?' "

What the hell happened was that in 1970, when North was a twenty-two-year-old playing for Quincy, Illinois, of the Single-A Midwest League, he had the misfortune of coming to the plate against Bird, then twenty years old and playing for Waterloo. The two batters ahead of North had connected for home runs, and Bird responded by brushing North back. After the hitter had words with Waterloo's catcher, Bird's next pitch drilled him in the helmet. North missed three days.

That was the last time the two shared a baseball diamond as minor-leaguers. North got called up to Oakland the following season, and two years later, when he saw the transaction wire indicating that Bird had joined the Royals, he began counting down the days until Kansas City came to town. Bird was inserted as a reliever in the first game of the series, and North didn't waste a moment. "I told [A's starting pitcher] Ken Holtzman, 'Watch this,'" said North. "I'm going to do some damage to this guy." Although North was ejected, his assault wasn't enough to knock Bird from the game—he finished the inning by striking out North's replacement, Gonzalo Marquez—but it did earn the outfielder a three-game suspension, which he felt was well worth it.

Not all his teammates agreed. To many of them, North's problem was less that he punched an opponent for reasons unrelated to the A's than that he did it in a game in which his team led only 5–4. Unlike a pitcher issuing a retaliatory beanball, of course, North's actions didn't result in extra baserunners for the Royals. Still, said Fosse, "we're all thinking, 'We're trying to win a championship, and this guy's doing something to redress a problem from the minor leagues. He's taking a chance that one of his teammates could get hurt helping out.' We couldn't believe it." North's Code violation wasn't in the execution but in the timing.

"Sometimes you get it next week, next month, next year," said Dusty Baker, who played with North on the 1978 Dodgers. "Sometimes it has to wait for an old-timers' game." Baker wasn't just talking—Bob Gibson once did that very thing. Gibson felt entitled, after giving up a grand slam to Pete LaCock in 1975, to knock the hitter down. The only problem was that Gibson, two months shy of his fortieth birthday, faced exactly one more batter, left the game . . . and retired. So, fifteen years later, the Hall of Famer did what he had been unable to do as an active player: When he faced LaCock in an old-timers' game, he hit him in the back with a pitch. ("Bob Feller was throwing when I came up to the plate," said LaCock. "All of a sudden Gibson comes running out of the dugout. He sends Feller back to the bench and starts warming up and I think, he's not really going to hit me. Sure enough, first pitch—whammo.")

It doesn't take an angry old man to play the waiting game, however. In 1942, a starstruck fifteen-year-old from Norristown, Pennsylvania, had his autograph request rebuffed by New York Giants outfielder Buster Maynard after a game at Shibe Park. He was crushed, and he didn't forget. The kid was Tommy Lasorda, who seven years later was himself a promising pitcher in the Single-A South Atlantic League, playing for Brooklyn's minor-league affiliate in Greenville, North Carolina. One day he found himself facing a fading former big-leaguer who was trying merely to hold his job with the Augusta Yankees: Buster Maynard.

Lasorda didn't hesitate. His first pitch sailed well inside, knocking Maynard off his feet. His second pitch did the same. When Maynard came up later in the game, the left-hander buzzed him again. After the game, Lasorda found their earlier roles reversed; this time it was Maynard looking for something from Lasorda—an explanation. "Why me?" he asked. "You don't even know me."

"Know you!" shouted Lasorda. "When I was a kid in the eighth grade, you used to play for the New York Giants. I used to save up for a whole year to get enough money to go to a game. When I got there, I asked you for your autograph and you just pushed me aside and kept walking. I wish I had hit you, you busher!"

It's as sweet a tale of retaliation as can be told. Most such strikes, however, especially the sort that inspire willingness to wait for the chance to deliver them, don't have childhood sensitivity at their core. Mostly it's just irritated guys looking for outlets for their rage—and nobody was better at waiting than Stan Williams.

At six-foot-five and 230 pounds, Williams—who pitched for the Dodgers alongside Don Drysdale and Sandy Koufax—was fearsome even without his flashes of anger, which flared at the slightest indiscretion against him. What made him truly terrifying to opposing hitters, however, was the List. Kept by Williams in a small notebook that he carried with him everywhere, the List consisted of the names of everyone who had ever offended his baseball sensibilities. Guys who hit him hard were noted next to those who showed him up. By keeping a log, the pitcher ensured that game situations never prevented him from meting out justice, and that he'd never forget a name when the time was finally right to strike. Being inscribed as a member of the List effectively turned a hitter into a dental patient—due for a drilling.

As Williams neared the end of his career, though, his character mellowed, and he slowly stopped adding names to his notebook, choosing instead to concentrate on crossing them off, one fastball at a time. By the time he pitched in his final big-league game in 1973, the only name left was that of Barry Latman, a pitcher for the Indians who had been added a dozen years earlier, in 1961, and who had himself left the majors in '72. The initial incident arose during a spring exhibition game in Las Vegas between the Dodgers and Cleveland, when Williams, bleary from a long night in Sin City, inadvertently bounced a pitch off the helmet of Indians third baseman Bubba Phillips. It was thrown so softly, said the pitcher, that "I wouldn't have hurt him if I'd hit him in the neck." Still, Phillips's pitcher stood up for him, and the next time Williams stepped to the plate, he was drilled in the ribs. The man who threw the pitch: Barry Latman.

"Stan never moved," said Dodgers first baseman Ron Fairly. "He didn't even try to get out of the way. The ball hit him and he stood there for about three or four seconds." Before finally heading toward first base, Williams turned to the mound and said ominously, "Hey, Barry, now it's my turn."

Dodgers manager Walter Alston, wanting to avoid needless escalation during a practice game, promptly pulled Williams. Denied his chance at immediate retaliation, Williams quickly added Latman's name to the List. But the two played in different leagues, so while Williams methodically cleared out everyone else in his notebook, he was unable to remove Latman.

Williams closed his career with the minor-league Seattle Angels, where he hoped to play his way back to the big leagues (a goal that never panned out). When he reported to Seattle he found, sitting across the locker room, another guy playing out his own string—Barry Latman. As soon as the big pitcher realized who he was teaming with, he laughed out loud. The two spent time sharing war stories, having become the old men in a clubhouse full of kids. They quickly developed a tight bond.

One day not long thereafter, Williams was assigned to pitch batting practice and didn't offer a moment's hesitation when his old foe stepped in against him, burying a fastball into Latman's rib cage. "That's for Vegas!" Williams yelled toward the plate. "If you don't like it, come on out—otherwise the List is done." Latman stayed put. Mission finally accomplished twelve years after the fact, Williams threw his notebook away.

12

The Wars

Ideally, retaliation is a straightforward affair: One team violates a statute of the unwritten rules, its opponent responds, the score is even, and each team moves on. As might be expected when tempers flare, however, reality is often quite different. Hotheaded pitchers add volatility to the mix, and cease-fire rules normally enacted after each team has had its shot are thrown out the window. In these cases, retaliation met in kind simply generates new anger and another round of inside fastballs. Hostilities are renewed—and often amplified.

There's no better example of this than the game between the Atlanta Braves and San Diego Padres on August 12, 1984, at Atlanta's Fulton County Stadium, which San Diego infielder Kurt Bevacqua later called "the Desert Storm of baseball fights." Total damage: six brushback pitches, three hit batters, four bench-clearing incidents, two full-on brawls that nearly spiraled out of control when fans rushed the field, nineteen ejections, five arrests, and a nearly unprecedented clearing of the benches by the umpires.

"It took baseball down 50 years," said umpiring crew chief John McSherry, who came close to awarding the game to San Diego via forfeit in the ninth inning. "It was the worst thing I have ever seen in my life. It was pathetic, absolutely pathetic."

It all started before the game even began, said Padres pitcher Ed Whitson, when Atlanta starter Pascual Perez looked toward San Diego's leadoff hitter, Alan Wiggins, standing in the on-deck circle, and promised to hit him with his first pitch. "Everybody on our bench heard it," said Whitson. Sure enough, Perez sent his initial offering into the small of Wiggins's back, landing the first blow in what would be a long afternoon of retaliatory strikes, and setting San Diego's dugout abuzz. Said Whitson: "By the time [manager] Dick Williams looked around at me, just as he started to speak, I said, 'Don't worry about it—we'll get him.'"

To that point in their fifteen-year history the Padres had lost an average of ninety-four games a season, had never finished higher than fourth in their six-team division, and ended up in last place more often than not. When San Diego sat atop the NL West with roughly six weeks to go in '84, many members of its closest competitor—Perez's Braves, which trailed by nine and a half games going into that mid-August meeting—felt that a stand was needed. The best way to do that, they decided, was to drain the upstart Padres of whatever confidence they may have built.

"They were trying to intimidate us, plain and simple," said Padres infielder Tim Flannery. "It was the first time we were in a situation to win anything in San Diego, and they probably figured they could get an edge. But what it did was rally our team together. We lost the game, but at the end of the day we came together as a ball club."

Perez's salvo against Wiggins sent Padres manager Dick Williams into attack mode. Whitson's proclamation of forthcoming justice notwithstanding, Williams wanted to hit back, and hit back hard. "He came from the stock of the old school," said Braves manager Joe Torre. "He was going to make sure that he got his pound of flesh." Williams's rationale was simple: Should his team withstand Atlanta's scare tactics, there was little to keep it from coasting to a division championship. "We can't be intimidated," the Padres skipper later proclaimed, and he set about using Perez to prove it.

As promised, Whitson quickly put a target on Perez. When Atlanta's pitcher came to the plate in the second inning, Braves shortstop Rafael Ramirez was on first with one out. Whitson threw his first pitch behind the hitter, with unmistakable intent that quickly emptied the benches. Though no punches were thrown, Whitson drew a warning from plate umpire Steve Rippley. His next pitch skipped away from Padres catcher Terry Kennedy, allowing Ramirez to advance to second. With a rally in the works and the lineup about to turn over, Whitson was compelled to alter his strategy; he struck the pitcher out and escaped the inning unscathed.

Perez next came to the plate in the fourth, whereupon Whitson again went after him. His first pitch ran inside, belt-high to the right-hander, and the benches again emptied into a parade of punchless shoving. That was twice Whitson missed his mark. His next offering came in higher and farther inside, nearly hitting Perez in the shoulder. Although it failed to connect, it was enough to earn ejections for both Whitson and Williams.

The manager was prepared for this eventuality, and had already prepped his line of succession. "Until Pascual Perez got hit, it wasn't going be finished," said Flannery. "Dick said to [coach] Ozzie Virgil, 'When I get thrown out, you're going to be the manager, and, [relief pitcher] Greg Booker, you're going to hit Perez. And if you don't get it done, Jack Krol, you'll be the manager because those two will have gotten thrown out, and, Greg Harris, you're going to be the pitcher."

Booker came in as planned but ended up walking Perez, then gave up two runs over the next two innings (one charged to Whitson). In Perez's next at-bat, leading off the sixth, Booker aimed two more pitches at him, both of which were deftly avoided. "He kept running from us—we couldn't knock him down," said Whitson. "Everybody was trying to throw the ugly-finder at him, and we still couldn't find him."

At this point, Booker and Virgil were tossed, and reliever Harris entered the game. But Harris, who had been acquired from the Montreal Expos less than a month earlier, inexplicably didn't stick to the game plan, throwing a series of breaking balls to Perez, not at him, and getting him to ground out. If watching Perez dance away from pitches through the first five innings was enough to drive the Padres batty, seeing one of their own pitchers refuse to execute what many on the club felt was his primary responsibility was enough to send them into full-fledged combat mode, devoid of logic or reason. Backup infielder Kurt Bevacqua started to berate his own pitcher at top volume from the dugout. Third baseman Graig Nettles approached the mound to ask exactly what it was Harris thought he was doing.

"It got nutty," said Flannery. "I volunteered to pinch-hit because nobody else was getting [Perez]. I told [Williams], 'If I ground out or fly out, I'll blindside him and hook him on the mound.' We became crazy. We became nuts."

Fortunately for Atlanta, Perez was pitching a great game, which ultimately earned him his eleventh win against only four losses. Unfortunately for Perez, he was pitching a great game, which meant that another at-bat was in the offing. Atlanta held a 5–1 lead in the eighth inning when the right-hander next came to the plate, this time to face San Diego's fourth pitcher of the day, Craig Lefferts.

Finally, mercifully, Lefferts managed to hit him with a fastball—which served to draw the Braves into San Diego's crazed mind-set. Players streamed from both dugouts, and the first real fight of the afternoon broke out on the field, erupting in clusters across the diamond. Atlanta's Gerald Perry charged Lefferts and landed several blows. Padres outfielder Champ Summers tried to hunt down Perez, who was lying low in the Braves dugout. The highlight came when Braves third baseman Bob Horner, watching the game with the broadcast crew while on the disabled list, sensed trouble, predicted the fracas on the air, raced to the clubhouse to pull on his uniform, and rushed out—cast on his arm—to intercept Summers near the top of the dugout steps. (He was later suspended for fighting while on the DL.) "It was the wildest thing I had ever seen . . . ," Horner said. "It seemed like it never stopped. It was like a nine-inning brawl." When this round ended, Lefferts and Krol, San Diego's replacement replacement manager, were tossed, as were Perry and Braves relievers Rick Mahler and Steve Bedrosian.

It wasn't finished. When the Padres came to bat in the ninth, Torre went so far as to specifically instruct his new pitcher, Donnie Moore—on the mound in relief of Perez—to avoid further escalation. "I said, 'Let's not continue this bullshit, let's just win this game,' " said Torre. "Then I looked him in the eye and I said to myself, 'I have no chance. I'm talking to a deaf man here.' I walked back to the dugout and he hit Graig Nettles. You can talk until you're blue in the face, but it's guys defending each other. That's what it's about."

As soon as Moore's fastball touched Nettles's ribs, it was as if the previous fight had never ended. Nettles charged the mound. Reliever Goose Gossage sprinted in from the bullpen and tried to get to Moore, but ended up fighting with Atlanta's Bob Watson (who, incidentally, later served as

Major League Baseball's vice president in charge of discipline). Five fans ran onto the field to join the fray, one of whom was tackled near third base by Atlanta players Chris Chambliss and Jerry Royster. Long-since ejected Gerald Perry, accompanied by the similarly tossed Bedrosian and Mahler, raced from the clubhouse to participate.

During the fight, Flannery, one of the smallest men on the field, was caught in a bear hug by Braves coach Bob Gibson, and pleaded desperately for his release so he could go after Gerald Perry, with whom he had already fought twice that afternoon. When Gibson finally complied, Perry quickly split Flannery's lip open. As a coda to the entire event, when things finally appeared to be settling down and the Padres were returning to their dugout, a fan hit Bevacqua in the head with a plastic cup of beer, spurring the player to jump atop the dugout and go after him.

"The donnybrook . . . was the best, most intense baseball fight I've ever seen or been involved with," wrote Gossage in his autobiography, *The Goose Is Loose.* "I realize it was the Sabbath, but guys were taking the Lord's name in vain. Fists flew and skulls rattled. Unlike most baseball fights, which are more like hugging contests than real fisticuffs, guys on both teams got pasted. Ed Whitson came running out from the clubhouse completely deranged. He and Kurt Bevacqua went into the stands and duked it out with some hecklers. Stadium officials had to send out for the riot squad to settle things down."

"Whitson was icing his elbow in the clubhouse without a shirt on, watching it on TV," said Flannery. "Later, Dick [Williams] says, 'The next thing I see, Whitson's on TV, no shirt, he's got a bat and screaming at the season-ticket holders, and Bevacqua was in the stands beating on them."

When round two was over, new ejections included Gossage and Bobby Brown from the Padres, and Atlanta's Moore, Watson, and Torre. To stem further damage, McSherry cleared the benches, sending all nonparticipating players into their respective clubhouses to await the game's final outs. ("They locked us in there with big wooden beams before they would finish the game," said Flannery.)

After Atlanta finally closed out the 5–3 victory, a disgusted Torre took the unusual baseball tack of comparing Dick Williams to Hitler, then called him an idiot—"with a capital 'I' and small 'w.' " Padres catcher

Terry Kennedy was a bit more clear-headed. "It would've been a lot simpler," he said, "if we'd hit Perez his first time up."

The sustained intensity of that Padres-Braves game was too much to be contained in just nine innings, spilling outside the field of play and all the way to the clubhouses. An equal concentration of malevolence featured prominently in a feud between the Red Sox and Devil Rays, but instead of a single game it was maintained over the better part of a decade. It seemed that nearly every time Boston and Tampa Bay got together between 2000 and 2008 they added another chapter to their collective book of spite.

It started in late August 2000, when Boston's Pedro Martinez hit Gerald Williams on the hand with his fourth pitch of the game. Martinez might have already been a bit testy, considering that, despite a 14-4 record and 1.77 ERA going into the contest, he was winless in his last three starts (two losses and a no-decision) against the moribund Devil Rays, dating back to 1999. Williams didn't take kindly to the pitcher's gesture and charged the mound, shoving the much smaller Martinez to the ground and landing a glancing blow to his face. There was no way to know it at the time, but this set the tone for the next eight years. Benches emptied into the middle of the field, the game was delayed for twelve minutes, and Williams was ejected. In the process, Boston's Brian Daubach dived into the scrum, where Tampa players accused him of taking cheap shots. After reviewing a tape of the fight, the commissioner's office ruled that Daubach had acted within the boundaries of acceptable behavior, but this decision came far too late to assist the first baseman. By the time the game ended, Daubach had been thrown at by a succession of Devil Rays pitchers, starting with Dave Eiland, who wanted to hit him so badly that, with two on and nobody out in the third inning, he sent his first pitch spinning toward Daubach's head. The hitter managed to avoid that one, but couldn't get out of the way of Eiland's next pitch, which drilled him in the body. After Carl Everett's two-run double scored the lead runners and sent Daubach to third, Eiland hit Nomar Garciaparra and was tossed from the game.

In the seventh inning, Eiland's replacement, Cory Lidle, was himself ejected after throwing a pitch behind Daubach. ("The only problem," said Tampa Bay manager Larry Rothschild, "was that our pitchers kept missing the guy.") Lidle's replacement, Tony Fiore, lasted all of two pitches before finishing the job, drilling Daubach with his third offering and spurring another confrontation between the teams in the middle of the field before being ejected himself. If Williams's first-inning mound charge set the tone for the game, Martinez followed it up with both actions (he took a no-hitter into the ninth inning) and words (saying ominously, "There will be another day"). Afterward, he sneaked out a rear exit to avoid the phalanx of Devil Rays waiting for him by the clubhouse's main door.

The day of Martinez's prediction wasn't far off. A quick rundown of events:

- September 29, 2000: Tampa Bay eliminates the Red Sox from the AL East race with an 8–6 victory. From the mound, Rays closer Roberto Hernandez waves a sarcastic bye-bye to the Tropicana Field visitors' dugout. The following day, when Hernandez gives up the game-winning homer in the ninth, Martinez stands on the top step of the Boston dugout and does some waving of his own.

- 2001: Over the course of the season, Devil Rays pitchers hit eleven Boston batters; Red Sox pitchers tag nine Tampa hitters.

- May 5, 2002: Devil Rays pitcher Ryan Rupe hits both Garciaparra and Shea Hillenbrand in the first inning of a game, a day after each was instrumental in helping Boston overcome a 5–2, ninth-inning deficit to beat Tampa in a 7–5 victory. (The key blow was Hillenbrand's game-winning, pinch-hit grand slam.) Rumors fly of stolen signs, which both Garciaparra and Hillenbrand deny. Boston's Trot Nixon responds by letting go of his bat on a second-inning swing, sending it flying toward the mound. (In classic fashion, he later denies intent.) Red Sox pitcher Frank Castillo responds further by hitting Tampa's Randy Winn. Both Castillo and Nixon are later suspended.

- July 18, 2002: The day after Manny Ramirez scorches the Devil Rays with a home run and a double, he's hit in the second inning by Tampa starter Tanyon Sturtze. Boston's Frank Castillo responds by hitting second baseman Brent Abernathy in the third, and reliever Tim Wakefield hits him again in the fifth. In the ninth inning, Devil Rays reliever Esteban Yan just misses Ramirez's head as the slugger ducks, and the ball glances off his shoulder. "You can't act like what happened never happened," says Derek Lowe in the *Boston Herald*. He also says, "Every year, why is it always this team?"

- September 9, 2002: Lowe keeps wondering after being ejected for hitting Devil Rays shortstop Felix Escalona with a pitch. The following night, Tampa Bay reliever Lee Gardner, pitching in the eighth inning of an 11–1 Boston runaway, is ejected for hitting second baseman Lou Merloni.

- September 27, 2004: Red Sox starter Bronson Arroyo keeps relations testy by hitting both Aubrey Huff and Tino Martinez in the third inning. Devil Rays pitcher Scott Kazmir retaliates by hitting Manny Ramirez and Kevin Millar in consecutive at-bats an inning later, emptying the benches. Kazmir is ejected.

- April 22–24, 2005: Five batters are hit in the first two games of a three-game series between the teams. In the sixth inning of the third game, Boston's Arroyo hits Huff—7-for-10 lifetime against him— with a pitch for the second time in as many seasons. An inning later, Devil Rays reliever Lance Carter throws a pitch behind Manny Ramirez's head, eliciting warnings for both benches. One pitch later, Ramirez belts a home run. Carter then throws at the head of the next hitter, David Ortiz, who has to be restrained by catcher Toby Hall. Both dugouts empty, and Carter, Trot Nixon, Tampa Bay manager Lou Piniella, and pitcher Dewon Brazelton are ejected. In the seventh, Arroyo hits leadoff batter Chris Singleton on the thigh with his second pitch, earning his own ejection. In a radio interview on WEEI after the game, Boston pitcher Curt Schilling blames Piniella: "Players on that team are saying, 'This is why we lose a hundred games a year, because this idiot makes us do stuff like this.' " A day later, also on the radio, Piniella says, "I have forgot more baseball than this guy knows."

- March 27, 2006: After tagging out Tampa's Joey Gathright at the plate during a spring-training game, Boston reliever Julian Tavarez stands on the baserunner's arm, he says, so that Gathright couldn't "throw a punch at me right away." Tavarez then hits Gathright in the jaw while the outfielder is down on one knee, and sparks a benches-clearing dustup. Gathright later says that Tavarez "hits like a woman." Devil Rays outfielder Carl Crawford subsequently challenges the pitcher to a post-game fight in the parking lot.

- June 5, 2008: The highlight of five hit batters on the night is Boston outfielder Coco Crisp's charge of the mound after being drilled by right-hander James Shields of the Rays, who by this time have dropped the "Devil" from their name if not their attitude. Shields is responding to Crisp's hard slide into second baseman Akinori Iwa-mura the previous night, which was itself a response to Tampa Bay shortstop Jason Bartlett using his leg to block Crisp's headfirst slide into second. Shields misses with a roundhouse right, and Crisp—with seventeen knockouts to his credit in seventeen amateur boxing matches as a youth—is able to land one shot of his own before being overwhelmed by a scrum of Rays, primary among them Crawford and Johnny Gomes, who shower blows upon him. (After the game, Crisp echoes Tavarez, saying the Rays were like "little girls, trying to scratch out my eyes." Shields had already hit Dustin Pedroia in the first inning, and Boston's Jon Lester responds by hitting Crawford, then Iwamura. Tampa Bay reliever Al Reyes closes the festivities by drilling Kevin Youkilis in Boston's final at-bat.

- October 10, 2008: In Game 1 of the ALCS, Rays reliever Grant Balfour sends a fastball toward the face of Boston outfielder J. D. Drew, which catches the slugger's shoulder as he spins to avoid it. Little more than barking ensues, and the seven-game series is so tight that even four more hit batters (two from each team) over the remaining games do little to raise the tension.

By the time Tavarez hit Gathright like a woman—let alone by the time the Rays tried to scratch out Crisp's eyes—the principals from the original skirmish in 2000 were long gone. That it didn't seem to matter was what gave legs to this rivalry. Boston's competition with the Yankees is driven primarily by fan involvement; the team's animosity toward Tampa

Bay, however, begins with the players themselves. Some of this ill will is firsthand, but there's no denying the tension that permeates each clubhouse when it comes to the other team, developed over years and lingering regardless of who's been involved or for how long. "With the way we hate them and the way they hate us," said Tampa Bay's Cliff Floyd, "this could be a great rivalry for a long time."

13

Hitters

Albert Belle is remembered for a lot of things: eight thirty-homer seasons; five All-Star games; his perpetually dour attitude; a habit of throwing baseballs at fans and photographers; his unprovoked verbal assault on Hannah Storm during the 1995 World Series; chasing egg-throwing teenagers in his pickup truck one Halloween.

The single event for which he's best remembered, however, is probably running over Fernando Vina as a member of the Cleveland Indians. The story was discussed for weeks afterward, and each player bore the details like an albatross for the rest of his career: In the eighth inning of a game against the Brewers in 1996, Belle—at six-foot-two and 210 pounds, towering above the five-foot-nine Vina—ran into and through the Milwaukee second baseman in an effort to break up a double play. With a well-placed forearm, he also broke up Vina's nose.

Belle took significant heat for his aggression, largely because it was so easy to believe the act to be another link in a chain of outrageous behavior—but that wasn't the case. Quite to the contrary, the outfielder had been chewed out by coaches earlier in that very game for being too passive, and was more or less under orders to wreak some havoc.

The scolding had come after the third inning, when Belle had been at first base, and Carlos Baerga on third. With one out, slugger Jim Thome topped a ball toward second; anything short of a double play would have allowed a run to score. Belle, though, slowed down and allowed Vina to make an easy tag, then throw to first for the inning-ending twin killing, which kept the run off the board. As Belle waited near second for delivery of his outfielder's glove, Cleveland coach Dave Nelson ran out to meet him, unable to wait through the end of the inning to deliver a piece of his mind. "Albert, dammit, what have I taught you?" he snapped at the young superstar. "You don't just stop and let the guy tag you—you either slide into him, you stop and back up . . . and if you can't avoid the tag you *run over him*! You know better than that!"

Nelson's words were ringing in Belle's ears when, five innings later, he again found himself on first base. Belle actually had double motivation to cut loose, having just been hit by Milwaukee reliever Marshall Boze. So when another ball was hit to Vina, nearly identical to the one in the third inning, Belle took off with intent. Vina naïvely positioned himself squarely in the base path to apply a gentle tag, just as he had done earlier in the game, but this time he was flattened. The play was, contrary to the subsequent charge of unmitigated brutality, for the most part, clean. "It was a violent hit," said Nelson, "but it was legal."

"The first time I could have crushed him," said Belle. "The second time he was open game. It was hard, clean baseball. You should be ready to get knocked down. It's an easy play to throw to the shortstop, and then I'll slide hard, okay?" There wasn't much excuse for the forearm to the nose, but even that fell within the boundaries of acceptable limits. First-base umpire Joe Brinkman went so far as to label the move a matter of "professional courtesy." It was enough, of course, for Milwaukee reliever Terry Burrows to drill Belle in his next at-bat, an inning later.

The situation certainly wasn't without precedent. Pitchers may control the vast majority of baseball's retaliatory strikes, but hitters aren't exactly powerless in that capacity; seeking revenge on infielders is their most common means for voicing displeasure. "You come in a little high with a forearm," said Dave Henderson, addressing not Belle's situation but retribution in general. "Those are what the unwritten rules say. The middle infielders should be very wary if a guy gets drilled and he's on first base."

"I've gotten on first base when I've been hit by a pitch and told the first baseman, 'If there's a ground ball hit I'm going to fuck up one of your middle infielders, and [pointing to the mound] you can tell him that it was his fault,' " said Bob Brenly. "That's a way you can get them to police themselves. A pitcher drills somebody just because he feels like it, and if one of the middle infielders gets flipped out there he's going to tell the pitcher to knock it off. Ultimately, that's all we want anyway—just play the game the right way."

Usually, such plays take the shape of clean slides augmented by an extra degree of vigor. Some, however, are so clearly intended to injure that the opposing team has no choice but to answer. Take White Sox slugger George Bell, who in 1992 responded to being hit by Brewers starter Chris Bosio by veering well out of the baseline to take out shortstop Pat Listach on a double-play grounder, roughly grabbing the infielder as he slid by— a play so blatant that umpire Darryl Cousins called the hitter, Robin Ventura, out at first for Bell's interference.

Both Bell and Belle earned skepticism from both fans and the national media for the violent extent of their plays, especially because the infielders at the business ends of the slides were not the men who touched off the bad blood. When a base runner has a chance to take out the offending player directly, things become much easier to reconcile. In 1952, for example, Cleveland's Al Rosen set his sights on rookie Red Sox shortstop Jimmy Piersall, who had collided with Indians second baseman Bobby Avila on a double play, barrel-rolling him backward several feet. Rosen got the opportunity to avenge his teammate when he was on first base against Boston and a ball was hit sharply up the middle. Forfeiting any pretense of sliding, Rosen crashed into Piersall with as much force as he could muster, sending both players flying toward the outfield grass. When Rosen looked over at his victim, however, he realized that Piersall hadn't been covering the base at all; he had unwittingly tackled Boston's second baseman, Ted Lepcio.

"Lepcio was such a great guy," said Rosen with regret, "and I was so apologetic." To make matters worse, Piersall became a full-time outfielder the following season, and Rosen's revenge never did materialize.

Belle's forearm shiver might have earned attention for its theatrics, but as far as infielders are concerned, the most blood-boiling action a runner can take is to go into a base feetfirst with spikes high. It's a time-tested method for inflicting pain, and has become less tolerated with every passing generation. (Ty Cobb had such a passion for the tactic that he not only would file his spikes down to razor sharpness, but would do so in the dugout before games so that his opponents could see exactly what he had planned for them. "I have dozens of spike scars, from my ankles to my thighs . . . ," wrote Cobb in his 1925 autobiography, *Memoirs of Twenty Years in Baseball*. "I also left a few marks of my own around the league. In staking my claim, people were bound to get hurt.")

Cobb represented the pinnacle of baseball's spikers; few of the tactic's less accomplished practitioners could come close to him in terms of style points. Take Cincinnati infielder Bill Werber, who was once so irate with Dodgers manager (and part-time shortstop) Leo Durocher for leaving starting pitcher Whitlow Wyatt in a game just to knock down Reds hitters that he tried to plant his spikes into Durocher's midsection in an ensuing play at second base. "The next thing I know," he said, "all the Reds players were gathered around me, laughing. I asked, 'What happened?' I thought maybe Durocher had hit me in the head with the ball. [Cincinnati manager] Bill McKechnie said, 'Well, you tried to kick him in the belly and your head came down before your feet did.' I had knocked myself out at second base. I hit my head on the ground and never touched Durocher. He got the ball from [second baseman Pete] Coscarart, stepped on the base and was gone before I got there."

Most spiking attempts were more successful, and the guys who carried them out gained notoriety. Before the practice was largely shunned into disuse through the 1970s and into the '80s, one of the game's final prominent slashers was Dodgers shortstop Maury Wills, whose victims, he wrote in a bylined article for Scripps Howard News Service in 2001, "had it coming." The peak of Wills's practice came during a game in 1964, in which Braves first baseman Joe Torre found that by dropping his knee in front of the bag he could effectively block Wills's headfirst returns on pickoff throws. "It wasn't anything illegal," said Torre, who as his team's primary catcher spent the bulk of his playing time executing similar moves in front of the plate. "I had the ball. If you block the plate or a base and you don't have the ball it's illegal. I *had* the ball."

Wills was dubious, but the umpire allowed it, so he decided to attack the problem in a different way. "I remembered in Cobb's book, sharpening his spikes," said the shortstop. "I got off the team bus after the game, about two blocks from the hotel, went to a hardware store and got me a file. I sat on the edge of my bed filing my spikes the way Ty Cobb must have been doing it." When Wills was finished, his spikes were glinting so brilliantly that he had to coat them with shoe polish to avoid drawing too much attention. Cautious, he wore a different pair to start the next day's game, but after he reached first on a sixth-inning single, Torre again dropped his knee—and again Wills was picked off. That was all he needed; Wills went straight to the clubhouse to get his honed spikes, which were so sharp they stuck to the clubhouse floor with every step he took. In the eighth inning, Wills again bunted for a single, and again took his lead. When the pitcher, Phil Niekro, threw to first, Wills went back feetfirst. As a measure of warning, he leaped over Torre's planted leg rather than into it, and his spikes ripped through the canvas of the base, sinking into the sole of the shoe. "I had to hold the bag down while I pulled the spikes out," Wills said. "Stuffing came out of the bag. Torre looked at me, he looked at the bag and he got the message."

At that point it became a guessing game. Wills didn't want to keep going back feetfirst, which necessitated a shorter lead, but neither did he want Torre to take advantage when he dived. So he mixed it up, diving on some pickoff attempts, leading with his feet on others. As Niekro kept throwing over—six times, then seven, then eight—all Torre had to do was guess what was coming and get his leg out of the way if he saw the bottom of Wills's shoe.

It worked well—until he guessed wrong. Unable to move quickly enough, Torre could only watch as Wills's spikes sank deep into the flesh of his leg. In Wills's 1992 autobiography, the shortstop likened the process of extracting them to pulling "the cork out of the bottle and blood starts running all over the place."

"I was cut pretty good," said Torre, who received treatment in the dugout. "I just wanted to make sure they taped me up so I wouldn't give [the Dodgers] the satisfaction of my leaving the game. But I did go to the hospital to get stitched up afterward."

As Torre was tended to, Wills figured that he was due for a pummeling. Torre was three inches taller and nearly forty-five pounds heavier, and had every reason to take a swing. Looking around, the startled baserunner realized that his closest line of defense was Los Angeles first-base coach Greg Mulleavy, who was nearly sixty years old and even smaller than

Wills. The shortstop then turned toward the Dodgers dugout, on the opposite side of the field, in hopes that his teammates were prepared to rush out and help him. Instead, he said, they were "all sitting back on the bench with their legs crossed, having a cigarette, looking up in the stands. La-de-da-de-da."

After being patched up, Torre trotted somberly toward first. Instead of punching Wills, however, he merely patted him on the leg in acknowledgment for winning the game of strategy. Why wasn't he madder? "Well," said Torre, years later, "I asked for it." As if that alone wasn't enough to prove his sincerity, that winter Torre went so far as to take in Wills's banjo-playing act at a Las Vegas nightclub. When Wills heard who was in the audience, he stopped his set and told the story to the crowd. Torre didn't mind a bit.

As satisfying as taking out a middle infielder might be, it's usually a piece of the pitcher that players truly want. Unless a hitter is willing to charge the mound, however, his options are limited when it comes to direct response. One tactic at his disposal involves dropping a drag bunt down the first-base line, which either draws the pitcher within reach as he fields the ball, or gets him to cover the bag should the first baseman take the play. Either way, he's directly in the line of fire for whatever it is the aggrieved hitter chooses to dish out.

One of the best practitioners of this tactic was Jackie Robinson, who, because few Dodgers pitchers were willing to defend him via retaliatory knockdowns in the early part of his career, made a habit of taking things into his own hands. When Robinson, one of the most feared bunters in the league, added the threat of direct impact to the equation, pitchers took notice. Among his favorite targets was New York Giants hurler Sal Maglie, a longtime antagonist of the Dodgers.

In Maglie's biography, *The Sal Maglie Story,* author Milton Shapiro describes Robinson pushing a bunt down the first-base line, then ramming the pitcher even after the ball went foul and Maglie eased up. Other accounts have Robinson warning Maglie after a knockdown pitch that there would be hell to pay, then beating out a bunt single because the pitcher opted against leaving the mound to field the ball. In 1951, Robinson talked to *Sport* magazine about this sort of play, admitting that he "did it deliberately, to force the league to step in and stop this beanballing before somebody gets hurt."

The best-known and most vicious of Robinson's bunts against Maglie occurred in April 1955. In response to a series of the pitcher's knockdowns aimed at several Brooklyn players, Robinson bunted to first baseman Whitey Lockman with the intent of bowling over the pitcher when he went to cover the base. At age thirty-eight, however, Maglie was no longer agile enough to make the play—or perhaps he knew what was coming and chose to pull up short. Robinson "even slowed down," said Willie Mays, watching from center field, "but Maglie wouldn't come over." Giants second baseman Davey Williams had to race to first and take the throw, ending up the unintended recipient of a hit leveled by Robinson— "a crushing shoulder block," as described in *The New York Times*—that equaled anything thrown by the future Hall of Famer during his collegiate career as a running back at UCLA. At age twenty-seven, Williams, an All-Star just two years earlier, struggled through the rest of the season, then retired.

"[Manager Leo Durocher] used to tell us every day, 'If they throw one at your head, don't say anything. Push one down and run right up his neck,' " said Robinson in 1951. "Leo's an expert at it. He was right."

Delmon Young drew national condemnation in 2006 when he threw his bat at the plate umpire in response to being ejected following a disputed called third strike in a Triple-A game. Young's subsequent suspension— fifty games, the longest in the 123-year history of the International League—may have been unprecedented, but the action he took to earn it certainly wasn't. Guys have been throwing bats since baseball's genesis, although most direct them at pitchers, not umpires. If a hitter is looking to achieve true equality in his response to being thrown at, after all, there's only one option: Throw something back. As long ago as 1913, *Baseball Magazine* published a description of George Van Haltren's reaction to a knockdown pitch from Silver King in 1890: "Like a streak of murderous slaughter the bat whizzed back at King, and only a tremendous leap saved Silver from death or serious injury."

The main downside to the tactic is that bats are considerably more difficult to control than baseballs, and tossed lumber rarely hits its mark. While throwing his bat at Cardinals pitcher Jerry Staley in 1950, for example, Carl Furillo instead came close to hitting his own manager, Charlie Dressen, who was stationed in the third-base coach's box.

One player to recognize this shortcoming was Billy Martin, who adopted an alternative bat-throwing strategy. In 1960, the second baseman, wanting to repay Chicago Cubs pitcher Jim Brewer for an earlier knockdown, let fly his bat on a swing. Instead of directly collecting it, however, Martin paused in the middle of the diamond and took the opportunity to cold-cock the pitcher, damaging Brewer's orbital bone seriously enough to require hospitalization. There is some dispute over whether or not Brewer said anything to provoke Martin; one report had him calling the hitter a "little Dago son of a bitch" and threatening to knock him on his ass if he came closer to the mound.

A dozen years later, this only added to the intrigue when, during the 1972 American League Championship Series, Oakland's Bert Campaneris sent his bat spinning toward Detroit Tigers reliever Lerrin LaGrow in response to a pitch that bounced off his ankle. Campaneris's anger was fueled by his belief that the pitch had been intentionally thrown, and in this he was correct—LaGrow threw it on orders from Tigers manager Billy Martin. Martin saw Oakland's leadoff hitter, who led the league with fifty-two stolen bases, as the catalyst for a powerful lineup, and felt especially vulnerable with Tigers catcher Bill Freehan unable to throw effectively because of a back injury.

The shortstop was quiet in the series opener, going 0-for-4 in an A's victory, but Martin could only cringe as he watched Campaneris single, steal second, steal third, and score on Joe Rudi's base hit in the first inning of Game 2. When Campaneris singled in the third and fifth innings as well, Martin decided to knock the shortstop out of action. "Billy told Lerrin LaGrow to throw at [Campaneris] and get him out of the game," said Charlie Silvera, the former Yankees catcher who served as a coach on Martin's staff. Before the pitch, Campaneris, expecting to be jammed, knew enough to stay loose in the batter's box. That didn't keep him from reacting with surprise, however, when LaGrow's fastball connected with his ankle. The shortstop looked toward the mound for a moment as if considering his options. Then, overhand, he threw his bat at LaGrow. The pitcher, at six-foot-five one of the taller men in the league, ducked and watched the stick helicopter harmlessly over his head.

Before Campaneris could even consider charging (not that he would have, dwarfed as he was by his opponent), plate umpire Nestor Chylak put him in a bear hug and walked him back to the A's dugout. Chylak couldn't stop Martin, however, who flew across the field to challenge the entire A's bench, only to be intercepted by a tag team of umpires Larry Barnett and John Rice. Martin was close enough for A's players to hear him, however, and loudly defied Campaneris to come out and fight, then offered the same challenge to the rest of the Oakland ball club. The A's opted to stay put, and only shook their heads sadly. After the game, first baseman Mike Epstein said, "Of course Martin was throwing at Campy. He's done it too many times. And coming out to fight, that's Martin's way of firing up his club. A lot of guys on his club have confided to me that they're tired of coming out on the field."

For his part, Campaneris was fined five hundred dollars and suspended by AL president Joe Cronin for the remainder of the ALCS and the first seven games of the following season. He was, however, allowed to participate in the World Series. He also brought the tactics of Furillo and Martin into the modern era, kicking off what could be the best decade for bat throwing in baseball history. Three years after Campaneris's effort, Rod Carew threw his bat at Gaylord Perry. The following season, in 1976, Bill Madlock targeted Giants pitcher Jim Barr. A year after that, Pittsburgh's Frank Taveras threw his bat at Reds reliever Joe Hoerner. In 1978, Reggie Jackson threw one at Milwaukee's Mike Caldwell. (Unlike his counterparts, Caldwell escalated things by picking up the bat and trying to break it.) Two years later, Philadelphia's Dickie Noles was suspended, like Delmon Young twenty-six years later, for throwing his bat not at an opposing player but at an umpire, Joe West.

The trend tapered off as the decade turned. It would be almost ten years before another such noteworthy incident, which came courtesy of Pedro Guerrero of the Los Angeles Dodgers, who flung his bat at Mets pitcher David Cone in 1988. Not much had changed, however, because, as in every incident above, Guerrero failed to make contact. "I think he had too much pine tar on his hands," joked Cone after the game. "The bat had good movement on it because it tailed away from me."

Ironically, had Albert Belle thrown a bat instead of a forearm, he'd probably have been better off in the eyes of the viewing public. It's the way of the Code: baseball thuggery (and make no mistake, bat throwing is baseball thuggery) is inevitably tolerated better than general thuggery. (After all, any barroom tough can punch a guy in the face.)

Just ask Fernando Vina.

14

Off the Field

There's retaliation from pitcher to hitter, from runner to fielder, from hitter to pitcher, and from fielder to runner. Baseball players of every temperament and position will, if sufficiently goaded, find a way to get back at opponents they feel have done them wrong. But all this sniping and slapping and sliding and tagging pales next to the most dangerous form of retaliation: Should management wish to retaliate against a player, as long as no contracts or laws are broken, there's not a hell of a lot that player can do about it.

In March 1972, Charlie Finley, the notorious A's owner loathed by many of those who played for him, set his sights on outfielder Tommy Davis. Davis had been one of Oakland's key reserves the previous season, hitting .324 over seventy-nine games, with a .464 mark as a pinch-hitter. Though Finley appreciated Davis's bat, he was less fond of the player's social dexterity; the previous winter, Davis had introduced A's pitcher Vida Blue, the reigning AL MVP and Cy Young winner, to attorney Bob Gerst, who took to representing Blue in contract negotiations. This was an unusual step in the era before player agents, and Blue's holdout through spring training sent Finley over the edge. Despite Davis's .563 Cactus League average, his owner plotted to get even, and as painfully as possible.

Finley waited until the A's made the three-hour bus trip from Phoenix to Yuma for a game against the Padres, waiting to inform Davis of his release until the team had pulled into the ballpark lot. Stunned, the player was left to his own devices to secure a trip back to town.

This sort of retaliation is hardly a one-way street, of course. Ballplayers have their own methods of exacting revenge against management; sometimes they can even be the same ones they use against opponents. In 1975, for example, Frank Robinson was the player-manager of the Indians when Cleveland claimed pitcher Bob Reynolds off waivers. Reynolds performed adequately for the team down the stretch, and the following year had high hopes of making the roster out of spring training. Instead, he was sent to the Triple-A Toledo Mud Hens of the International League.

That June, Cleveland played an exhibition game against Toledo, with Reynolds drawing the start for the minor leaguers. When Robinson came to the plate in the fifth inning, the pitcher made it clear how he felt about his springtime demotion, sending his first pitch over his former manager's head. To remove any possible misinterpretation of the act, he then yelled, "Thanks for saying something to me before you sent me down to Triple A—I found out from a newspaper reporter!" Robinson's response wasn't standard fare for most management types: After grounding out, he walked to the mound and punched Reynolds twice, felling him with the second blow. Indians general manager Phil Seghi was on hand to see the fisticuffs but said that Robinson would not be punished, reasoning that "things like this happen in baseball from time to time."

For Frank Robinson, of course, "from time to time" occurred with some degree of frequency. The previous season, 1975, was his first at Cleveland's helm, and was marked by an acrimonious relationship with pitcher Gaylord Perry—a man who, like Robinson, lacked appreciation for those whose opinions diverged from his own. His solution was to trade Perry to Texas on June 13, which proved problematic in that, just two days later, the pitcher's first start as a member of the Rangers came against none other than Robinson and the Indians. The target on the manager's back couldn't have been more clear.

Robinson, as smart as he was tough, pre-empted the showdown by removing himself from the lineup. "No way I was going to give Gaylord the satisfaction of knocking me down," he said afterward. Perry responded, saying he was looking forward to the opportunity to "stick a ball in his fucking ear. Tell him I said so." As it turned out, he never got the chance; Robinson held himself out of all three of Perry's starts against his team through the end of the 1976 season, then retired.

. . .

Dick Bartell was a fiery shortstop, good enough to start for the National League in the first All-Star Game, in 1933. He was as scrappy a player as could be found on a baseball diamond, but he finally met his match in 1939—and the guy to give it to him didn't even play the game. Bartell was going into his eleventh year in the league and his first with the Chicago Cubs; as he and teammate Dizzy Dean arrived at the ballpark one morning for spring training, Bartell spied an overweight man struggling to get through a turnstile. His ensuing snide comment—"What time does the blimp go up?"—ended up haunting him for the rest of the season.

The fat man was Ed Burns, a writer for the *Chicago Tribune* and one of the team's official scorers. Though Bartell didn't yet recognize Burns, Burns was familiar with his antagonist. He stopped, turned toward the infielder, pointed his finger, and delivered an ominous message: "You'll hear from me all summer." The writer's meaning soon became clear.

"The season started and I was being charged with errors on plays where there was no error, like a double play we didn't finish . . . ," said Bartell. "And anything that might have been called a hit for me, he'd charge the other team with an error. So the headline the next day in *The Tribune* would read: 'Cubs Win. Bartell Makes Error No. 14.' " The error parade got to be such an institution that at that winter's baseball writers' dinner, a baby bootie was brought onstage with the pronouncement "A boot for Bartell." Throughout the evening, a parade of shoes was presented to the audience, each slightly larger than the last, and all with the same statement: "Another boot for Bartell." "It was," recalled the shortstop, "the biggest hit I made all year."

Bartell ended up batting .238 that season, forty-eight points below his career mark, and for the first time in eight seasons his fielding percentage was below the league average. Burns later apologized, said the shortstop, "for coming down so hard on me." It didn't make much difference—after just one season, Chicago traded Bartell to Detroit for Billy Rogell, a clearly declining shortstop who played a single lackluster season for the Cubs before retiring. Bartell played four more years and helped the Tigers to the AL pennant in 1940, introducing one final level of retaliation to the relationship.

PART THREE

CHEATING

15

Sign Stealing

It started with a thirteen-run sixth. Actually, it started with a five-run fifth, but nobody realized it until the score started ballooning an inning later. It was 1997, a sunshiny Wednesday afternoon in San Francisco. By the end of the game, it was 19–3 Expos, and the Giants—the team at the wrong end of that score—were angry, grumbling that the roster of their opponents was populated by thieves.

San Francisco's thinking stemmed from the belief that it likely takes more than skill or luck to send seventeen men to the plate against three pitchers in a single inning. There was no disputing the numbers: Montreal had six players with three or more hits on the day, and in the sixth inning alone, five Expos picked up two hits apiece, including a pair of Mike Lansing homers. Montreal opened its epic frame with eight consecutive hits, two shy of the big-league record, and it was a half-hour before the third out was recorded.

San Francisco's frustration boiled over when manager Dusty Baker spied Montreal's F. P. Santangelo—at second base for the second time in the inning—acting strangely after ten runs had already scored. One pitch later, the guy at the plate was drilled by reliever Julian Tavarez. Two batters later, the inning was over. "They were killing us," said Baker. "F.P. was looking one way and crossing over, hands on, hands off, pointing with one arm. I just said, 'That's enough. If you *are* doing it, knock it off—you're already killing us.' "

What Baker was referring to was the suspicion that Santangelo and other members of the Expos had decoded the signs put down by Giants catcher Marcus Jensen for the parade of San Francisco pitchers. From second base a runner has an unimpeded sightline to the catcher's hands. Should the runner be quick to decipher what he sees, he can—with a series of indicators that may or may not come across as "looking one way and crossing over, hands on, hands off"—notify the hitter about what to expect. Skilled relayers can offer up specifics like fastball or curveball, but it doesn't take much, not even the ability to decode signs, to indicate whether the catcher is setting up inside or outside.

If the runner is correct, the batter's advantage can be profound. Brooklyn Dodgers manager Charlie Dressen, who was as proud of his ability to steal signs from the opposing dugout as he was of his ability to manage a ball club, said that the information he fed his players resulted in nine extra victories a year.

Baker sent a word of warning to the Expos through San Francisco third-base coach Sonny Jackson, who was positioned near the visitors' dugout. Jackson tracked down Santangelo as the game ended and informed him that he and his teammates would be well served to avoid such tactics in the future. More precisely, he said that "somebody's going to get killed" if Montreal kept it up. The player's response was similarly lacking in timidity. "I just told him I don't fucking tip off fucking pitches and neither does this team," Santangelo told reporters after the game. "Maybe they were pissed because they were getting their asses kicked."

The Giants' asses had been kicked two nights in a row, in fact, since the Expos had cruised to a 10–3 victory in the previous game. It was while watching videotape of the first beating that Baker grew convinced something was amiss, so he was especially vigilant the following day. When Henry Rodriguez hit a fifth-inning grand slam on a low-and-away 1-2 pitch, alarm bells went off in Baker's head. Former Red Sox pitcher Al Nipper described the sentiment like this: "When you're throwing a bastard breaking ball down and away, and that guy hasn't been touching that pitch but all of a sudden he's wearing you out and hanging in on that pitch and driving it to right-center, something's wrong with the picture." The Expos trailed 3–1 at the time, then scored eighteen straight before the Giants could record four more outs.

Baker knew all about sign stealing from his playing days, had even practiced it some, and the Expos weren't the first club he'd called out as a manager. During a 1993 game in Atlanta, he accused Jimy Williams of untoward behavior after watching the Braves' third-base coach pacing up and down the line and peering persistently into the San Francisco dugout.

For days after the drubbing by Montreal, accusations, denials, veiled threats, and not-so-veiled threats flew back and forth between the Giants and the Expos. Among the bluster, the two primary adversaries in the battle laid out some of the basics for this particular unwritten rule.

Santangelo, in the midst of a denial: "Hey, if you're dumb enough to let me see your signs, why shouldn't I take advantage of it?"

Baker: "Stealing signs is part of the game—that's not the problem. The problem is, if you get caught, quit. That's the deal. If you get caught you have to stop."

Signs have been stolen in major-league baseball for as long as there have been signs to steal, and players and managers generally accept that opponents will try to gain every possible advantage. It's why signals from the catcher to the pitcher, from the dugout to the field, and from the third-base coach to the hitter can be so complex. And as Santangelo said, if the team from which they're being stolen isn't doing enough to protect them, whose fault is that?

"[Sign stealing has] been there since the beginning of time, and it should be," said Sparky Anderson. "If you can't hide your signs, you've got problems." First baseman Mike Hegan put it this way: "Everything is okay in baseball as long as you don't get caught."

Hall of Famers like Paul Molitor and Robin Yount were notorious for their sign-stealing prowess with the Brewers. Yankees stars Joe DiMaggio and Mickey Mantle were delighted when an alert runner would flash tips. Alex Rodriguez and Ted Williams were both respected for their ability to see and decode their opponents' signs from the base paths. Cal Ripken, Jr., was once reprimanded by Blue Jays pitcher Woody Williams for stealing signs from second base. Jim Price, who played for the Detroit Tigers from 1967 to 1971, said that Al Kaline was his only teammate during that time who *didn't* want to know what was coming.

When Chris Speier came to the Giants as a twenty-year-old in 1971, Willie Mays pulled him aside for a lecture. "Listen, we get everybody's signs and we relay those signs," he informed the rookie, "so you better start thinking about it and doing it." Legend has it that Mays was alerted to the pitch for every one of the four home runs he hit against the Braves on April 30, 1961, thanks to Giants coach Wes Westrum, who had broken Milwaukee's code and was signaling the slugger with a towel. Mays in turn taught his secrets to Bobby Bonds, and Bonds passed them on to the next generation of Giants youngsters, like Gary Matthews. "We were the best [sign-stealing] team I'd ever seen at the time," said pitcher Steve Stone of the 1971 squad. Westrum, he said, "would have all the [opponent's] pitches down" within three innings.

Hall of Famer Hank Greenberg proclaimed himself the "greatest hitter in the world" when he knew what was coming. Tigers manager Del Baker would signal him vocally from the third-base coach's box with a system of "all right"s and "come on"s—"All right, Hank, you can do it" indicated that a fastball was on the way, whereas "Come, on Hank" meant curve. If it was a teammate signaling from second base, Greenberg liked to keep things simple. "He told me, if it's a fastball, just turn your head toward right field," said Hall of Famer George Kell, Greenberg's teammate in Detroit in 1946. "If it wasn't a fastball I'd look straight at him. And he loved to jump on that fastball."

Of course, the hitter has to be confident that the baserunner has the signs and isn't just fidgeting on the base paths. One way for the runner to communicate this is to touch the brim of his helmet should he pick up information to relay. "Then [the hitter] would brim back," said Mark Grace, "which meant, 'You got 'em, I want 'em.' "

If a member of the defense suspects that a baserunner is trying to signal the hitter, a range of action can be taken. The mildest response is simply to change the signs; a more aggressive approach involves verbal dissuasion. "I'd just go up to them and say, 'Come on, now, you've got to be a little bit more discreet—it's too obvious,' " said shortstop Shawon Dunston. "They just give you a dumb look, but the next time the behavior changes. You've got to get every edge and I don't have a problem with that, but don't be too obvious. And be prepared to get drilled if you get caught. Period. That's how it is."

If the warning works, there's rarely reason to escalate things. Some pitchers, however, like to ensure that their message has been received. In 1993, when Blue Jays pitcher Jack Morris was clued in to the sign-tipping efforts of a baserunner at second, he spun on his heel, walked toward his opponent, and, pointing toward the plate, said, "I'm throwing a fastball and it's going at him. Make sure you tell him that." Then he delivered the pitch, as promised, knocking the hitter down. At that point, Morris made a second trip toward the runner. "Did you tell him?" he yelled. "Did you?"

Morris's approach wasted no effort on subtlety. A less obvious—though no less effective, and often more dangerous—technique involves a pitch in which the catcher signals for a curveball away but the pitcher delivers a fastball high and inside. It can be prearranged during a mound conference or through a switch signal (an indicator from the catcher, such as a bare hand over the mitt after the signs have been delivered) that tells the pitcher to throw the opposite of whatever was just called. Sometimes pitchers simply mix it up on their own. "That tactic lit them up pretty good," said 1967 NL Cy Young Award winner Mike McCormick. "It was a cat-and-mouse game. You could tell by the hitter's reaction what he was expecting—a curveball and a fastball are significantly different, because hitters are waiting for the curve to break. You throw a fastball up and in and you could see some pretty good eyes."

"After that, you ask the hitter, 'You still want the signs?'" said Ron Fairly. "No one ever says yes."

Trying to hold a 4–2, ninth-inning lead over Minnesota in 2005, Indians closer Bob Wickman came upon an uncomfortable realization: Michael Cuddyer had been at second base for two consecutive batters, which to the pitcher was an eternity. About two weeks earlier, Wickman had blown a save in Anaheim when Garrett Anderson hit a low outside pitch for a bloop single to drive in Darrin Erstad from second. The stout right-hander was convinced that the only reason Anderson made contact was that the pitch had been tipped by the baserunner. (When faced with Wickman's accusation, Erstad just smiled. "I guess we'll never know, huh?" he said.)

Wickman had no inside knowledge that Cuddyer or the Twins had done anything untoward, but he wasn't about to be burned twice by the same tactic. Rather than take a chance, the pitcher opted for an unorthodox approach. If Cuddyer was on third base, reasoned Wickman, his view to the catcher would be significantly hampered. So Wickman invented the intentional balk. Before his first pitch to the inning's fourth hitter, Shannon Stewart, the right-hander lifted his left leg as he wound up, then froze. After a long beat, he returned to his starting position. "As I did it, I'm thinking to myself, 'There it is, dude, call it,' " said Wickman. Plate umpire Rick Reed did just that, and sent Cuddyer to third. Wickman's decision was based on perverse logic—given Cleveland's two-run lead, Cuddyer's run didn't matter, but Stewart's did. Stewart, said Wickman, was "a semi–power hitter, and he possibly could have hit one out on me if he knew what pitch was coming." It was the first balk of Wickman's thirteen-year career.

Of course, the pitcher nearly shot himself in the ERA by subsequently walking Stewart, who promptly stole second, giving him the same vantage point from which Wickman had just balked Cuddyer. The pitcher, however, managed to strike out Matt LeCroy on a full count to earn his sixth save of the season. "Some guys couldn't believe it, but to me as the closer my job is to finish the game without giving up the lead," Wickman said. "There are so many things that come into play. I'd have no problem doing it again if a guy's standing there too long."

Wickman is in the majority of pitchers, whose primary consideration when it comes to signs is preventing them from being stolen by other teams. There's another category, however—guys like New York Yankees starter Bob Turley, who in the 1950s was more concerned with stealing them himself. The pitcher was frequently used as first-base coach by manager Casey Stengel on days he wasn't scheduled to pitch, for the simple reason that there was nobody on the team who could steal signals as effectively. It was a trick Turley learned with the St. Louis Browns at the beginning of his career, as he tried to stay involved in games in which he wasn't participating. "I started watching the pitchers, trying to pick up little habits and movements, and match them to the pitches they threw," he said. "Pitchers want consistency in what they do; it's a key to success, but it also creates patterns you can pick up." Whenever his seat in the dugout afforded him a clear view of the opposing catcher, his prowess became even more potent.

Shortly after being traded to New York following the 1953 season,

Turley was sitting on the Yankees' bench, talking softly to himself about each pitch that was about to be thrown: "Here comes curveball. . . . Here comes fastball. . . ." Mickey Mantle overheard him, and inquired about what it was exactly that Turley was doing. Once Mantle found out, word quickly spread among the team's hitters about Turley's skills, and it wasn't long before many of them—Gil McDougald, Elston Howard, and Johnny Blanchard included—enlisted him to assist in their at-bats. Turley once estimated he "probably called the pitch on half the home runs [Mantle] hit."

Turley's relay system was simple—he'd whistle whenever a pitch was different from the last one. Hitters would start every at-bat looking for a curveball, and if a fastball was coming, so was Turley's whistle. He'd then stay silent until something else was called. The pitcher was so good that when he went on the disabled list in 1961, manager Ralph Houk wouldn't let him go home, instead keeping him with the team to decipher pitches. (Roger Maris, in fact, hit his sixty-first home run of 1961 on a pitch he knew was coming because third-base coach Frank Crosetti, doing his best Turley imitation after watching the pitcher for years, whistled in advance of a fastball.)

Eventually, people began to catch on. Among them was Detroit Tigers ace Jim Bunning, who grew increasingly angry as Turley whistled and the Yankees teed off during one of his starts. Finally, with Mickey Mantle at bat, Bunning turned to Turley in the first-base coach's box and told him that another whistle would result in a potentially painful consequence for the hitter. Sure enough, Turley whistled on Bunning's first pitch, a fastball at which Mantle declined to swing. With his second offering, Bunning knocked Mantle down. The on-deck hitter, Yogi Berra, could only watch in horror. When it was his turn to bat, Berra turned toward the mound, cupped his hands around his mouth, and shouted, "Jim, he's whistling, but I ain't listening."

Bunning was vigilant, but even vigilance has its limits; sometimes there's nothing a team can do to keep an opponent out of its pantry. Take Marty Barrett, who played second base in Boston for nine seasons in the 1980s, every one of them with right fielder Dwight Evans. Even while playing the field Evans liked to know the pitch that was coming in advance, to help him get an early break on balls hit his way, so Barrett would make a fist and put it behind his back. If his hand didn't move, a fastball was on the way. If his arm wiggled, it would be something softer.

In Fenway Park, the bullpens for both teams are located in right field, allowing visiting relievers a clear view of Barrett's machinations. The only club to pick up on his tactic, though, was the Toronto Blue Jays. Through much of the 1980s, bullpen coach John Sullivan would look over the fence at Barrett's arm, then signal the hitter with a towel (draped over the fence meant fastball, off the fence meant curve). Sometimes, so as not to draw too much attention, Toronto pitchers would simply stand up or sit down, depending on the pitch type, in accordance with prearranged signals. During Barrett's final two seasons as a full-time player in Boston, the Blue Jays went 13-0 in Fenway Park (as compared with 6-7 when the teams played in Toronto). "Haywood Sullivan [the Red Sox general partner] came down a couple of times and said, 'I think they're getting our pitchers' pitches,'" said Bill Fischer, the Red Sox pitching coach at the time. "We would look at the videotape for hours, and we couldn't find anything."

"You're taught to catch things on the field," said Blue Jays manager Bobby Cox, who helmed the sign-stealing operation. "You watch body language with coaches at first and third, and runners with their body language when the hit-and-run and squeeze is on. There's tip-offs and tells throughout a nine-inning ballgame. If you pay attention, you might catch something."

Fischer eventually discovered the secret, but only after he joined Cox's Braves staff in 1992, at which point the manager fessed up and told him that Toronto "had every pitch" the Red Sox had thrown.

Really, the only way for a pitcher to be certain that the other team isn't picking up his signs is to do away with them entirely. In 1973, Nolan Ryan responded to what he felt were the prying eyes of Detroit coaches by ignoring everything Angels catcher Art Kusnyer flashed, then calling his own pitches—touching the back of his cap meant fastball, the bill a curve. As a onetime experiment it worked out okay; the opposition never caught on, and Ryan ended up with the second no-hitter of his career.

·   ·   ·

Much of Bob Turley's ability to read the opposing team was due to his expertise at at picking up pitchers' tells, or inadvertent movements that indicate the type of pitch about to be delivered.

Tells can be as simple as a pitcher keeping his glove snapped tight when throwing a fastball but flaring it out for a breaking ball, or coming set with his glove at his belt for one type of pitch but at his chest for another. Matt Morris, for example, was lit up by the Braves during his rookie season in St. Louis after they noticed that the exposed index finger on his glove hand pointed upward whenever he threw a fastball, but lay flat for curves. Once he pinpointed the trouble, Morris quickly fixed it by attaching a flap to his glove that covered the finger.

Examples like this litter the game's history. When Babe Ruth first came to the American League as a pitcher with the Red Sox, he curled his tongue in the corner of his mouth whenever he threw a curveball—a habit he was forced to break once enough hitters became aware of it. Kansas City's Mark Gubicza was cured of his tendency to stick out his tongue when throwing a breaking ball under similar circumstances. Ty Cobb regularly stole bases against Cy Young, abetted, said the outfielder, by the fact that Young's arms drifted away from his body when he came set before throwing to first; when he was preparing to pitch, he pulled his arms in.

Pitcher Todd Jones dished similar dirt on several competitors in an article he wrote for *Sporting News* in 2004: "When Andy Benes pitched, he always would grind his teeth when throwing a slider. In Hideo Nomo's first stint in L.A., he'd grip his split-finger fastball differently than his fastball. Randy Johnson would angle his glove differently on his slider than on his fastball. I've been guilty of looking at the third-base coach as I come set when gripping my curveball. When hitters see this, word gets around the league. In fact, my old teammate Larry Walker was the one who told me what I was doing. He said he could call my pitches from the outfield."

Even position players get in on the action. In 1986, Toronto slugger George Bell noticed that in the process of calling for breaking balls, Red Sox catcher Marc Sullivan moved his right elbow away from his body, something he didn't do for a fastball. So notified, someone on the Blue Jays bench called out to the batter whenever it happened. Similarly, there wasn't a first baseman in the league Yogi Berra wouldn't talk to as a baserunner—until the moment he got a hit-and-run sign, at which point he began to concentrate and grew quiet. Teams noticed, and Berra found himself the consistent victim of pickoff throws until he learned to keep up the chatter.

Then there was Brooklyn Robins second baseman Pete Kilduff, whose tell cost his team a victory against the Indians in the 1920 World Series. As Brooklyn's noted spitballer Burleigh Grimes threw a complete-game shutout in Game 2, Cleveland scout Jack McAllister noticed that Kilduff picked up a handful of dirt before each pitch. "If he saw our catcher signal for a fastball, he dumped the dirt," said Grimes, who found out about it after the fact. "For a spitter, he hung on to it. Didn't even know he did it." The dirt, of course, afforded Kilduff a better grip should a wet ball be hit to him. In Game 5, it also allowed Indians hitters, alerted to keep their eyes on second base, to lay off Grimes's best pitch and focus instead on crushing his fastball. The right-hander gave up seven runs in three and a third innings—including the first grand slam in series history, to right fielder Elmer Smith—and the Robins (who later changed their name back to the Dodgers) lost 8–1.

The Robins deciphered Cleveland's strategy before Grimes's start in Game 7, and though Cleveland won the game 3–0, the pitcher did his part to keep things close, holding the Indians to two earned runs over seven innings while throwing nearly all spitballs.

However much Billy Martin appreciated stolen signs as a player, by the time he became a manager it had turned into full-fledged fanaticism—and he was as obsessed with protecting his own signs as he was with stealing those of his opponents. While managing the Texas Rangers in 1974, Martin came up with what he felt was a surefire way to safeguard his signals—he installed a transmitter in the dugout that broadcast his orders to earpiece receivers worn by each of his base coaches, eliminating signs entirely. Such technology has since been outlawed, but even then it wasn't always useful. With a runner on third and Cesar Tovar at the plate against the Red Sox, for example, Martin told third-base coach Frank Lucchesi to give the suicide-squeeze sign. The transmission was fuzzy, however, and Lucchesi couldn't make out Martin's order.

"Billy says, 'suicide squeeze,' " recalled Rangers catcher Jim Sund‑berg, "and Frank hits his ear like he can't hear Billy's command. Billy says it a little bit louder: 'Suicide squeeze.' And Frank's tapping his ear again and shaking his head like he can't hear." Finally, Martin yelled into the microphone, "Suicide squeeze!" It didn't matter; Lucchesi couldn't hear a word. Red Sox pitcher Luis Tiant, however, could. He stepped off the mound, looked at Lucchesi, and said, "Frank, Billy said he wants the sui‑cide squeeze."

16

Don't Peek

Imagine—a major-league baseball player who had never come to the plate as a professional. It doesn't happen often, but by his second big-league season Jose Nunez, a pitcher for the Toronto Blue Jays, had played only on teams—in the majors, minors, and winter ball—that used the designated hitter. When Nunez was finally called upon to pick up a bat, during a spring-training game against the Phillies in 1988, he made his estrangement from the offensive end of the game all too clear.

It started even before Philadelphia's Kevin Gross could throw a pitch. When Toronto third-base coach John McLaren noticed that Nunez had failed to remove his warm-up jacket before coming to the plate, he called time and had the hitter return it to the dugout. Jacket-free, Nunez again returned to the batter's box, but for the second time, play was halted before Gross could throw a pitch. This time it was plate umpire Dave Pallone, who informed the right-handed hitter that he was wearing a lefty's helmet, with the protective flap covering the wrong ear. In an effort to avoid another trip to the dugout, Nunez simply spun the helmet around, with the bill facing the rear of his head but the ear flap properly positioned. Though amused, Pallone wouldn't allow it, so Nunez opted to step over the plate and bat left-handed. By this point, both Pallone and Gross were laughing out loud.

For the third time, Gross looked in for the sign from catcher Lance Parrish, but was shocked to see that he wasn't the only one with eyes on Parrish's fingers—Nunez had his head swiveled around and was himself peering in to see what the catcher was calling. "What are you doing?" asked a surprised Parrish, looking up. "I want to see the signs," said the unabashed batter.

It was only spring training, and with Nunez's comedy act already well under way, Parrish played along. "Okay," he said. "What pitch do you want?" Nunez requested a fastball, if Parrish didn't mind. The catcher accommodated him, and Nunez fouled the pitch off. He then turned toward Parrish for his second request. "That was too fast," he said sweetly. "Could you make it a changeup this time?" That was all it took. Pallone was shaking so hard with laughter that he was unable to call balls and strikes—which was fine, because Gross was also doubled over. Nunez even acquitted himself at the plate, hanging in for five pitches before grounding out. "Did you see me swing?" he asked reporters proudly after the game. "Just like George Bell."

Nunez's at-bat may have been a highlight of big-league comedy, but it was also noteworthy as one of the few instances in which a major-league hitter has been caught peeking at the catcher without a shred of repercussion. If on-field sign stealing is generally considered a gentleman's challenge, peeking is its evil twin. "You do that," said Mark Grace, "you're going to get squashed."

There are many ways to go about it. Players can glance back while stepping out for a practice swing, or make a pronounced act of getting into their stance. "I hit .350 in the Pacific Coast League one year," said infielder and longtime manager Gene Mauch, who made a habit of the former during his playing days. "If I couldn't have read signs, I couldn't have hit .350 in batting practice."

Modern peekers often wear wraparound sunglasses to hide their wandering eyes—which, glasses or not, don't have to wander far. A successful peek doesn't even require head movement—just a quick drop of the eyeballs. Picking up the sign is beneficial but hardly essential; all a hitter really needs is a general survey of the landscape—if he sees any part of the catcher in his peripheral vision, he can reasonably assume that he's setting up outside; seeing nothing indicates an inside pitch.

Catchers have different ways of dealing with this. There's subterfuge, such as slapping a glove on the inside corner loudly enough for a hitter to notice, then moving outside once the pitch is released. In some instances, catchers don't set up at all until the last possible moment, when the hit-ter's full concentration must be focused on the mound. These approaches are common, but throwing peekers off the scent too effectively can prove disastrous.

In 1979, the Rangers fingered Royals outfielder Al Cowens as a peeker. "He stands in the batter's box," said Texas catcher Jim Sundberg, "and his eyes would just glance back." When Cowens saw Sundberg position himself outside, he made a habit of leaning over the plate as he swung, extending his reach for better contact with pitches that were tailing away from him. That was the upside. The downside came courtesy of pitcher Ed Farmer.

Both Farmer and Sundberg denied intent, but when Cowens looked back to see an outside setup and leaned accordingly, there was little he could do to avoid the fastball that rode up and in. Intentional or not, the pitch had all the markings of a peeker-deterrent, wherein the catcher calls for a pitch away, knowing that the pitcher will be sending one high and tight. The ball crashed into Cowens's jaw, crumpling the hitter instantly. Pete LaCock, who had been standing in the on-deck circle, was the first member of the Royals to arrive. "His glasses were still on and his eyes were bouncing up and down and I didn't know if he was still breathing or not," said LaCock. "I reached into his mouth and grabbed his chew, and right behind it came pieces of teeth and blood. It was an ugly scene."

"I have to say he was throwing at me, maybe not in the face, but it was intentional," Cowens said angrily after the game, through a wired-together jaw. "That was his first pitch, and the two times before, he was throwing outside. He pitched me so well before. I can't figure out why he pitched on the outside corner, struck me out, and then hit me."

Farmer's reply was equally pointed, though he avoided a direct accusa-tion. "[Cowens] thinks I'm guilty of throwing at him," he said shortly afterward. "I think he's guilty of looking for an outside pitch and not moving." It may not have been the result he intended, but the pitcher felt justified in protecting his own interests. "It's a fine line out there," he said. "You don't want to hurt anybody, but you don't want anybody to take advantage of you."

It's a rule by which most pitchers live. Even Jose Nunez—the original peeker of this chapter—played by it. After being traded to the Cubs prior to the 1990 season, he had to pick up a bat in games that counted, and he didn't once look back at the catcher. Of course, without the privilege of a free peek, he didn't fare well. Nunez was hitless in eleven trips to the plate that season. It's likely that his 6.53 ERA had more to do with his never again pitching in the majors than his lack of hitting, but he can always say it was the rest of the peekers around baseball who drove him out.

17

Sign Stealing (Stadiums)

Allan Worthington was a quality pitcher, a right-hander who came up with the New York Giants in 1953 and moved with them to San Francisco five years later. By 1959, he was not only one of their most trusted bullpen members, but one of the most reliable relievers in the major leagues.

Then, over the course of a single season, everything changed. He was traded twice within a span of six months, playing for three teams in 1960 alone, and shortly thereafter quit the game altogether, at age thirty-one. Worthington was neither a bad character nor a headcase. He was throwing as well as he ever had. In fact, he had only one problem, which was enough to sour him in the eyes of more than one ballclub: Al Worthington wasn't a cheat.

At the tail end of the 1959 season, San Francisco was battling the Dodgers and Braves for the National League pennant, holding first place into the season's final week. In an effort to gain an edge on its competition, the club asked former coach and proven sign stealer Herman Franks, who had left the Giants the previous year, to return and set up an espionage system. His resulting handiwork had various members of the organization, armed with binoculars, placed in the far reaches of San Francisco's Seals Stadium to pick up signs and relay them to the dugout. When Worthington first heard about the operation, he was appalled.

The pitcher had seen a similar system over the first four years of his career, when the Giants played in New York's Polo Grounds before moving west. Although it bothered him, he was never certain enough about his standing on the team to speak his mind. In 1958, however, Worthington found religion at a Billy Graham rally at San Francisco's Cow Palace and from that point forward refused to tolerate inequities on the field.

When he found out about Franks's scheme in '59, Worthington pulled Giants manager Bill Rigney aside and demanded that the practice cease, threatening to abandon the team if it didn't. Rigney was stuck: Worthington was a valuable member of the bullpen, and losing him would be a blow. The binoculars were shelved, and the Giants immediately lost three straight to the Dodgers (and seven of their last eight), to finish four games back in the National League.

At that point, of course, Worthington's fate hardly hinged on the team's success; when the season ended, the Giants couldn't get rid of him fast enough, trading him to the Red Sox for spare parts prior to the 1960 campaign. Boston in turn shipped him to the White Sox that September. Chicago, only three games behind the Orioles, was looking to bolster its bullpen, but nobody in the organization bothered to ask the Giants about their new acquisition. This would have been beneficial, considering that the White Sox used a sign-stealing system even more complex than the one in San Francisco. When the team played at home, Chicago's pitching instructor and former Tigers standout, Dizzy Trout, watched the opposing catcher from inside the recently installed Comiskey Park "exploding" scoreboard—a pyrotechnic exhibition unlike any seen in baseball up to that time. Trout then triggered a light hidden amid many others in the center-field display, that signaled hitters to the type of pitch about to be thrown—blinking meant breaking ball, solid meant fastball. It could be seen from both the plate and the White Sox dugout along the third-base line, but not from the visitors' dugout near first. The scheme was incredibly effective, helping the Sox build a 51-26 record (.662) at home that year, even as they struggled to a 36-41 mark (.468) on the road.

The benefit hardly outweighed the detriment in Worthington's eyes. It was illicit behavior, and by the time he arrived in Chicago, the pitcher was already practiced in his response. Shortly after learning of the system, the right-hander informed manager Al Lopez in a hotel lobby in Kansas City that he wanted nothing to do with it, that he "didn't want to play for a team that cheats."

"As a player it was none of his business what we were doing," said

Lopez. "But I did say, 'Show me in the rule books where it's wrong.' I told him I respected his religious beliefs. I said I hoped he would respect mine, and that my religious beliefs would not permit me to do anything I thought wrong."

"Al Lopez said that it wasn't cheating . . . ," said Worthington. "I thought later, Well, if it's okay to do it, why don't they tell everyone?"

Lopez sent Worthington to speak with general manager Hank Greenberg, which only made things worse. Greenberg, after all, freely admitted to his own preferences for receiving pilfered signs during his Hall of Fame playing days with Detroit. "Baseball is a game where you try to get away with anything you can," he said. "You cut corners when you run the bases. If you trap a ball in the outfield, you swear you caught it. Everybody tries to cheat a little."

After less than a week with the White Sox, Worthington was fed up enough to quit, going home to Alabama and enrolling at Samford University. The team's official explanation was that he left over a salary dispute. This was the first time the White Sox had been challenged about a system that had been in use for years. It had originally been implemented by Frank Lane, the team's general manager four years before Greenberg came along, as a response to the abundant stories about other clubs' use of similar schemes. According to Sam Esposito, a utility infielder with the Sox, it started when Lane brought his complaints to two of the team's third basemen—future Hall of Famer George Kell and his backup, Bob Kennedy. Esposito said that the pair devised a system far more devious—not to mention effective—than the then standard practice of having a coach peer at the opposing catcher through binoculars from the bullpen, then manually signal the hitter by placing (or removing) a towel atop the fence.

That type of system was easily identified. The way Esposito tells it, Kell and Kennedy's plan to use the scoreboard light couldn't have been more effective. "It was hump city . . . ," he said. "You'd be sitting in the bullpen or dugout, the pitcher would be winding up, in his motion, and our hitter would still be looking up at center field, waiting for the light to come on. Sherm Lollar loved the light, Walt Dropo loved it. Nellie Fox wouldn't use it. Nellie was a slap hitter, and he was afraid if he knew it was a fastball that he'd muscle up on the pitch and end up hitting a long fly ball, one of those warning-track outs."

"I doubt if there is one club that hasn't tried it at one time or another in recent years," wrote White Sox owner Bill Veeck in his autobiography, *Veeck—As in Wreck*. "There is absolutely nothing in the rules against it."

Though most ballplayers admit that the stealing of signs is pervasive within the game and accept it as an unavoidable facet of a complex sport, even those who embrace the practice have a difficult time defending those who go beyond the field of play to do it. Any sign deciphered via a mechanical device (usually binoculars or hidden video feeds) is roundly denounced. Don Lee, a reliever with the Los Angeles Angels in the early 1960s, could stand up in some well-placed bullpens and, with his naked eye, read the catcher's signs from beyond the outfield wall. When he relayed those signs to hitters by placing his hand (or not placing his hand) atop the fence, it was generally considered acceptable because he was picking them up unaided. ("Sounds impossible, but he was able to do it," said his teammate, catcher Buck Rodgers. "I was there. I was a beneficiary.") Stick a telescope in Lee's hands, however, and he'd have a roster full of enemies in the opposing dugout the instant he was caught. "Bootling information to the batter through a hidden observer equipped with field glasses is a dastardly deed," wrote Red Smith in 1950. "But the coach who can stand on the third-base line and, using only his own eyes and intelligence, tap the enemy's line of communication, is justly admired for his acuteness."

Even Al Worthington was willing to admit as much. "Sign stealing is as old as baseball," he said. "You watch a coach from the dugout and you try to figure out the signs he's giving to the batter. But it's the coach's job to hide them from you. . . . There's nothing wrong with that. But to spy with binoculars . . . that's cheating."

Numerous methods have been used to communicate illicitly pilfered signs, with indicators ranging from the digital clock at Kansas City's Municipal Stadium ("You know the two vertical dots which separate the hour from the minutes?" asked groundskeeper George Toma. "One dot for a fastball, two for a curve") to dummy TV cameras reportedly placed in center-field wells at places like Candlestick Park and Dodger Stadium that would signal hitters with phony "on air" lights. The practice is nearly as old as the game itself.

At the turn of the twentieth century, spyglass espionage was all the rage in baseball. Teams would regularly place operatives not just inside the scoreboards of stadiums but in apartments across the street. Signals would be relayed by waving towels, opening and closing windows and curtains in accordance with the upcoming pitch, hanging feet or arms out of scoreboard openings, and even using mirrors to reflect signals to the batter.

One of the most notorious early cases involved the Philadelphia Phillies, who in 1900 attempted to bypass the risk of having their spy discovered by positioning their third-string catcher, Morgan Murphy, in Baker Bowl's center-field clubhouse, where he used binoculars aimed through a spy hole to read the catcher's signs. To notify the team, Murphy used a Morse-code key that was wired to a receiver buried under the third-base coaching box, so when coach Pearce Chiles stood in just the right spot he could feel vibrations through the sole of his shoe—one dash for fastball, two for curve, three for changeup—and would signal the batter appropriately.

It took some time, but opponents finally got wise. In the season's final month, Reds shortstop Tommy Corcoran tried to figure out why Philadelphia continually battered pitcher Ted Breitenstein when the rest of the league had such trouble against him. The Phillies had already aroused widespread suspicion because their record at home (36-20) was the league's best, whereas they weren't even close to .500 (24-35) on the road. Some accounts, such as the one offered by Hall of Famer Christy Mathewson in his 1912 book, *Pitching in a Pinch,* have Chiles drawing attention to himself by standing with his foot in a puddle left after a recent rainstorm. Others say the coach was noticed for simply failing to ever move from the same spot on the field. A few have Corcoran tripping over an exposed cable. No matter how it happened, the shortstop, fed up, invaded Chiles's coaching box and began digging, first with his cleats, then dropping to his hands and knees to scoop dirt away by the fistful. Curious players crowded around, as did umpire Tim Hurst. Most of them were certain that Corcoran had lost his mind—until he pulled from the hole a small wooden box attached to underground wires. The evidence seemed irrefutable, but the Philadelphia front office issued blanket denials, identifying the device as leftover detritus from a circus that had used the stadium several months earlier. At the very least, it was enough to spur the Phillies' opponents to keep a watchful eye on them, even on the road.

One of those opponents was the Brooklyn Superbas, who, while hosting the Phillies just before the end of the season, again caught Murphy stealing signs with binoculars—this time from a Brooklyn apartment across the street from the ballpark—then signaling Chiles with a rolled-up newspaper.

Corcoran soon discovered that the Phillies weren't the only club practicing such schemes. There was also a system in Pittsburgh, in which the Pirates' sign stealer signaled pitches from inside the fence via a letter "O" painted into an advertisement on the field side of the wall. Inside the "O" was a crossbar; when it pointed up, a fastball was coming, and horizontal meant curve.

For Corcoran, having his team's signs stolen was troublesome enough, but the true indignity came when it was discovered that Pittsburgh and Philadelphia were in cahoots, having agreed not only to keep mum about each other's systems, but to refrain from using them when their teams met. Philadelphia went so far as to have Murphy sit on the bench as a show of goodwill when facing the Pirates.

The practice faded in and out of use over the ensuing decades. In one noteworthy instance, the 1948 Indians turned to a military-grade gun sight brought back from World War II by pitcher and anti-aircraft gunner Bob Feller that was sixty times stronger than the naked eye. Cleveland had fallen into a late-August swoon that saw it drop from first place to third, four and a half games behind Boston, in a span of less than two weeks. With twenty-six games to play, the team was growing desperate, so a spy station was placed in the scoreboard of Cleveland's Municipal Stadium. Among the people manning the scope were Feller himself, fellow Hall of Fame pitcher Bob Lemon, and groundskeeper Emil Bossard's two sons, Marshall and Harold. Theirs was the system that would one day drive Frank Lane, the White Sox GM, to implement his own practice at Comiskey Park and subsequently drive Al Worthington from the game.

For Cleveland third baseman Al Rosen, the stretch of games in which the Indians first put their system to the test proved monumental, not least because, aside from a handful of games in which he had appeared the previous season, it served as his big-league debut. Just before Rosen stepped to the plate for one of his five at-bats on the year, player-manager Lou Boudreau offered instruction on what to look for against Yankees right-

hander Bob Porterfield. "He said, 'You see that scoreboard out there?' "
said Rosen. "I said, 'Yes.' He said, 'Look up where it says Runs, Hits, and
Errors. If you see an arm hanging out of there it's the signal for curveball.'
Well, that arm came down and Bob Porterfield did throw me a curveball,
which I hit into left-center field for a two-base hit. I thought, 'Boy, this is
easy. No wonder you guys are so good here in the big leagues.' "

"I myself called a grand-slam homer for Joe Gordon on a 3-and-0
count against the Red Sox," said Feller. "As soon as it landed, [Boston
manager] Joe McCarthy came out on the top step of the dugout and
looked at the scoreboard. He knew he had been had."

Aided by Feller's scope, the Indians stormed back into the pennant
race, winning nineteen of their final twenty-four games—all but four of
which were at home—to force a one-game playoff with the Red Sox.
Cleveland won that, too, even though it was in Boston, and went on to
meet the Boston Braves in the World Series. Whether Cleveland cheated
in the Fall Classic, with the eyes of the baseball world upon them, is
largely conjecture, but the team's acknowledged activities from earlier in
the season put a slight tarnish on its October accomplishments. Indians
outfielder Larry Doby had to spend the rest of his days insisting that his
pivotal home run in Game 4 was legitimate, unaided by stolen signs.
Cleveland ended up winning in six.

With that kind of success, there wasn't a lot of motivation to curtail the
practice. Baseball fans perked up their ears in 1950, when Red Sox manager Steve O'Neill publicly aired his suspicions. Rather than lie low, however, the Indians rubbed it in his face, calling him to home plate before a
game in August for a formal presentation of a gift box. Among the inflammatory items O'Neill found inside was a set of toy binoculars.

Looking back on it all, Rosen came to the realization that Cleveland's
system was not something to which he should have adhered, even as a
green rookie; that it was, as he called it, "out and out cheating." His conclusion was partly informed by ethical considerations, but personal safety
was also a factor. "I decided I'd rather use my own instincts at the plate
rather than have somebody tell me what's coming," he said. "If there was
a take-off [last-moment sign switch] or something of that nature, I
thought the danger was much greater than it would be if I was using my
own judgment."

. . .

Without question, the game's most infamous sign-relay system—which inspired countless newspaper accounts and its own book-length examination—was the one used at the Polo Grounds in 1951, which allowed the Giants to storm back to take the pennant from Brooklyn, culminating with Bobby Thomson's "Shot Heard 'Round the World."

The windows of the stadium's center-field clubhouses faced the diamond, giving a spotter a perfect sightline to the plate. The positioning was so favorable that even visiting teams used the setup to their advantage. Gene Mauch recalled that, as a little-used infielder with the Cubs in 1948, he'd pick up signs with binoculars and signal Chicago's hitters with a large can of peach nectar that he'd move back and forth across the sill—to the left for one type of pitch, to the right for another.

A beverage can, however, wasn't nearly sophisticated enough for Giants manager Leo Durocher, who installed a switch in the home clubhouse that triggered a buzzer in the bullpen. The system was simple and effective—no matter how hard people looked for an illicit signal coming from behind the center-field window, they wouldn't see a thing.

After falling thirteen and a half games behind Brooklyn as of August 11, the Giants went on a tear, winning sixteen straight and then going 20-5 in September to end the season tied with the Dodgers. A three-game playoff was won by the Giants on Thomson's home run; although he's acknowledged the sign-stealing scheme, the slugger has long denied—if sometimes halfheartedly—that he was tipped off to the pitch he hit out.

Thomson and the Giants might be a bad example, though, because not every team that stole signals in such a manner enjoyed as much success. Take Mauch's Cubs, a perennial second-division club despite sustained efforts at espionage. In 1959, Chicago finished in fifth place even though the team had a spy in the Wrigley Field scoreboard for much of the season. He was traveling secretary Don Biebel, who, armed with binoculars, signaled hitters by sticking his shoe into an open frame used to post scores. Even through the losing, however, the Cubs still managed to arouse suspicion. Most skeptical were the Giants, whose ace, Sam Jones—the runner-up in that year's Cy Young voting—got lit up every time he pitched in Chicago. (Against the rest of the league that year, Jones was 21–12, with a 2.54 ERA, and struck out a hitter every 1.25 innings; at Wrigley Field, he was 0–3 with an 8.53 ERA, and struck out a hitter every six innings.) It wasn't long before San Francisco players identified the cause of the discrepancy.

"We just got wise and looked up, and sure enough in the scoreboard there was a big empty square," said pitcher Mike McCormick. "Same scoreboard they have today, where they hand-place the numbers. There was somebody sitting up there in an empty square—one foot in the window was a fastball, two feet was a curveball, no feet was a changeup. You let a major-league hitter know what's coming, and he might not hit it all the time, but it certainly makes him a better hitter."

Jones was particularly affected by the Cubs' system, said Biebel, because he had trouble handling anything but the simplest signs, which kept Giants manager Bill Rigney from stymieing would-be thieves with a more complicated system. Instead, he dealt with the matter in a different way: six-foot-four, two-hundred-pound outfielder Hank Sauer, who was sent to the scoreboard to get some answers.

"Between innings I saw [first-base coach Wes] Westrum and Sauer and Bill Rigney get over in the corner of the dugout, and they were chatting," said Biebel. "Sauer went out of the dugout and up the ramp, and I told the groundskeeper who was in the scoreboard with me, 'You better lock this thing up—I think we're going to have some company.' About ten or fifteen minutes later, here comes Sauer along the back fence of the bleachers. He walks all the way out there and he starts pounding on our little door, shouting, 'Let me in!' He pounded for a while, but when he finally knew he wasn't going to get in, he turned around and left."

Biebel was good for more than stealing signs, of course. He was also proficient in catching opponents who were doing it. In 1960, Braves pitchers Bob Buhl and Joey Jay were dressed in street clothes and stationed in the Wrigley Field bleachers with a pair of binoculars, lounging in the sun as if they had just popped in from a North Side apartment. The pair vigorously waved their scorecards whenever a breaking ball was on its way, and Biebel caught them immediately. "It was easy to spot them," he said. "I knew who they were. You have a good view in that scoreboard, and back then the bleachers were pretty empty." Biebel informed the dugout of his discovery, and ushers soon escorted the pair from their seats.

Though it's neither safe nor fair to assert that the sign stealers are the bad guys in this tale and that those who stop them are the good guys, for just a moment assume that's the case. It's a contrivance that enables this story to come full circle, because one member of the San Francisco Giants the day that Sauer went banging on the door of the Wrigley Field scoreboard was an oft-used reliever named Al Worthington, who the next season would play briefly for the White Sox. And we all know what happened after that.

18

If You're Not Cheating, You're Not Trying

We do not play baseball. We play professional baseball. Amateurs play games. We are paid to win games. There are rules, and there are consequences if you break them. If you are a pro, then you often don't decide whether to cheat based on if it's "right or wrong." You base it on whether or not you can get away with it, and what the penalty might be. A guy who cheats in a friendly game of cards is a cheater. A pro who throws a spitball to support his family is a competitor.

—Former major-league manager George Bamberger

There's cheating in baseball like there's cheating in all sports, because competitive instincts direct players toward any possible advantage. Some are able to corral those instincts to within the limits of the rulebook, but for many, the field of play is open to possibilities.

When it comes to cheating in baseball, however, many tactics that go against the letter of the law are viewed as perfectly acceptable, both by those who utilize them and those against whom they're used. It's a soft-focus that turns lines that are sharply delineated in the view of an outsider into so much gray area at the level of the playing field. Think about it this way, because others certainly do: Deceiving an umpire is cheating, but deceiving an opponent (say, by stealing his signs) is simply hard-nosed competition.

Take it from no less an authority than Frank Robinson, who, in addition to his Hall of Fame career as a player and manager, served as Major League Baseball's discipline czar from 2000 to 2001. "Some of that stuff might be against the rules or against some code, but none of it is against the law," he said. "There's nothing wrong with trying to find an edge. That's smart—that's not cheating."

That said, there are numerous ways to go about "not cheating," all of which offer their own subtleties and intrigue.

Take, for example, an instance from 1987. George Steinbrenner was watching his Yankees play the California Angels on television, and was shocked when the camera zoomed in to show close-ups of what appeared to be a small patch, or even a bandage, on the palm of Angels pitcher Don Sutton's left hand. The WPIX broadcasters brought it up whenever the pitcher appeared to grind the ball into his palm between pitches. It was, they said, probably why Sutton's pitches possessed such extraordinary movement that day. He was in all likelihood scuffing the baseball.

Outraged, Steinbrenner called the visitors' dugout at Anaheim Stadium and lit into Yankees manager Lou Piniella. Was he aware, asked the owner, that Sutton was cheating? "Our television announcers are aware of it," yelled Steinbrenner. "I'm sure the Angels are aware of it. You're probably the only guy there who doesn't know it. Now, I want you to go out there and make the umpires check Don Sutton!"

This wasn't exactly breaking news about Sutton. He had been thrown out of a game in 1978 for scuffing. In 1981, a secret feature he was scheduled to shoot for NBC in which he detailed many of the ways pitchers cheat was scrapped when word about it leaked. (To protect his identity, Sutton was to have worn a ski mask and the image was to appear reversed, so he would appear to be a lefty.) By the time the Yankees' broadcasters started musing over the possibility that Sutton might be scuffing, the pitcher was already among the most discussed ball-doctors in the game.

"George," Piniella responded, "do you know who taught him how to cheat?" Steinbrenner confessed that, in fact, he did not. "The guy who taught Don Sutton everything he knows about cheating is the guy pitching for us tonight," Piniella said. "Do you want me to go out there and get Tommy John thrown out, too?"

America is built on the shoulders of its honest icons—George Washington and the cherry tree; Honest Abe. We're raised to believe that cheating is bad, that truthfulness and integrity make the man. We warn against cheating in school, look with indignation at cheating spouses, and above all proclaim that cheaters never win.

That last part, of course, is factually inaccurate. Cheaters do win. They win a lot. It's why they cheat. And in professional sports, where every athlete seeks every advantage that can be comfortably tolerated (and some that can't), the concept of cheating is continually stretched to its maximum breadth.

If baseball is a business, cheating has become little more than a business practice, and, like sign stealing, is generally abided as long as it stops once it's detected. This covers a wide range of endeavors: pitchers applying foreign substances to the ball, and hitters doctoring their bats; outfielders acting as if they've caught balls they actually trapped, and hitters pantomiming pain from balls that didn't hit them. It's why, when Sammy Sosa was caught using a corked bat in 2003, Cubs president Andy Mac-Phail said, "There is a culture of deception in this game. It's been in this game for 100 years. I do not look at this in terms of ethics. It's the culture of the game." MacPhail might be easy to dismiss as a company guy protecting his star, but he spoke the truth.

"Everyone cheats," said White Sox manager Ozzie Guillen. "If you don't get caught, you're a smart player. If you get caught, you're cheating. It's been part of the game for a long time. If you're doing whatever you're not supposed to do and you don't get caught, keep doing it."

This is why Tigers star Norm Cash, in the rare instance when he was on base when a rain delay was called, would try to advance illicitly before play resumed, returning to third if he had been on second, or second if he had been on first. That he never got away with it hardly matters—it's the effort that counts.

Or take the time in 1941 when a loaded pitch from notorious Tigers spitballer Tommy Bridges broke so severely that it squirted away from catcher Birdie Tebbetts. When Yankees manager Joe McCarthy asked the umpire to check the ball, both Tebbetts and the batter, Joe Gordon, raced after it. Tebbetts got there first and, with the bases empty, promptly threw the ball into the outfield, where it was tossed from fielder to fielder before being returned to the umpire, clean. Unimpeachable, Bridges continued his ways.

In the pantheon of cheaters, Bridges was merely an All-Star; Rogers Hornsby was a legend. Owner of a lifetime .358 batting average and three .400 seasons, Hornsby is widely considered to be the greatest second baseman of all time. In 1961, after his playing career and fifteen years managing six big-league teams were behind him, he authored a story for *True* magazine titled "You've Got to Cheat to Win in Baseball." In it, he wrote, "I've been in pro baseball since 1914 and I've cheated, or watched someone on my team cheat, in practically every game. You've got to cheat. I know if I had played strictly by the rules I'd have been home feeding my bird dogs a long time ago instead of earning a good living in baseball for 47 years." By Hornsby's own estimation, cheating was all that stood between the Hall of Fame and a lifetime of kennel work.

Or take it from Orioles manager Earl Weaver, who, upon visiting the mound to talk to pitcher Ross Grimsley during a bases-loaded situation, offered a simple suggestion: "If you know how to cheat, this would be a good time to start."

With the preponderance of such low-level dishonesty in the game, it's surprising that more players aren't called out by ex-teammates who know every detail of their methodology. The reason is simple: If Player A calls out Player B, he can be assured that Player B will return the favor—if not directly, then against one or more of Player A's teammates, who will then also respond in kind. This can get messy quickly, with players forced to offer perfunctory answers to boneheaded questions from an obligated media. There's little to be gained from forcing a colleague to decry a practice that, in his heart, doesn't bother him a bit.

It's why Indians pitcher Jason Grimsley (no relation to Ross) was willing to crawl through the Comiskey Park ductwork and break into a locked room to spirit away a corked bat that umpires confiscated from teammate Albert Belle. It's why the Yankees allegedly made a secret after-hours practice during the late 1980s of checking the bats in the Yankee Stadium visitors' clubhouse for cork, but never acted on whatever information they might have picked up. It's why Lou Piniella, looking after the best interests of his own pitching staff in 1987, didn't want Don Sutton checked by the umpires.

Leave the definitive sentiment to Dick Williams, the Hall of Fame manager who won two championships with the A's, and pennants with Boston and San Diego. "Anything short of murder," he said, "is okay."

*Pitchers have always cheated. They're crooks and scoundrels. I don't trust
any of them.*

—Richie Ashburn

Casey Stengel wasn't a rookie manager in 1949, but he was about to
start the most important job of his life, at the helm of the New York Yankees. In nine seasons managing the Boston Braves and Brooklyn Dodgers
he had never finished higher than fifth, so when he was plucked from the
Oakland Oaks of the Pacific Coast League to lead the mighty Yankees—
winners of fifteen pennants and eleven championships over the previous
twenty-six seasons—the pressure was on. Stengel inherited a third-place
club returning all its key players, and another flag was expected to soon be
raised atop Yankee Stadium.

By July 24, New York held a three-game lead over the Cleveland Indians, but something was missing. The pitching staff, led by veteran hurlers
Vic Raschi, Allie Reynolds, and Eddie Lopat—all over thirty—was solid
but aging. Perhaps the forward-looking manager started to fear for his
own future job security should his valuable arms falter in coming seasons.
His solution: pitcher Ralph Buxton.

Managers bring up promising young pitchers from the minors all the
time, but Buxton was hardly that. Thirty-five years old, the right-hander
had appeared in all of five big-league games in 1938, then spent more than
a decade bouncing from minor-league outpost to minor-league outpost.
His most recent stop had been with the same Oakland Oaks club that
Stengel had managed to the PCL title a year earlier. Buxton's 13-3 Triple-A
record under Stengel in '48 was certainly a factor in ending his eleven-
year minor-league exile, but the manager's decision to summon him to
New York was at least partly based on his nickname: "Pine Tar."

The sobriquet originated during Oakland's championship run, during
a game in which Buxton was a strike away from beating the cross-bay rival
San Francisco Seals. Before he could deliver the decisive pitch, however,
Seals manager Lefty O'Doul shouted from the dugout for the umpires to
check Buxton's glove. O'Doul's suspicions weren't exactly new: Clubs
around the league had long presumed that the reliever regularly loaded up
the baseball. "He stuck [the pine tar] on his pants along the crease," said
former big-leaguer John Babich, the Oaks pitching coach. "All he'd do is

rub his hands on his pants." With a quick search the umpires quickly found the substance, which led O'Doul to protest the game. The league suspended the pitcher for ten days and ordered the final inning to be replayed at a later date. (The Oaks won the replay, as well.)

Buxton's arrival in New York in July 1949 was ostensibly aimed at shoring up the Yankees' bullpen, but the twenty-six innings he threw didn't help much in that regard. The best service Buxton performed was explaining his trade secrets. By the end of the year, said Buxton, "the whole Yankee staff was using my pine tar."

New York went on to win the World Series that year, as well as the following four, for a still-unmatched five-year streak of titles. It would be inaccurate to attribute that success to the lessons of Ralph Buxton, but his brief appearance in pinstripes did show that even the winningest team in baseball history made a point of looking for every edge it could get.

What does pine tar do for a pitcher? How about Vaseline? Spit? They're all considered to be foreign substances, and banned from use under two of baseball's official rules: 3.02, which states that "No player shall intentionally discolor or damage the ball by rubbing it with soil, rosin, paraffin, licorice . . . or other foreign substance," and rule 8.02(a)(6), which says, "The pitcher shall not deliver what is called the 'shine' ball, 'spit' ball, 'mud' ball or 'emery' ball."

Generally speaking, the prohibited substances fall into two categories: those that add friction and those that remove it. Tacky substances like pine tar or even mud are used by pitchers to improve grip in cold weather, but can also add snap to a breaking ball and, by weighing down one side of the baseball, can lend an extra degree of sink. The slick substances like petroleum jelly create what's generally known as a spitball. They allow pitchers to deliver offerings at near-fastball speed but with substantially less rotation, because the ball squirts out of the hand rather than being spun across the fingers upon release. This lack of backspin provides significant late drop. "Vaseline is the best and K-Y Jelly is next," said former Giants, Expos, and Cubs manager Charlie Fox, reviewing the pantheon of spitball substances. "The advantage to K-Y Jelly is that it doesn't adhere to the ball and can't be detected by the umpire. Balls with Vaseline on them will be hit on the ground and a big glob of dirt will be stuck to the ball."

Substances can be hidden virtually anywhere on a pitcher's body, on his uniform, or under his cap. Dodgers manager Charlie Dressen cut pieces of slippery-elm bark—which produces copious amounts of saliva when chewed—into sticks and wrapped it like gum so that his pitchers could pop it into their mouths without suspicion during games. Pirates pitcher Dock Ellis, an African American, withstood significant grief for wearing hair curlers on the field, but knew that the beads of sweat collecting at the ends of his straightened tresses would be ripe for harvesting. In the 1980s, several of Billy Martin's pitchers on the Oakland A's were said to regularly slather their legs in baby oil, which would soak through their uniforms for easy access during the course of a game, while others applied heating ointment to whichever part of their body sweated most copiously, producing faster and more reliable perspiration. Yankees pitcher George Frazier kept a supply of a Chicago-area shampoo that made his hair exceptionally oily, saying, "During a game I'd just reach back behind my neck for some [of the ensuing] grease." A's closer John Wyatt went so far as to keep a stash of Vaseline inside his mouth.

Many sources credit Frank Corridon with inventing the spitball in the early 1900s, though a 1931 *Baseball Magazine* article quoted Phonney Martin, a pitcher with the 1872 Brooklyn Eckfords, lamenting the spitter thrown by his contemporary, Bobby Matthews of the Lord Baltimores. Foreign substances were outlawed in the game's earliest days, but saliva was not, and the spitter soon caught on around the league. White Sox star Ed Walsh, among others, rode his expectoratory success into the Hall of Fame, using a pitch that went by many names: the "spitball," "brown spitter," "country sinker," "damp sling," "wet ball," and "wet wipe."

By 1920, pitchers were using the spitter to such great effect that it was outlawed by Major League Baseball, which claimed that because the pitch was difficult to control, it put hitters at risk. Seventeen recognized spitball pitchers were grandfathered into the rule and allowed to ply their trade legally through the end of their careers; the last of them, Hall of Famer Burleigh Grimes, was also the best, and threw baseball's last legal spitter in 1934.

Outlawing a practice doesn't stop people from doing it, however, and the ruling simply meant that those determined to throw spitballs needed to increase their secrecy. The first man to be ejected for the practice was Browns pitcher Nelson Potter in 1944, for wetting his fingers before touching the rosin bag, in defiance of the umpire's warning against doing exactly that. Potter, however, was an exception; others received far more leniency. Cardinals pitcher Red Munger, who played at the same time and in the same city as Potter, was known by opponents and umpires alike to load up balls with tobacco juice. After umpire Larry Goetz called the second strike of an at-bat on one of Munger's doctored pitches, the hitter complained that the pitch had been a spitter. "Yes it was," Cardinals catcher Joe Garagiola recalled Goetz saying. "Strike two."

The 1950s, said Dodgers pitcher Claude Osteen, was "the [decade] of the spitter, and everyone took a turn at trying it." It grew so pervasive that in 1955 Commissioner Ford Frick lobbied for the pitch's relegalization; a *Sporting News* poll found that only 30 percent of 120 players, coaches, and managers surveyed would have a problem with this. ("Restore the spitter?" asked Dodgers shortstop Pee Wee Reese. "When did they stop throwing it?") Still, the groundswell was insufficient to spur action, and the spitball stayed banned. Nonetheless, it continued to evolve.

Doing his predecessors one better, in the 1960s, Yankees great Whitey Ford mixed up a concoction of turpentine, baby oil, and rosin that he stored in a roll-on deodorant container that he freely brandished in the dugout during games. (After Yogi Berra grabbed the wrong container in a search through Ford's locker for some antiperspirant, his armpit hair had to be cut away to free him from the stuff.)

The pandemic only grew through the 1960s and '70s, to the point where Pete Rose claimed Angels pitcher Bill Singer threw him four straight spitters in the 1973 All-Star Game, one of which hit American League catcher Carlton Fisk in the knee before bouncing away. Recounted Rose: "He looked up, rubbed his knee, and said, 'He didn't even tell me the damn thing was coming.' "

That April, Yankees outfielder Bobby Murcer had exploded to the press after facing Cleveland's greaseball king Gaylord Perry in the pitcher's second start of the season, yelling: "Just about everything he throws is a spitter. . . . The more he knows you're bothered by him throwing it the better he is against you. He's got the stuff behind his ear and on his arm and on his chest. He puts it on each inning. I picked up the balls and they're so greasy you can't throw them." Murcer went so far as to call commissioner Bowie Kuhn "gutless" for refusing to respond—and this was after the outfielder had recorded a three-hit game against Perry. When the pitcher was confronted with Murcer's accusations, however, he said that Murcer hit "fastballs and sliders," not spitballs. It would have been a more credible excuse had Perry been on the same page as his catcher, Dave Duncan, who in a separate, contrived denial said that Murcer had hit "off-speed stuff."

To further the argument, *The New York Times* hired an unnamed Yankees pitcher to chart Perry's every pitch throughout the game, marking those he thought to be spitballs. When the resulting pitch chart was compared with a replay of the game, the *Times* noted that, before every pitch identified as a spitter by the Yankees operative, Perry tugged at the inside of his left sleeve with his right (pitching) hand—an action he did not take for the rest of his repertoire. Yankees second baseman Horace Clarke, according to the chart, struck out on a spitter that, on replay, was seen to drop at least a foot. In the fourth inning, Thurman Munson asked to see the ball twice during his at-bat—during which, said the chart, Perry threw four spitters.

But Perry wasn't just a practiced spitballer—he was also a practiced spitball deceiver. One of the strengths of the pitch, according to virtually everybody who has been suspected of throwing it, is that making a hitter believe it's coming is nearly as valuable as actually throwing it. "The more people talk and write about my slick pitch, the more effective I get," wrote Perry in his autobiography, *Me & the Spitter.* "I just want to lead the league in psych-outs every year." To this end, Perry turned into his era's version of 1950s spitball artist Lew Burdette—all fidgets, wipes, and tugs once he stood atop a mound.

"Perry's big right hand started to move and people started to boo," wrote Gerald Eskenazi in the *Times*, about its charted game. "First he touched his cap, sliding his fingers across the visor, bringing them down along the right side of his head, stopping behind his ear. Then the hand went across his uniform, touching his chest, his neck. Was all this to create a diversionary action? Was he simply having fun? . . . 'I did the same things I always did,' Perry said later, suppressing a smile. 'If people want to read things into it, so be it.' "

Partly in reaction to the uproar Perry caused, a rule was implemented in 1974 that removed the mandate for hard proof in an umpire's spitball warning, saying that peculiar movement on a pitch provided ample evidence. It didn't take long—all of six innings into the season—before Perry earned his first warning under the new rule. Not that it mattered; by the end of the season he had won twenty-one games, was voted onto the All-Star team, finished fourth in the Cy Young balloting, and was thrown out of exactly zero games for doctoring baseballs.

It wasn't until 1982, when Perry was forty-three and in his twenty-first season in the big leagues, that he was finally disciplined for loading up a baseball, when he earned a $250 fine and ten-day suspension after throwing two allegedly illegal pitches as a member of the Mariners—the first such punishment for this type of activity since Nelson Potter in 1944. By that point, Perry had become the most frequently accused spitballer in big-league history, and did little to dispel the notion: Not only was his autobiography suggestively titled, but it came out in 1974, nearly a decade before he retired; his North Carolina license plate read SPITTER; when his five-year-old daughter was asked by a TV reporter in 1971 whether her daddy threw a greaseball, she quickly replied, "It's a hard slider."

Although Perry claimed, upon his book's release, that he didn't throw the spitter any more, Twins manager Gene Mauch was quick to respond, saying, "But he doesn't throw it any less, either."

In 1991, after 314 wins over twenty-two seasons, Perry was inducted into the Hall of Fame. George Owens of the *Utica Observer-Dispatch* described the ceremony: "When Rod Carew was inducted into baseball's Hall of Fame, Panamanian flags waved. When Ferguson Jenkins was inducted, Canadian flags were flown. When Gaylord Perry was inducted, it began to rain."

Though cheating has been a steady practice throughout baseball history, rarely has a player endured quite the humiliation of Seattle's Rick Honeycutt upon being caught. In a game at Kansas City's Kauffman Stadium in 1980, members of the Royals thought the break on the pitcher's offerings was too extreme, especially after the left-hander had held them to two runs over eight innings just six days earlier. Kansas City manager Jim Frey collected an assortment of blemished baseballs, then requested that Honeycutt be examined. The pitcher clearly wasn't prepared for this eventuality. When umpire Bill Kunkel reached the mound, he found the pitcher, glove off, violently snapping his hand back and forth. He was trying, it soon became clear, to detach a flesh-colored Band-Aid from his index finger, through which was protruding the thumbtack he'd been using to cut the baseball.

Not only did Honeycutt fail to remove the damning proof, but he went so far as to inadvertently prick Kunkel—himself a former big-league pitcher who was once accused of throwing spitballs—when the umpire grabbed his hand. "The evidence at that point was pretty irrefutable," said Mariners general manager Lou Gorman. To that point, Honeycutt's humiliation was only moderate. Things became truly embarrassing when the ejected pitcher, on his way to the showers with the tack still affixed to his finger, went to wipe the sweat from his brow and gashed his own forehead.

The following day, Seattle manager Maury Wills handed Kunkel a one-square-inch piece of sandpaper that the umpire had failed to detect on Honeycutt before tossing him, saying, "You might as well get the whole kit."

"If you were good at it, you wouldn't get caught," said Honeycutt, long after his career ended. "To have something as blatant as a tack to scuff a baseball . . . it was just total inexperience and stupidity on my part." (When Honeycutt was traded to the A's seven years later, his clubhouse greeting included a passel of thumbtacks and a Band-Aid across the space where the nameplate over his locker belonged.)

There's no mystery to why players cheat, but Gorman suspected that Honeycutt simply wanted to return to form after an elbow injury decreased the effectiveness of his breaking ball, which helped lead to sixteen losses over his final nineteen decisions after a 7-1 start to the season. "Sometimes you can be so frustrated," said the GM, "that you will practically do most anything."

Honeycutt's deceit hardly made him a baseball pariah—far from it. He was hired as the pitching coach for the Los Angeles Dodgers in 2006, after spending four years as the team's minor-league pitching coordinator. If he stands out from the field at all, it wasn't because he cheated—it was because he got caught.

Honeycutt's methods of choice, scuffing and cutting, are well documented through the game's annals, and have been utilized by some of the greatest pitchers baseball has known, from the admitted (Whitey Ford) to the assumed (Nolan Ryan). A ball's raised seams provide air resistance (the higher the seams, the bigger the break); similarly, a scuffed ball adds movement to a fastball and drop to a breaking ball. "It's a huge difference," said Lary Sorensen, who took to scuffing in the latter stages of his career to compensate for his diminishing fastball.

Taping a tack to one's hand is hardly the only method to achieve such dramatic effect. There's a piece of sandpaper or emery board hidden within a baseball glove, or a sharpened belt buckle upon which the ball can be subtly rubbed—a tactic, it's been reported, used by Hall of Fame Tigers pitcher Jim Bunning. A pitcher for the Milwaukee Brewers in the 1980s had a jigsaw blade sewn into his glove between the thumb and index finger. Another pitcher went so far as to change the insignia on his glove—a Rawlings logo consisting of a white "R" inside a red circle—to hide his tools. "He cut out the red material, slipped in the sandpaper and spray-painted the glove the same color red," said his teammate, outfielder Billy Sample. "It looked believable. He wouldn't scuff the ball on every pitch, just when he needed an out in a big spot."

Pitchers can also enlist the assistance of teammates. Infielders intentionally drop balls as they toss them around, marking them up in the process. Sharpened eyelets on a glove can produce extreme gashes in a leather surface. Catchers can hone their shin-guard buckles to give balls a quick working over in the process of cocking their arms for return throws to the pitcher.

After Astros pitcher Mike Scott leaped from obscurity to win the 1986 NL Cy Young Award, then dominated the Mets in the NLCS (one earned run over the course of two complete games)—all amid accusations that he was a consistent scuffer—the league decided to crack down. In 1987, Phillies pitcher Kevin Gross was ejected after umpires found sandpaper in his glove. Also that season, Joe Niekro was caught on the mound with an emery board. (He insisted it was for filing his nails; two of his prominent defenders were ex-teammates Scott and another reputed scuffer, Dave Smith.) Yankees pitcher Rick Rhoden was put under suspicion, called to task by AL president Bobby Brown after umpires kept "more than three and fewer than 10" balls he used in a game against Baltimore, each of which bore thin two-inch scuff marks. (Rhoden was not disciplined.)

"Rick Rhoden and Tommy John are reasons 1 and 1A for the Yankees' presence in first place," wrote Thomas Boswell in 1987. "If they don't abrade the horsehide, then maybe the whole thing is just a UFO scare and nobody cheats."

Of course, the Yankees did end up finishing fourth in their division that season, which just goes to show that cheaters don't necessarily win—or at least that they need some help along the way.

Properly doctoring a baseball can achieve wondrous results, but it can take a significant amount of preparation. The easiest way for a pitcher to cheat is simply to inch down the mound. The closer he gets to the plate, the less time the batter has to react to his pitches and the less velocity the baseball loses in arriving. This happens more frequently than most people realize.

"On occasion I've pitched from about six inches in front of the rubber when I've needed the big strikeout. And I know I'm not the only one who's done that," wrote Nolan Ryan in his book, *Throwing Heat*. "You just rock up, step in the hole, and you're half a dozen inches closer to the plate. Normally there's enough dirt and stuff on the mound late in the game to cover things up, but you have to work the area to dig a hole to get your foot in."

"If you covered the rubber up with dirt, it was easy to do," said Whitey Ford. "It's just something nobody's ever looking for. When I coached first base for the Yankees, I never remember checking to see if the pitcher had his foot in contact with the rubber when he delivered the pitch. Sometimes you could stand with both feet on the rubber, get your sign, and then when you pitched, your first step could be about three feet in front of the rubber. Talk about adding a yard to your fastball."

For all the ways pitchers can cheat, hitters are pretty much limited to their lumber. The industry standard for bat augmentation involves drilling a hollow core into the barrel, about a half-inch wide and up to eight inches deep—any more would affect the basic integrity of the wood—then packing the hole with cork (a much lighter substance than the ash or maple that has been removed) or various forms of shredded rubber, which can remove up to two ounces from a two-pound bat. A plug is then inserted, and the bat end is sanded to look as much as possible like a whole piece of wood. "I played with a guy who saved the last inch-and-a-half of dozens of broken bats," said Bob Brenly. "When he was ready to plug that hole, he would take all the little caps and match them up so the grain lined up exactly perfect with the plug. That's a master craftsman."

The practice has been going on for generations, but its effectiveness is still up for interpretation. Lighter bats equal faster swings, which, according to Lawrence Fallon and James Sherwood's "A Study of the Barrel Construction of Baseball Bats," could make up to a 1 percent difference in the distance a ball travels, or about four feet on a four-hundred-foot home run. Skeptics counter that the bat's decreased mass negates most of that advantage.

The most prominent example of this argument comes courtesy of admitted bat corker Norm Cash, a four-time All-Star with the Detroit Tigers, primarily in the 1960s, who went so far as to demonstrate his bat-doctoring technique for *Sports Illustrated* after he retired. In 1961, using a bat he later admitted was filled with cork, sawdust, and glue, Cash led the American League with a .361 average, hit forty-one home runs and drove in 132 runs.

Still, it's difficult to explain the first baseman's slump the following year, in which his .243 average represented the largest single-season drop-off ever for a defending batting champion (118 points). Teammates insisted the reason for Cash's diminishing returns was his ongoing effort to become more of a power hitter, but it's a specious argument; Cash connected for 377 longballs over his seventeen-year career, but never again reached the forty-homer plateau. Minus his '61 season, his lifetime batting average was just .264. Why Cash stopped corking—or *if* he stopped—is largely conjecture. It's difficult to believe, however, that the slugger went cold turkey on altered bats after the success of his monster 1961 season, especially as he struggled through his follow-up campaign. If corked bats led to consecutive averages of .361 and .243, it probably wasn't the bats that were running hot and cold.

One thing to which corked bats can contribute, however, is a positive mental attitude. Put simply, because a player thinks his bat is quicker, it might actually be. "Quickness is everything, but thinking about quickness usually makes you lose quickness," said one big-leaguer with experience in the subject. "If you think your bat makes you quicker, then you stop thinking about being quicker and you probably are—not because of the bat, but because you're not thinking about it."

Efficacy of the argument aside, there's no disputing that many players buy it. The list of guys who have been caught using doctored bats contains prominent names, such as Sammy Sosa, Albert Belle, and Graig Nettles; others, such as Mets All-Star Howard Johnson, were long accused but never caught. Johnson, in fact, went so far as to leave one of his bats behind after his team concluded a series in Montreal in 1987, specifically for Cardinals manager Whitey Herzog—one of his primary complainants—whose team was due into town the following day. Attached to the bat were twenty wine corks dangling from strings. St. Louis pitcher Bill Dawley, who had served up a homer to Johnson less than a week earlier, wasn't laughing.

"Very funny," he said when the bat was discovered. "He's going to get drilled."

The most unsung cheaters on a baseball diamond are often the groundskeepers, who don't break rules so much as perform their tasks with an eye toward benefiting the home team. The possibilities are virtually limitless: baking the ground around home plate to help a slap-hitting team or watering the dirt into a stew to help a sinkerball pitcher; gently sloping the baselines either fair or foul, depending on which club is stocked with bunters; growing the infield grass long to slow the ball for a team with speed, while keeping the outfield grass short to help balls squirt into the gaps; deforming the mound just where the visiting pitcher tends to land, and making the batter's box either too hard or too soft in the spot that the opposing slugger likes to set up.

Groundskeeper assistance occurred as far back as the 1890s, when the great Baltimore teams of John McGraw and Wilbert Robinson won their games with the help of an unsurpassed collection of speedsters. The Orioles stole a ridiculous 342 bases in 1891 alone, and augmented their baserunning dominance by originating tactical maneuvers such as the hit-and-run. That, though, wasn't enough. Creating a home-field advantage in the truest sense of the term, they mixed the soil near home plate with clay and left it unwatered through the summer months, until it hardened into a concretelike consistency. This became useful when implementing one of their inventions, the Baltimore chop, in which a fleet-of-foot hitter would drive the ball straight down, then race to first as the catcher waited helplessly for the bounce to return to earth. (Visitors could attempt chops of their own, but the swing took a fair amount of practice to perfect and proved beneficial only for the fastest runners.)

Baltimore's groundskeepers didn't stop there; they also sloped the outside of the third-base line to push bunts fair (a tactic later used at Shibe Park for the Phillies' bunter par excellence, Richie Ashburn) and mixed soap flakes into the downslope of the mound, which made it difficult for visiting pitchers to find solid footing unless they knew where to plant. The Orioles even went so far as to hide extra baseballs in the high outfield grass, for those times when chasing a hit all the way into an alley proved inconvenient. (This trick worked well until the day that two outfielders both picked up balls and threw them in simultaneously.)

Except for the hidden baseballs, every trick mentioned above is legal. Some field alterations, however, go specifically against the rulebook, such as moving first base a foot closer to home plate to assist teams built on speed, or a foot backward, to hinder them. Groundskeepers have been known to extend the rear of the batter's box, to give the home-team hitters more time to swing against a particularly hard thrower, or the front of it, to let them get at a curveballer's offering before the pitch can fully break. The most famous instance of the latter happened under instruction from Seattle Mariners manager Maury Wills, who in 1981 ordered the Kingdome's batter's box to be lengthened toward the mound in an effort to help outfielder Tom Paciorek, who stood so far forward that earlier in the season he had a home run nullified because his foot left the box when he swung. (Oakland manager Billy Martin, who noticed Wills's batter's box irregularity, surmised that the reason was that the A's had a curveball pitcher, Rick Langford, on the mound.)

"I think the majority of teams probably hedge an inch or so for their clubs," said White Sox groundskeeper Roger Bossard. Only Wills, though, was suspended for it—for two games. His primary complaint after the fact wasn't even that he got caught, but that his own grounds crew gave up the goods on him after Martin alerted the umps. "I'm shocked and dumfounded," he said afterward. "This never happened to me in 22 years of baseball." It never would again. Wills was fired nine days later, and never managed again.

19

Caught Brown-Handed

In the moment of his being caught red-handed—or brown-handed, as it was—it seemed for all the world that the most interesting thing about the smudge on Kenny Rogers's left palm was that it put up for discussion the notion that not only do ballplayers cheat, but occasionally they don't cheat very well.

The situation was brought to national attention early in Game 2 of the 2006 World Series between St. Louis and Detroit, when television broadcasters Joe Buck and Tim McCarver spotted what appeared to be a muddy substance on Rogers's hand. McCarver immediately noted its resemblance to pine tar, and the announcers discussed it at length—even after it vanished an inning later, leaving a marked skin discoloration. The question was quickly raised: Had Rogers, key to Detroit's pitching staff, been cheating?

The points of those who argued in the affirmative were bolstered by the pitcher's disastrous postseason history. In five wretched playoff starts prior to 2006, Rogers was 0-2, with a 10.26 ERA (plus another loss pitching in relief for the Mets in 1999, when he walked in the winning run of the NLCS), not once making it out of the fifth inning. So it was something of a surprise when, in 2006's earlier rounds, Rogers ran off fourteen consecutive scoreless frames against the Yankees and Athletics. When footage from those starts was reviewed, the same brown smudge showed up on the same spot on his palm. What else could it be?

Shortly after Buck and McCarver began discussing Rogers's hand,

Cardinals manager Tony La Russa—apparently tipped off by someone watching TV in the clubhouse—engaged in a protracted conversation with the umpiring crew, who then ordered the pitcher to go wash up. Conspicuously missing from La Russa's end of the conversation was a request that Rogers be checked for a foreign substance, even though he clearly appeared to be in possession of one. Had the umpires found anything on him, baseball's rulebook called for an automatic ten-game suspension. Rogers could well have missed the rest of the World Series.

Afterward, both La Russa and Tigers manager Jim Leyland refused to condemn the act. Digging through the aftermath, the viewing public was left to wonder why.

Rogers had long been known as one of baseball's premier red-asses, the guy who had punched a cameraman as a member of the Texas Rangers in a widely broadcasted dustup just a season earlier. His smudged hand in the World Series wasn't even the first time he had been accused of cheating; in 2002, Cleveland's Milton Bradley said that Rogers was scuffing the ball after the left-hander came within six outs of a perfect game against the Indians. In the face of such controversy in the World Series, the Gambler did the only thing he could reasonably do—he cleaned his hand and continued to pitch well. Fifteen postseason shutout innings with an obvious foreign substance were followed by seven shutout innings without it. Alleged pine tar or no alleged pine tar, the Cardinals, who scratched out only two hits against Rogers in eight innings, fared no better than the Yankees or the A's had in earlier rounds. Had Rogers's tour de force helped swing the series to Detroit rather than simply provided the Tigers with their lone victory, it would have reaped even greater scrutiny.

Still, why didn't La Russa put up more of a stink?

Pundits immediately turned to the manager's relationship with Leyland, positing that the Cards' skipper wouldn't do anything to embarrass his longtime friend, a theory dismissed out of hand by both La Russa and Leyland. Closer to the truth was La Russa's general acceptance of a base level of cheating in his sport. A baseball man through and through, the manager harbored clear notions of on-field propriety, spending significant time considering the integrity of his actions and those of others. To him,

baseball's Code allowed for subtle bending of the rules. Just as sign stealing is rarely a retaliation-worthy offense, La Russa saw pine tar—as
benign a foreign substance as can be found illegally coating a pitcher's
palm—as an acceptable violation of the rules.

After all, the manager's own players bent certain rules to get whatever
edge they could, as did those on every club in major-league baseball. Only
two seasons earlier, Cardinals pitcher Julian Tavarez had been caught by
umpires with pine tar slathered across his notoriously dirty hat, after
three teams—the Phillies, Braves, and Pirates—accused him of doctoring
the ball. He was suspended for ten days, and La Russa called it "an example of bullshit baseball."

With this in mind, the manager's play-and-let-play credo shouldn't
have been surprising. "There was a time when there was a rage of corked
bats in the American League," he said in response to a question about why
he failed to have Rogers checked. "And the only time I ever challenged a
corked bat was when somebody did some B.S. on the other side. You want
to mess around? Hey, go check his bat."

There's also the fact that many people within the game view the use of
pine tar as perfectly valid. "The only [illegal substance] I ever saw was
pine tar, and I guarantee 80 percent of the pitchers still use it," said Cy
Young Award winner Jack McDowell, who insisted that its primary purpose is "to get a grip for a breaking ball." McDowell recalls balls thrown
by Dennis Martinez that were discolored "right where his curveball grip
was," leaving "two black finger-marks."

In his press conference following Game 2, La Russa was blunt in
describing his reaction to Rogers's palm. "I said, 'I don't like this stuff,
let's get it fixed. If it gets fixed let's play the game,' " he said. "It got fixed,
in my opinion. . . . I detest any B.S. that gets in the way of competition."

The fact that Leyland knew every intricacy of the Cardinals, having
spent the previous six seasons scouting for them, helped make this a can
of worms that La Russa had little inclination of opening. Just as he'd
excuse a sign thief who stopped pilfering upon being caught, once Rogers
washed his hand the problem of cheating ceased to exist for the St. Louis
manager. "Tony's been through a lot himself," said Tigers legend Jack
Morris after the incident, "so I don't think he wanted to push that enve-
lope."

One didn't have to look far for precedent illustrating how ugly things can get in this type of situation. Just a year earlier, members of the Angels had been convinced that Washington Nationals manager Frank Robinson was tipped off to pine tar on the glove of reliever Brendan Donnelly by outfielder (and former Angel) Jose Guillen, who had recently left Anaheim under acrimonious terms. Robinson used the information to the fullest extent of the rules, having Donnelly checked as soon as he entered the game; the right-hander was ejected before he could even throw a pitch. Furious, Angels manager Mike Scioscia confronted Robinson on the field and threatened to "undress" Nationals pitchers in response.

"There's etiquette and there's lack of etiquette," said Donnelly at the time. "And the other day, you saw the latter." The pitcher was ultimately suspended for ten games.

To listen to pitchers like Donnelly tell it, the question is less about why players use pine tar than why the punishment for using it is so steep. Much of its desired effect is, as McDowell said, to gain a better grip on the ball, especially on cold, wet nights. The substance isn't so far removed from rosin (another tacky substance used to increase grip), which is so legal that a supply of it is kept in a bag atop every big-league mound. Technically, rosin is a powdered form of resin, which comes from the sap of pine trees—essentially making it powdered pine tar. When a pitcher picks up a bag filled with the stuff, tacky residue coats his hand; when wet, the two substances can be remarkably similar. "Pine tar is accepted practice for pitchers," said Scioscia after Donnelly was caught.

At the time of Rogers's first World Series pitch against St. Louis, it was forty-four degrees and raining. In his victory over the A's in the previous round, it had been forty-one degrees. Against the Yankees in the Division Series it was fifty-four. All of these numbers were great reasons to want a better grip. The pitcher also claimed that even if the substance on his hand was pine tar—which it *wasn't*, he said—it wouldn't lend anything to the ball's movement. "I don't put anything on the baseball," he said. "I really don't see how that would benefit it, except to maybe throw it twenty feet short." This is mostly accurate, except for the part about benefit; if utilized properly, extra tack can have a profound impact. "Better grip means better spin on the ball," wrote former pitcher Jim Brosnan in a bylined article in *The New York Times*. "Better spin means better movement on the pitch." This means that, through the use of pine tar, an average curveball can conceivably become an outstanding curveball.

What is it about pine tar that makes people so crazy? It's been in use at least since the early 1900s, and had made several prominent appearances in games of significance well before the 2006 series. The most noteworthy of these was the 1983 contest in which Yankees manager Billy Martin had George Brett's go-ahead, ninth-inning home run negated because the future Hall of Famer had pine tar twenty inches up his bat (a common practice to improve grip) when rules mandated an eighteen-inch limit. Upon hearing the umpires' ruling, Brett came tearing out of the Royals dugout at full speed and in a state of near insanity, arms flailing, his face a twisted mask of rage—"about as much of a lunatic act as you've ever seen on a field," he said. (Ironically, the one guy on the Kansas City bench with enough foresight to try to hide Brett's lumber was none other than Gaylord Perry, who grabbed the bat from umpire Tim McClelland, initiating what was essentially a relay race to try to get it off the field and away from the authorities. It didn't work.)

Of course, even Martin had to admit that too much pine tar did nothing to help Brett put distance on a batted ball, and, days later, American League president Lee MacPhail ordered Brett's homer reinstated, which eventually led to a Royals victory. More like Kenny Rogers was Jay Howell, the Dodgers reliever who in 1988 was found to have pine tar on his glove during Game 3 of the National League Championship Series against the New York Mets.

In Darryl Strawberry's autobiography, *Darryl!,* the outfielder wrote that Mets manager Davey Johnson grew suspicious when he saw the extreme break on Howell's pitches, though other sources say Johnson heard about the pitcher's use of the substance from Tucker Ashford, a minor-league manager in the Mets system who played against Howell in the mid-1980s. Either way, Johnson ordered all eyes on Howell as soon as he entered the game. First-base coach Bill Robinson noticed the pitcher tugging at the leather strings on the back of his glove, and Johnson waited until the eighth inning to pounce. With Howell trying to hold a 4–3 lead and a full count on leadoff hitter Kevin McReynolds, Johnson asked the umpires to search the pitcher; they found the pine tar, ejected him, and continued the game. New Dodgers pitcher Alejandro Pena served up ball four to McReynolds, which helped ignite a five-run rally for New York. Howell was ultimately suspended for two days by National League president Bart Giamatti, the first time any player had been suspended from postseason play for cheating.

Dodgers manager and former pitcher Tommy Lasorda, who admitted to his own occasional use of pine tar during his playing days with Brooklyn, brought up a point that would become a staple eighteen years later in conversations about Rogers. "I don't think (Howell) was cheating," he said. "What he did was simply to get a better grip."

Whether or not Rogers cheated, there are holes in his story. Plate umpire Alfonso Marquez said that he talked to the pitcher about removing the "dirt" as Rogers came off the field. Crew chief Randy Marsh said he told La Russa that Rogers was being instructed to wash his hand. Both these accounts were confirmed by umpiring supervisor Steve Palermo. In Rogers's version, however, the pitcher noticed the dirt himself and wiped it off on his own accord, and said that his discussion with Marquez concerned the amount of time between innings, not pine tar or his pitching hand. He also said the smudge was the result of his rubbing up warm-up baseballs with mud and rosin before the game. "It was a big clump of dirt," Rogers opined. "I like the dirt on it, mud on it, spit, rosin, whatever you want to talk about. I use all that stuff to get the ball to where you can feel it."

Not everyone bought it. "I don't believe it was dirt," said La Russa the next day. "Didn't look like dirt."

If both the conversation and the foreign substance are conjecture, the reaction Rogers received upon returning to the Tigers dugout in the second inning was indisputable: The pitcher was caught on television being ordered into the clubhouse by Tigers first-base coach coach Andy Van Slyke. Although Van Slyke said that he told Rogers only to "get down in the tunnel and stay warm," there was a brown clump on the pitcher's palm when he disappeared, and nothing but residue from whatever had just been washed away when he returned. As Tim McCarver asked on the air: "If it wasn't illegal, why was it washed off?"

"What they're doing," said Palermo after the game, explaining why the umpires had Rogers clean his hands but didn't discipline him, "is that they're trying to remove doubt in that situation."

But if an illegal substance Rogers claims wasn't on his hand wouldn't help him, how about the other noted liberty he took during the game? Instead of a regulation Tigers cap, as was worn by every one of his teammates, Rogers sported a batting-practice cap. The difference? The hat on his head was darker under the bill—the better, said skeptics, to hide a foreign substance. The pitcher's explanation made about as much sense as anything else he said: The regular cap gave him headaches.

After the Rogers incident, the person to whom reporters repeatedly turned for comment was eight hundred miles away, on his fifty-eight-acre North Carolina farm. Gaylord Perry was used to it, having made a career of applying various lubricants to baseballs. The day after the Rogers incident, Perry had to interrupt work to field no fewer than sixteen calls seeking his opinion on the matter.

He told everyone who asked that he concurred with most of the principals in the affair, ceding that pine tar is used primarily to help a pitcher's grip when the weather is cold and the ball is damp. Then he added, "Pine tar in North Carolina is clean. . . . It doesn't show up. [Rogers has] to get some of *that*."

PART FOUR

TEAMMATES

20

Don't Talk About a No-Hitter in Progress

If baseball ranked practical jokers like it ranked home-run hitters, Bert Blyleven would be the all-time leader—by a mile. His was a relentless pursuit of the perfect clubhouse prank, with his teammates living in a perpetual state of giddy terror, horrified at the notion that they might end up on the wrong end of what he continues to describe as a sense of humor. But, as beloved as Blyleven may have been, and with as much leeway as he was afforded for being both slightly addled and from the Netherlands, he still found a way to take things too far. Hotfoots, buzzers, firecrackers, and liniment oil were his staples, but it wasn't with any of them that the right-hander overstepped his limits when he broke one of baseball's most hallowed unwritten rules.

It was September 22, 1977, in Anaheim. Blyleven, the ace of the Texas Rangers, was dominating the Angels with the best curveball in the game. Through seven innings, the only baserunner he allowed had come on an error by Rangers shortstop Bert Campaneris. As Blyleven sat in the dugout next to catcher Jim Sundberg, he looked up at the scoreboard and started pondering. "Hey, Jimmy," he said as casually as if he was complimenting Sundberg's sweatbands. "You know we got a no-hitter going?" The catcher was speechless. He looked at Blyleven. He thought about an appropriate response. He looked at Blyleven again. In the end, he could manage only to walk away in silence.

"He wouldn't even talk to me," said the right-hander quizzically. "I don't know why. [Bringing it up] kind of relaxed me a little bit, but it made

Jimmy very nervous. I thought I had friends on the team until I got to a situation like that, and then they leave you pretty much alone. That's just the way it is." Despite the faux pas, Blyleven got his no-hitter.

Not talking about a no-hitter in progress is among the oldest of baseball's traditions. It's relatively unique among the unwritten rules, in that, whereas the majority of the Code has to do with respect, this one is sheer superstition. Some players take their totems very seriously—from never touching a baseline as they walk on or off the field, to refusing to wash their clothes when they're riding a hot streak—but this is the only one to garner virtually unanimous consensus.

Don't talk to the pitcher. Don't sit near the pitcher. Don't interact with the pitcher. Don't look at the pitcher. Don't change the pitcher's routine in any way. Don't change *your* routine in any way. The same rules apply to the pitcher himself, who is expected to avoid his teammates with the same fervor they use in avoiding him. The subclauses of the rule are plentiful, and if one of them is broken and a hit is subsequently surrendered, it's the fault of the jinxer, not the pitcher. "Don't ever do that," said Phil Garner. "You don't ever say anything. It's just something you don't ever do. Don't ever mention it. Never."

"If you even think about telling him he's got a no-hitter going, somebody's going to smack you one," said Mark Grace.

Superstition aside, the concept is designed to protect pitchers from outside influence, removing unnecessary pressure in case they hadn't yet taken note of their accomplishment. The question, of course, is whether that's even possible.

"I knew it. I mean, shit, anybody who says he didn't know he had a no-hitter, he must have been worse than Dock Ellis was on the one that he threw," said Dick Bosman, who threw a no-hitter for Cleveland in 1974, referencing Ellis's famous LSD-fueled masterpiece in 1970. (Even Ellis claimed he was aware of what was happening at the time.)

"There's no way he can't know," said Dodgers pitcher Rex Barney, who no-hit the Giants in 1948. "Every time he looks at the scoreboard for the outs or the count he sees that 0-0-0 up there."

In the modern era, players also have television. Starting pitchers regularly make between-innings trips to the clubhouse, where it's virtually impossible to avoid game broadcasts in which their performance is likely the primary topic of discussion. (During David Cone's perfect game in 1999, for example, the right-hander listened to Yankees broadcaster Michael Kay talk about it from the fifth inning on, which is when the superstition usually kicks in.)

If, beyond all odds, the feat still manages to escape the pitcher, he can pick up a clue from incrementally decreasing interactions with his teammates. "You start to see the guys easing away," said Oscar Gamble. "When they get that no-hitter you start to notice a little bench space on both sides of the pitcher getting bigger and bigger."

"Same seats, same thoughts—that's the mantra," said Bob Brenly, manager of the Arizona Diamondbacks when Randy Johnson threw his perfect game in 2004. "From about the fourth inning of that ballgame on I found myself sitting on the bat rack at Turner Field. [Second baseman] Matt Kata's bat was sitting right next to my right leg, and before every pitch I would tap that bat just to knock wood for luck. The deeper we got into the game, I was afraid to stop doing it. I'm a firm believer in the baseball gods—you show them their due respect and they will reward you. So I didn't move off that bat rack. I knocked on that bat on every pitch. My knuckles were raw by the end of the game, but I just felt that you can't change anything."

Ignorance of the rule is no excuse. When David Wells was with the minor-league Syracuse Chiefs in 1987, he struck up a fifth-inning conversation with teammate Todd Stottlemyre, who was charting pitches on his off-day. That one of their teammates was in the process of throwing a no-hitter didn't affect him a bit. "Hey, Stott," he said, "how many walks does he have?" Stottlemyre replied that an opponent had yet to draw a base on balls. "Wow!" said Wells. "He's throwing a perfect game!" Chiefs trainer Jon Woodworth recalled Stottlemyre looking "like he was going to kill" Wells. The left-hander's defense: In his twenty-four years on the planet, five of them in professional baseball, he had somehow never before heard the rule prohibiting discussion of no-hitters. The very next inning, the Syracuse pitcher gave up a two-out bloop single.

It's a lesson Wells didn't need to learn twice. In fact, he went so far as to become an evangelist for the idea. In his book, *Perfect I'm Not*, the pitcher laid out in the starkest possible terms the rule of which he once claimed ignorance:

Rule number one in baseball is that you never, EVER mention that a guy's throwing a perfect game or a no-hitter until it's over. If you mention it during the game, it's a major jinx, the ultimate whammy. The pitcher on the mound will give up a hit to the next batter, and it WILL be your fault—guaranteed.

Some people find religion; David Wells found superstition. Like Blyleven before him, however, Wells held his view only in regard to other pitchers; he didn't care a bit when it was him at the center of the maelstrom. During his perfect game in 1998, in fact, as Wells's teammates on the Yankees edged farther away with each passing inning, he decided to take things into his own hands. Changing his undershirt in the clubhouse after the seventh inning, Wells saw David Cone, one of his best friends on the team. Highly in tune with the pressure of the moment, the left-hander approached his teammate, uncertain of what exactly he needed. "Can you believe what's going on here?" he asked.

In retrospect, Cone feels that Wells simply wanted someone to talk to. In the moment, however, he was all too aware of the implications and at something of a loss for words—so he blurted out the first thing that came to mind, daring Wells to break out the knuckleball he liked to throw in practice but wouldn't dare try in a game.

Wells laughed and returned to the dugout. After he finished his eighth perfect inning, Cone got on him again, this time in the dugout. "You showed me nothing," he yelled as the nervous pitcher came off the field. "You didn't use your knuckleball—you've got no guts!"

The tactic might have been taboo, but Cone knew his pal needed conversation more than he needed tradition, and Wells went on to finish the fifteenth perfect game in big-league history. "To me, that kind of stuff is more important than some superstition that says you can't get near the guy," Cone said later.

Cone was more than just talk, however. A year later, in the middle of his own perfect game, against the Montreal Expos, he handled a similar response with aplomb. Yankees catcher Joe Girardi was in the on-deck circle when the sixth inning ended, and had to scramble back to the dugout to don his equipment. With backup catcher Jorge Posada in the bullpen, there was nobody to catch Cone's warm-ups. Designated hitter Chili

Davis quickly assessed the situation and, not wanting Cone's rhythm to be thrown off, grabbed a mask and filled in until Girardi could get properly armored.

The change hardly rattled Cone, who retired three Expos in order, but shortly after he returned to the bench, Davis sat down next to him. "Hey, man," he said to the surprised pitcher, "I was a catcher in the minor leagues." Cone was simultaneously perplexed and relieved as Davis began to recount his own bush-league glory wearing shin guards and a chest protector. "You should have seen me catch, man, I was great," said the slugger, who pitched in more games as a major-leaguer—one—than he caught. "Don't baby it up there next time I warm you up," he teased. "Let it go. I can handle it."

"It worked," said Cone. "It was nothing profound, but at the time it was a real tension-breaker."

The most famous no-hitter ever, of course, was Don Larsen's perfect game in Game 5 of the 1956 World Series, which made his breach of etiquette in the middle of it all the more shocking to his teammates. As the game wound down, the New York bench was a silent picture of no-hitter decorum. Backup infielder Billy Hunter made sure to maintain his position on the bench, and when he returned from a seventh-inning sojourn to the water cooler to find Mickey Mantle there, he politely asked the superstar to move. Mantle far outranked Hunter in the clubhouse hierarchy, but he hardly outranked Bob Brenly's baseball gods, and quickly obliged. With nowhere to sit, Mantle strolled by the dugout tunnel, where he saw Larsen hanging back in the shadows, cigarette in hand. The pitcher looked up. "Well, Mick, do you think I'll make it?" he asked.

Mantle, stunned, could formulate no reply. For a moment he did nothing. Then he decided that, if the Code was strong enough for him to concede his spot on the bench, it was strong enough for him to keep his mouth shut. He didn't say a word.

"Some people believe in jinxes, some don't," said Larsen later. "I don't. If it's going to happen, it's going to happen. I mentioned it, but nobody would talk to me. I didn't care about that, either. I was just trying to win the ballgame."

Bob Brenly might embrace the "same seats, same thoughts" mantra when it comes to no-hitters, but during Randy Johnson's perfect game in 2004, he wasn't allowed simply to sit still, tapping his knuckles raw on Matt Kata's bat. As the manager, he had decisions to make.

Late in the 2–0 contest, Brenly wanted to insert a defensive substitute for left fielder Luis Gonzalez, but was hesitant to disrupt the game's rhythm. He also considered having a pitcher warm up as the forty-year-old Johnson's pitch count climbed in the late innings, but didn't want the pitcher even to glimpse such a thing. "What should have been one of the easiest games to manage, I was losing my hair over," he said. "I had never been involved in a game like that before, and I just didn't want to do anything to screw it up. That was one of the most stressful games I've ever been involved with in my life." Brenly and his coaches ultimately opted to maintain the status quo, and it worked out to everybody's advantage.

Conversely, White Sox manager Ozzie Guillen paid no attention whatsoever to the rule when he inserted DeWayne Wise into center field as a ninth-inning defensive replacement during Mark Buehrle's attempt to close out a perfect game against the Tampa Bay Rays in 2009. Buehrle may actually have been spooked by the change; the first batter after the substitution was Gabe Kapler, who hit a ball over the left-center-field wall that a leaping Wise managed to pull back into the park for the first out of the inning. No harm, no foul; Buehrle didn't allow another ball out of the infield, recording two more outs and finishing off the seventeenth regular-season perfect game in big-league history.

For an example of what can go wrong when a manager begins to tinker, look no further than Cincinnati's Davey Johnson. It was 1995, and the pitcher was David Wells, three seasons before he achieved perfection with the Yankees. The left-hander had taken a no-hitter into the seventh inning in Philadelphia, which was broken up when outfielder Tom Marsh connected for a one-out double. Wells, though, never blamed Marsh for the hit. He blamed Johnson.

With left fielder Ron Gant suffering from leg problems, Johnson decided to realign his outfield before the inning, shifting center fielder Thomas Howard to left, inserting Darren Lewis into center, and removing Gant from the game. Wells just about blew his top, and in the process lost focus, giving up two hits and a run by inning's end. When the pitcher returned to the bench, he was beside himself with rage. Without a word he threw his hat to the ground and head-butted Johnson, who barely flinched. "What the fuck are you doin'?" asked the manager, as if Wells had merely tousled his hair. "You don't ever mess with the lineup during a no-hitter!" Wells screamed. "That's a cardinal rule, dude! You don't do it!"

Wells is lucky he never played for manager Preston Gomez, who not only juggled the lineup while his pitcher was throwing a no-hitter—the guy he juggled was the pitcher himself. It was 1970, and Gomez was managing the San Diego Padres when Clay Kirby held the Mets hitless through the first eight innings of a game. The problem was that Kirby had allowed a first-inning run on two walks and three stolen bases, and trailed 1–0. Kirby and all ten thousand paying customers couldn't believe it when pinch-hitter Cito Gaston emerged from the dugout to bat in the pitcher's spot. "My father was there," said Kirby. "It was the first game he'd ever seen me pitch in San Diego. He was madder than I was." Reliever Jack Baldschun took over in the ninth, and took all of four pitches to give New York its first hit in a game it would win 3–0.

As if to prove it wasn't a strategic fluke, Gomez did the same thing four years later while managing the Houston Astros, pulling Don Wilson after eight no-hit innings for a pinch-hitter with his team trailing 2–1. Never has a man been more inclined to prove the theorem that winning takes precedent over any part of the Code.

Short of being pulled from a game, no pitcher had to endure more while chasing a no-hitter than Kenny Rogers. In 1994, the Rangers ace was hurling a perfect game against the California Angels when, in the fifth inning, a full-fledged bonfire broke out in his team's dugout. It had been set by Rangers players Chris James and Gary Redus, and was directed not at Rogers but at designated hitter Jose Canseco. For kindling, the duo used the red, ratty high-top cleats Canseco refused to relinquish in favor of new ones. James absconded with the shoes before the game, forcing Canseco to don another pair, and when the slugger responded by hitting two home runs in the first three innings, the decision was made to ensure that his old shoes would never return. A bottle of rubbing alcohol was procured from the trainer's room, and somebody found a match. Right there by the bench, the immolation began—all while Rogers pitched.

As the flames grew, members of the Rangers bench started dancing around the pyre. "I looked over there from first base and said, 'What the hell's going on?' " recalled Texas first baseman Will Clark. "Then I heard what they had done. I couldn't see, I was laughing so hard." On the mound, however, Rogers was so focused that he never noticed the plume of smoke emerging from the dugout, and remained oblivious until he was told what had happened once the game was over. "I like that," he said. "We'll burn the rest of his shoes if that's what it takes."

Players on the bench might be required by code to refrain from discussing a no-hitter in progress, but logic dictates that broadcasters be held to a different standard—after all, it's their job to describe the action. For some, though, that's not motivation enough. "I won't even mention it," said Angels broadcaster and former player Rex Hudler. "I'll let my partner do it."

Hudler has copious precedent on which to base his opinion. During the first televised World Series, in 1947, Yankees right-hander Bill Bevens pitched hitless ball into the ninth inning of Game 4 against the Dodgers; with virtually no precedent on which to rely, broadcaster Mel Allen refused to reference the feat. "Obviously, what I said or didn't say in the booth wasn't going to influence anything that happened on the field," he said. "But I've always known that players on the bench don't mention a no-hitter; they respect the dugout tradition. And I've always done the same. It's part of the romance of the game. It's one of the great things that separates it from the other sports, like the seventh-inning stretch or 'Take Me Out to the Ballgame.' "

For the purists in the audience this was just fine, save for one fact: Allen worked only the first half of the game. The later innings were given to Dodgers broadcaster Red Barber, who wasted no time in altering the tone. Among the first things out of his mouth when he entered midway through the fourth was the line score: "Dodgers: one run, two errors, no hits." Allen, said Barber, "nearly fell out of the booth." Barber continued to report the feat throughout the game, his comfort level possibly buoyed by the run Brooklyn scored in the fifth without benefit of a hit, courtesy of two walks, a sacrifice, and a fielder's choice. In the ninth, long after Barber gave up the goods on the air, Bevens issued two more walks (one intentional) and a two-out double by Cookie Lavagetto to score both runners, the difference in an improbable 3–2 Brooklyn victory.

As the winning run scored, Barber's on-air comment was, "Well, I'll be a suck-egg mule." His audience certainly thought so. "There was a hue and cry that night," said the broadcaster. "Yankee fans flooded the radio station with angry calls and claimed I had jinxed Bevens. Some of my fellow announcers on sports shows that evening said I had done the most unsportsmanlike broadcast in history."

It's not like he had no experience with the subject—Barber encountered a similar situation during the first major-league game he ever worked. It was opening day for the Chicago Cubs in 1934, and pitcher Lon Warneke hadn't allowed a hit into the ninth inning. At the time, Barber didn't actively disdain the ban on mentioning a no-hitter—he'd simply never heard the rule. "I broadcast Warneke's mastery as he performed it," he wrote in a bylined article for the *Christian Science Monitor* in 1988, and no one seemed any the worse for it—save, of course, Warneke himself, who gave up a hit in the ninth. Barber was also behind the microphone four years later for the first of Johnny Vander Meer's back-to-back no-hitters. True to form, he talked about Boston's dearth of hits against Cincinnati's right-hander at least once each inning as the game unfolded, this time jinx-free.

All that was merely an opening act, however, for the most famous contest in World Series history—Don Larsen's perfect game in 1956. During that game, Mel Allen worked alongside Brooklyn's young announcer, Vin Scully. As Scully watched the game unfold, the public reaction to Barber's handling of Bevens's failed no-hitter was at the forefront of his mind. "In those days people did not mention 'no-hitter,' " Scully said. "And Mel, he did the first five innings, said, 'He's retired 10 in a row, 12 in a row,' so I picked up the thread and in the second half, I was doing the same thing: 'Twenty-two in a row, 24 in a row.' . . . Today, I would have come on in the fifth inning and said, 'Hey, call your friends, he's pitching a no-hitter.' "

Broadcasters who insist on omitting the small detail that a no-hitter is in progress are often forced to come up with increasingly creative workarounds. Take Bob Wolff, who handled the national radio broadcast for Larsen's perfect game. Like Scully, Wolff knew all about the deluge

Barber had faced after chatting about Bevens's no-hitter in '47, and did not want it repeated on his account. "I thought that if I ever did a no-hitter, I could avoid all that if I used synonyms," he said. "If you keep saying 'no-hitter,' what's your punch line? I wanted to tell the whole story, but I was superstitious myself. So I said things like, '18 up, 18 down,' 'The only hits so far are by the New York Yankees,' and on and on. There was no question [to listeners] what was going on. Not one phone call, not one letter. I didn't use the words until the climax, and then I said, 'A no-hitter, a perfect game!' "

"It's just those three words," said Allen during Dave Righetti's no-hitter for the Yankees in 1983. "He's pitching a . . . you know."

Among the ranks of modern broadcasters, those who refrain are usually ex-players, but even among them opinion is divided. "Because I came from the playing field, my partner told me that it's our job to share what's going on in the game, to alert the viewers to what's happening," said Hudler. "But if the pitcher gave up a hit I'd say, 'Awww, I jinxed it,' because I still have that player's attitude."

Jim Kaat, another ex-player, took things a step further when broadcasting Dwight Gooden's no-hitter for the New York Yankees in 1996. Kaat's partner, David Cohen, refused to mention what was going on; Kaat, treating it like he did as a player, would not even leave his seat. "I usually make a couple pit stops [during the course of a game]," he said, "but I never moved." Phillies broadcaster Scott Graham was even more extreme during Kevin Millwood's no-no against the Giants in 2003. When Graham's wife, sitting in the stands with their two young sons, told him that their boys were getting antsy and needed to go home, he gave her specific instructions . . . that were remarkably short on specifics. "Listen to me," he said, pointing to the scoreboard and issuing as direct an order as he felt able. "You can't leave here until that number under the 'H' changes." Even in casual conversation, the broadcaster was unable to risk a jinx.

The counter to this sort of superstition, of course, is common sense. "It certainly is not a rule in broadcasting to not talk about it," said player-turned broadcaster Steve Lyons. "If you want people to stay tuned, it's almost the opposite. If you want people to stay tuned, you should probably mention, 'Hey, hang in there, don't go anywhere—guy's throwing a no-hitter.' " This is especially true on the radio, said longtime A's broadcaster Ray Fosse, where "you can't see a line score."

By the time Sandy Koufax threw his perfect game in 1965, Scully had completely turned the corner on the rule, and his poetic description of the ninth-inning pressure stands as one of the enduring calls in the game's history, largely because he counted down inevitability while acknowledging exactly what was happening:

There's 29,000 people in the ballpark and a million butterflies. . . . I would think that the mound at Dodger Stadium right now is the loneliest place in the world. Sandy fussing, looks in to get his sign, 0 and 2 to Amalfitano. The strike-two pitch to Joe: fastball, swung on and missed, strike three! He is one out away from the promised land. . . . You can't blame a man for pushing just a little bit now. Sandy backs off, mops his forehead, runs his left index finger along his forehead, dries it off on his left pants leg. All the while, Kuenn just waiting. Now Sandy looks in. Into his windup and the 2-1 pitch to Kuenn: swung on and missed, strike two! It is 9:46 p.m. Two-and-two to Harvey Kuenn, one strike away. Sandy into his windup, here's the pitch: Swung on and missed, a perfect game!

When Scully called Jack Morris's no-hitter for Detroit on the *NBC Game of the Week* in 1984, he came out in the middle innings with the following gem to introduce the topic: "[Tigers catcher Lance] Parrish, needless to say, is not superstitious. He wears No. 13. We have a reason for bringing that up, because we're in the business of telling you what's going on here, and not getting cute and superstitious. So the big story, really, with Detroit leading 4–0, is the fact that Jack Morris has not allowed a hit, and it's going to start to build."

If that's not enough to disprove the notion that talking up a no-hitter is a surefire jinx, what explains the fact that Yankees broadcasters Michael Kay and John Sterling have called four no-hitters, two of them perfect games, and discussed each one along the way? "I'm not a big believer in jinxes, but I heard 'perfect game' about 100 times for four or five innings," said Cone, who listened to Kay in the clubhouse during his own masterpiece. "Believe me, there is nothing to that jinx."

"It doesn't mean a damn thing," agreed Hall of Fame broadcaster and former player Jerry Coleman. "If you're going to pitch a no-hitter, you're going to pitch a no-hitter. If you don't want to mention it, don't. That's a very personal kind of thing." Coleman made that comment from the perspective of the booth, but there are indications that when he was still a Yankees second baseman in the 1950s he felt differently. According to legendary sportswriter Jimmy Cannon, Coleman had such trouble dealing with the pressure of Larsen's perfect game that he had to leave the bench and pace the tunnels under the stands. A groundskeeper saw him there and informed him that Larsen still had not given up a baserunner. "Coleman didn't reply," wrote Cannon, "just glared at the guy."

21

Protect Yourself and Each Other

Because baseball clubhouses are insular by nature, an extraordinary amount of protection takes place within their walls, aimed mostly in three directions: from the media (don't let slip potentially compromising personal tidbits, or anything about internal conflicts), from management (the less the boss knows about last night's bender, the better), and from women (never let someone else's wife or girlfriend in on road-trip indiscretions).

It doesn't take much effort to refrain from spilling clubhouse secrets to the media, since most players inherently prefer to avoid the press whenever possible. Standing up to management, however, is a different matter. The first step is to understand whom one's dealing with. Clubhouse secrets are known to filter their way upstairs; the trick for players is figuring out how it happens, and putting an end to it. The conduit of sensitive information between clubhouse and the executive offices is known informally as "the pipeline," and, to the consternation of players everywhere, most teams have one. "There's one on every team I've gone to," said pitcher Matt Herges. "When I came to the Marlins I called [catcher] Paul Lo Duca and asked what's up with the team. He said, 'So-and-so is the pipeline, this guy is a jerk, this guy comes to the park drunk every day,' and so forth. You get the whole rundown, and the pipeline is always the first guy mentioned."

The pipeline can be a trainer, a coach, or an equipment man—anyone with an ear to the clubhouse wall. Trainers are especially notorious, holding the potent combination of being beholden to management and possessing unassailable information about the health of the roster. Say a player is injured enough to merit taking several days off. He's struggling, though, and maybe not on the best terms with the manager, so rather than risk earning a reputation as being soft, he decides to play through it—with some help. He approaches the trainer with a dual request: something to treat his ailment, and secrecy.

Some trainers deliver this; some go straight upstairs. Their information becomes useful for management when it comes to things like roster decisions and arbitration hearings. It's hardly limited to the trainer's room, however.

On the A's teams of the early 1970s, the pipeline was said to be broadcaster Monte Moore, the only radio man team owner Charlie Finley allowed to last as many as two seasons. ("I was fired by Finley after my first year," said play-by-play legend Jon Miller, the longtime voice of ESPN's *Sunday Night Baseball*. "I didn't take it badly. Everybody was fired by Charlie.") There seemed to be a primary reason that Moore outlasted sixteen play-by-play partners in as many years with the team: He reportedly passed inside clubhouse information to the owner—in one case specifically, details of a drunken incident on a team flight in 1967, which likely led to the release of first baseman Ken Harrelson and the dismissal of manager Alvin Dark. Moore long denied the allegations, but as with most men suspected of serving as a pipeline, the rumor hardly endeared him to the players—to the point that protections were put into place: "It's an automatic $500 if anyone punches Monte," said A's catcher Dave Duncan at the time.

Suspicions run so deep in this arena that when the Mets hired Allan Lans to be the team psychiatrist in 1987, he was immediately pegged by a number of players as a clubhouse spy. It didn't matter a bit that as the associate director at the Smithers Center for Alcoholism and Drug Treatment Lans had cared for Dwight Gooden, and had clearly been brought in to ease the pitcher's return to the game after the right-hander missed the first third of the 1987 season while in rehab.

Pipelines were a regular feature of the George Steinbrenner–era Yankees, though over his thirty-plus years in charge of the team, the owner seemed to use them against his managers as often as against his players. Of particular interest to him in this regard was Billy Martin. In *The Bronx Zoo*, Sparky Lyle's day-by-day account of the 1978 season, the pitcher noticed that coach Gene Michael was forced to locker separately from the rest of the staff. Lyle guessed that he had been exiled by Martin on suspicion of spying for Steinbrenner. "It's a good example of what the love of baseball can make a person do," Lyle wrote. "He loves the game so much that this is what he'd do to stay in it."

During his later tenures as Yankees manager, Martin also had suspicions about players such as Lou Piniella and Bobby Murcer, and another coach, Jeff Torborg, who was probably suspected because he didn't fit in with the late-night, hard-drinking crowd with which the manager surrounded himself. Although it was Martin who initially brought Torborg to the team, their relationship soured quickly. Torborg, however, became a favorite of Steinbrenner's, and managed to outlast Martin's protestations for a decade, being retained on staff four of the five times Martin was fired by the club.

Gene Michael took over two seasons after Martin was fired by Steinbrenner for the second time, at which point another coach, Clyde King, was rumored to have become a spy for the owner. (And just as the accused spy Michael took over when Martin was fired, King took over the ball club upon Michael's dismissal midway through the 1982 campaign.) When Buck Showalter led the team in 1994 and 1995, he was convinced that coach Bill Connors served as Steinbrenner's ears in the clubhouse. "He kept his own book with pitchers' and hitters' matchups, and kept it all to himself," Connors said. "He actually got pissed off at me for looking at it one time. 'What's that?' I asked him. 'I thought we were on the same team.' "

As late as 2007, New York's bullpen coach, Joe Kerrigan, was purported to be a mole for Steinbrenner—after filling that role while on the coaching staffs in Montreal, Boston, and Baltimore, said Hall of Fame writer Tracy Ringolsby—in the process damaging a previously strong relationship between manager Joe Torre and general manager Brian Cashman.

"It's a give-and-take thing," said one player who wished to remain anonymous. "If someone in the front office is desperate to know what really goes on down here [in the clubhouse], they have their ways. But they take the chance on splintering apart what could already be good chemistry. Proceed at your own risk."

·   ·   ·

There are times when management doesn't need a mole to find out what's going on. Take a story from the Tampa hotel owned by George Steinbrenner that was used by the Yankees during spring training. In 1979, numerous players—by multiple accounts, virtually the entire roster—broke curfew one night by tying bedsheets together and rappelling to the ground from their second-floor rooms in order to visit a local after-hours establishment. (The team couldn't walk out the front door on account of the sentry posted there, who recorded the names of everyone who came and went.) Things were especially delicate at the time, because the team was off to a rocky start to the exhibition season; it may only have been spring training, but this was the Yankees and expectations were high.

When the team returned to quarters near dawn, pitcher Ron Guidry was first up the bedsheet ladder, then helped his teammates into the building. People returned to their rooms via outdoor balconies, since Steinbrenner also had guards posted in the hallways. It was a perfect plan, and would have gone undetected had only someone remembered to pull the sheets back through the window. This became relevant when Steinbrenner decided, in a rare occurrence, to join his team on the bus to the ballpark the following day. Looking toward his hotel, he saw the sheets flapping in the wind and flew into a fury.

"He wanted to know whose room that was," said pitcher Dick Tidrow, who was especially nervous owing to the fact that it was his room. As the owner dressed down his roster from the front of the bus, Tidrow weighed his options. A solid member of the bullpen but hardly a star, the pitcher was probably expendable should Steinbrenner want to make an example of him. He also knew that if he kept his mouth shut it was a simple matter for the Boss to get all the relevant information with a phone call to hotel security, at which point things would only get worse.

On the hook either way, Tidrow spoke up. "Um . . . I think it might be mine," he said softly. Steinbrenner's eyes fixed sharply on the right-hander, and as the owner opened his mouth Tidrow contemplated the possibility that he had pitched his last game for the Yankees. Before Steinbrenner could speak, however, Guidry's hand shot up. "No," he said emphatically. "It's mine."

Now the owner was confused. Tidrow might have been expendable, but Guidry, the reigning AL Cy Young Award winner, certainly was not.

Steinbrenner closed his mouth and quietly pondered the situation. After a moment's hesitation, he perked up and shouted, "I like the initiative that shows!" The subject was never raised again.

In many ways, it's not so difficult for players to protect themselves from management. They usually know whom to talk to and whom not to talk to, and the social circles of the two groups rarely intersect. Protecting teammates from the women in their lives, however, can be significantly more complex, especially when it comes to trysts on the road. The crux of the problem with this particular endeavor is that it involves ballplayers— the most visible people in virtually any public environment—trying to stay as *in*visible as possible. The bond between players is strong, however, and they do what they can to maintain each other's anonymity. It's why players whose wives show up during road trips make clear to their teammates where on the town they'll be that night, so they can avoid the chance of running into a married player on a "date" with someone other than his wife. (Mets pitcher Doug Sisk was once guilty of this when he brought his wife, Lisa, to the team's hotel bar, where she saw a number of his married teammates getting friendly with ladies unknown to her.)

It's why some players implement an ignorance rule at home. "My policy with my wife is this: Don't ask me," said one longtime pitcher who claimed fidelity but didn't want to incriminate his teammates. "First of all, I don't want to lie to you. Second of all, I don't want to tell you that this guy's cheating on his wife. You're her friend, you're going to be sitting next to her at games, your heart will be breaking for her—you can't do it. Please, just don't ask me. Don't ask me, because I don't want to put you in that situation."

Not everybody is so virtuous. Players have been known to prattle to their wives about the extramarital adventures of their teammates in an effort to mask their own infidelities. Wives inevitably talk to each other, and if word gets out about where it all started, clubhouses can fracture. When a player is inexplicably traded over the off-season for less than full value, there's a reasonable chance that he betrayed his teammates in this or some other regard (or, in turn, that he was betrayed by a less expendable star).

Perhaps the best story of teammate protection in this category was told by Negro Leagues star Buck O'Neil, who found himself one day in the middle of a Satchel Paige love triangle that involved Paige's fiancée and a woman named Nancy, who at the pitcher's request had traveled to Chicago to visit the team.

We're in Chicago, on the South Side, at the Evans Hotel. We're housed on the third floor, but Satchel and me are down in the restaurant sipping on a little "tea," right near a bay window. We could look right out on the street. A cab drives up and out stepped Nancy, as pretty as a picture. Satchel jumps up and gets the bellman, goes out and gets Nancy, takes her stuff upstairs, and gets all situated. As soon as they get through, they're going to be coming back down.

I go back to the table and was sipping on my tea—it wasn't twenty minutes—and here comes another cab. And out steps Lahoma. Lahoma was Satchel's fiancée. I said, uh-oh. I jumped up, ran out, and greeted Lahoma. I said, "Lahoma, Satchel ran off with some reporters but he'll be back presently. Come on in." I went to get the waiter and sat her down and told him, "Get her whatever she wants."

Then I went to the bellman and I said, "Hey, man, you go upstairs and you tell Satchel that Lahoma's here." I'm sleeping next door to Satchel, but next door to me is a vacant room. I tell him, "You take Nancy and her stuff and put them in the vacant room, and when you get everything straight, you come and let me know." Then I go back with Lahoma, and about twenty-five minutes later he gives me the signal everything is okay.

Now, from the third floor, Satchel has to come down the elevator, come down the stairs, and he's got to come by us, but he can't do that because he's supposed to be off with some reporters. So, from the third floor, Satchel comes down the fire escape and walks all the way around the hotel and walks in the front door. "Oh, Lahoma, what a pleasant surprise, I'm so glad to see you."

We had a good time that evening too. Joe Louis stopped by and dined with us, and Jesse Owens stopped by—we had a good time.

Now it's eleven o'clock. I said, "Well, we've got a doubleheader tomorrow. I guess it's time we better go to bed." Well, Satch and Lahoma and me, we go up. I get in bed but I can't sleep, because I know Satchel has to see Nancy and give her some money to get back home.

After about a half-hour, Satchel's door opens. I say, "Mm-hmm, it's going down right now." Satchel goes to Nancy's door and knocks soft, whispers, "Nancy." Nobody answers. He knocks louder and says, "Nancy," under his breath, and nobody answers. "Now he knocks loudly, and says "Nancy!" And I hear Satchel's door open again. I go, "Uh-oh, this has got to be Lahoma, and Satchel's at Nancy's door." I run out into the hall and say, "Satchel, you lookin' for me?" And he says, "Yes, Nancy!"

And I've been Nancy ever since.

22

Everybody Joins a Fight

Troy Percival was pissed. It was 1999, and the Angels closer had blown a lead to Cleveland, hanging a 1-2 curveball that Indians first baseman Richie Sexson had crushed for a three-run, game-winning homer. Percival was pissed that Sexson's blast was the capper on an eighth-inning rally that brought the Indians back from what had, at the beginning of the frame, been a 12–4 deficit. He was pissed that Sexson and the Indians rejoiced on the field before the next batter came to the plate. He was pissed that he was lousy that night. He was pissed that his team lost what had, a half-hour earlier, looked like an unlosable game. He was pissed that the Angels were 10-36 since the All-Star break. But mostly he was pissed at Mo Vaughn.

Percival had responded to Sexson's homer by hitting the next batter, David Justice, in the midsection with a ninety-six-mile-an-hour heater. The pitch was clearly fueled by a reckless blend of frustration and anger, and its intent was unmistakable. Suddenly, Percival was no longer the only one stewing on the field; Justice, incensed, charged the mound, throwing his helmet at the pitcher when he got close. (Percival later called it "a Little League move.") The benches emptied, and though there weren't many punches thrown, the few that were seemed to connect with Percival's face; the pitcher was cut when the strap from Justice's batting glove whipped across his cheek, and he sported a bruise under his right eye.

When Percival returned to the bench following the skirmish, he found Vaughn, Anaheim's designated hitter, standing in the corner of the dugout, having never set foot on the field.

It seemed a fitting cap to Percival's wretched day. The pitcher went straight into the trainer's room after the game and didn't emerge for more than an hour, while the media lurked in the adjacent clubhouse. When he did, he made it worth their wait. "I'll tell you one thing," he said to those who had bothered to stick around. "I gained respect for certain people, and there are certain people that I have to question. You can watch the video and figure it out. I was pretty impressed with some people, I can tell you that much." It just so happened that TV cameras caught Vaughn in the dugout, looking on as the fight came to a close, and Percival, watching replays in the trainer's room, knew it. "I've got respect for my infielders—they were out there," he continued. "Gary DiSarcina, Darin Erstad, [Troy] Glaus. That's where you learn who the people are on your team who are standing behind you 100 percent. In the future, you know what guys will go to battle with you and which ones won't."

It was another divisive issue in a clubhouse that had already been splintering for months. After initially declining to comment, Vaughn addressed the matter the following day, in the most conspicuous way possible—at high volume, in the middle of the Angels locker room, and within easy earshot of both media and his teammates, Percival included. "I'm sick and fucking tired of this shit!" Vaughn bellowed. "I can give a fuck what somebody else says! I've been fighting in brawls all my career, and if I was down on the bench I would have been in that one. But I was in the clubhouse, watching the game on TV and feeling like I was in the fucking Twilight Zone!"

Percival, playing cards nearby, looked up at the tirade, then nonchalantly returned to his game. "I've been telling these assholes the same thing all year—keep that shit out of the papers!" Vaughn continued. "You got a problem with somebody, say it to his face and keep it inside [the clubhouse]!"

At that point, Vaughn, realizing that the best defense is a good offense, turned the tables and made it personal. "Take your beating like a man," he said, in comments obviously pointed toward Percival's defeat a day earlier. "You get your shit wrapped around the pole, don't throw at the guy—get the next guy out and get out of the inning." Next, Vaughn tore into the notion of teammate protection, which for Percival meant on-field brawn during a fight, but for Vaughn meant something different. "I've been getting drilled all year. Anyone protecting me?" he screamed. "We've been getting drilled all year. Ain't nobody doing shit! Nobody's been on their backs once, not one time. You call that a fucking team?"

It was a lot of anger for any player to put on open display, let alone someone who was brought in during the off-season to be a team leader, at a price tag of eighty million dollars. It was the clearest-cut example of a deeply fractured clubhouse, and though the Angels' problems certainly ran deeper than Vaughn versus Percival, the spat serves to illustrate one of the most universally observed of the unwritten rules: Everybody joins a fight.

Most of the Code is about respect for the opponent, but this rule is about respecting teammates. It's the most basic of sacrifices, and the fact that the majority of baseball fights don't involve much actual fighting is almost incidental; it's a matter of loyalty that can't be ignored. Hall of Famer Ernie Banks called a player's failure to join a fight "the ultimate violation of being a teammate."

"The player that didn't come out would lose a lot of respect from his teammates, not being there to help them out," said outfielder Dave Collins. "It's probably not a situation where he could ever work his way back into good graces. It's one of those things like cheating on your wife—it may be forgiven, but it will never be forgotten."

It's one of the things that ran George Foster out of New York in 1986. Foster's rapidly declining performance and highest-in-baseball salary also had something to do with it, but on July 22, Foster lost most—if not all—of whatever teammate support he had in one swift display of inaction. It started when Cincinnati's Eric Davis inadvertently knocked into Mets third baseman Ray Knight during a play at third base. Shoving became punching, the dugouts emptied, and one of the rare baseball fights in which actual blows were thrown was under way. It would be the most brutal brawl in which many of the players ever participated, with violent skirmishes breaking out across the diamond for a sustained period of time. "I have three guys on me, people are trying to kill each other, it's all-out mayhem," said Mets outfielder Kevin Mitchell, a rookie that season. "And one guy is on the pine, watching it all happen."

That guy was Foster, sitting on the bench, arms folded. He had been there all along.

"I know what was expected of me," said Foster shortly thereafter, "but there were two reasons I didn't run on the field. For one thing, you can easily get hurt. And if there's a fight, the umpires are supposed to break it up. Another thing, I believe that violence has no place in the game. I'm against the violence factor, and I'm against fighting on the field when it's not necessary. I'm a Christian man, and I also take serious the idea of being a role model. When there's a fight, you can just imagine kids saying, 'Hey, wasn't that great, all those punches thrown in the game yesterday?' . . . I don't want to be a part of the negative side of baseball if I can help it." Just over two weeks later, in August, Foster was released. Two months after that, the Mets won the World Series.

Foster wasn't the only man in baseball with a low opinion of violence, but the important thing about ballplayers taking to the field in defense of teammates is not that they throw punches, it's that they simply make an appearance. Many even go out as peacemakers in an effort to keep a fight from escalating. "A guy can walk out there, find somebody he knows, and try to look upset," said Andy Van Slyke. "I did that. If it didn't involve me, I'd try to find somebody I knew and just go up and grab him by his shirt collar and say, 'Hey, how's the family doing?' Let the guys who were upset beat each other up." Derek Jeter once took heat from teammate Chad Curtis for laughing with Seattle's Alex Rodriguez as the field cleared after a fight between the Yankees and the Mariners in 1999. The pair's main mistake wasn't joking around instead of fighting—it was failing to look more serious as they did so.

"Participants on the outer barrier of these things, guys who are basically just talking to somebody, are acceptable," said longtime big-leaguer Darrin Jackson. "As long as they aren't still sitting in the dugout or out in the bullpen."

"If you don't have the respect of your teammates," said outfielder Dave Roberts of those who fail to participate, "it's a recipe for disaster."

The thrill that accompanies baseball fights can be felt throughout the ballpark, but nowhere more keenly than in the dugouts. For relievers in a bullpen, on the other hand, any simmering animosity that serves as the prelude to a brawl is largely lost. Before a game's middle innings, relievers are often doing nothing more involved than spitting sunflower seeds and passing time; when called upon to join a fight, they enter cold, usually with little idea about what's actually going on.

There's also the matter of getting there. Should a scrum form in the middle of the diamond, bullpen-bound relievers must traverse the breadth of the field to reach it, often running alongside the men they'll soon be expected to fight. "That's the strangest thing about baseball fights," said Jack McDowell. "Relievers will jump out of the bullpen and run together until they get to the pile, and within two minutes they may be brawling, but it's not like they stop right there and fight. How stupid is it that you're running in with these guys?"

When the Phillies and Padres brawled in 1985, the San Diego bullpen was no exception. As soon as John Denny and Tim Flannery began slugging each other near third base, San Diego's backup catcher Bruce Bochy and closer Goose Gossage hopped the bullpen fence and ran for the infield, the rest of the relief corps a step behind. The problem in this situation wasn't lack of desire, or even lack of proximity—it was Bochy's legs. After ten seasons of professional squatting, seven of them in the big leagues, Bochy's feet tended to kick out when he walked, an endless source of amusement for his teammates. Unfortunately for the Padres relievers, the combination of having to navigate both the bullpen mound and the catcher's extremities while keeping their eyes on the fight proved to be too much; pitchers Tim Stoddard and Greg Booker clipped Bochy's ankles, and all three tumbled to the ground. "I raced toward the infield, but I arrived there alone," said Gossage. "I looked back toward our bullpen and saw Bochy, Stoddard, and Booker all tangled up, a cloud of dust billowing over them."

"I give myself credit because I was the first one out of the bullpen," said Bochy. "Unfortunately, I couldn't run very well, so everyone was catching up. . . . Those two guys who went over me are probably five hundred pounds alone, and then myself, so the guys behind them all went down also. We were all just laying there on the ground, laughing. Meanwhile, Flannery's getting beat up awhile, so he's wondering where we were."

It could have been worse. Had that happened in a place like Milwaukee County Stadium, which featured adjacent bullpens, members of both teams could have tripped over Bochy as they streamed from the same gate in the fence. One time, after the third benches-clearing incident in a mid-

1970s game there between the Brewers and Indians, Cleveland reliever Dave LaRoche tried to approach the situation from a practical standpoint as players filtered back from the field. "This is getting to be a joke," he told the slowly moving mass of ballplayers. "Why don't we, one time, save some energy and start a fight here, and make *them* come running all the way out to *us*?"

Alas, said LaRoche: "It never happened."

In the broadcast booth at Jacobs Field in Cleveland, Angels announcer Rex Hudler watched Troy Percival hit David Justice—spurring the fight that led to Mo Vaughn's tirade—and got fired up himself. A rookie radio man, he had been a major-leaguer until just the season before. As ballplayers streamed from the dugouts to join the fight, Hudler felt the tug of the contest and started yelling on the air for Angels players to "go ahead and get after it, guys!"

"I wanted to fight along with them," he said. "I was looking for the Indians' broadcaster, Rick Manning. Broadcaster to broadcaster—that was my initial reaction. I couldn't throw down with the players, and I saw Rick down there a couple of booths over, and you know what? I wanted to throw down with him. I didn't have a clue on how to broadcast."

Hudler's radio partner, Steve Physioc, offered some timely instruction on appropriate behavior, but the best lesson the broadcaster learned about baseball fights that day was rooted entirely on the field. Watching the drama unfold in the Angels dugout, he came to one primary conclusion: Vaughn's problem wasn't that he failed to join his teammates on the field for the fight, it was that he only made it as far as the dugout. "I learned that if you're in the clubhouse and a fight breaks out, *stay there*," Hudler said. Had the slugger done that, his absence might never have been noticed.

Of course, some clubhouse-bound players refuse to let a little thing like proximity to the field deter them from joining a fight. "In my day, even guys who were inside and out of the game came out in shower shoes with their shirts off," said Ray Fosse. "Everybody came out—that's one rule you'd better not violate. I don't care if you come out five minutes after it started, you had better be there."

Yankees pitcher Luis Tiant did precisely that, emerging from the shower to join a fight with the Milwaukee Brewers wearing nothing but a towel, with a cigar clamped firmly in his teeth. Said Brewers outfielder Gorman Thomas: "It wasn't a pretty sight."

"It's the worst feeling," said former Astros pitcher Jim Deshaies, about being in the clubhouse when violence erupts. " 'Oh shit, a brawl broke out and I'm up here.' It was a long run down the hallways in the Dome."

All of which undermines Vaughn's assertion that he was simply unable to reach the field in time. The Angels slugger eventually implicated the ankle that he injured on opening day, nearly five months earlier, saying it slowed him just enough to miss the battle. Vaughn did have a history of standing up for teammates: With the Red Sox in 1992, he stared down the entire New York Yankees bench after teammate Roger Clemens hit Matt Nokes; when White Sox outfielder George Bell charged Aaron Sele, Vaughn was the first one at the scene and knocked Bell to the ground with a vicious forearm before damage could be done to his pitcher; and when Toronto's Todd Stottlemyre hit Andre Dawson, Vaughn was the first one out of the dugout.

In the end, though, it didn't matter. Whatever good standing the first baseman held within the Angels clubhouse evaporated, and the issue further divided the team. Two days after the fight, Angels manager Terry Collins quit. Exactly four weeks later, general manager Bill Bavasi turned in his own resignation. At the end of the season, the team's farm director, scouting director, twelve senior scouts, and nearly every coach were dismissed.

Vaughn played two more seasons for Anaheim and was traded to the New York Mets with two years and about thirty-five million dollars left on his contract. He was sixteen years too late to join George Foster on the bench, which is too bad—the two might have had something to talk about.

23

The Clubhouse Police

Maintaining harmony within any sizable assemblage is always a challenge. Camaraderie is a finely tuned mechanism, and keeping people spirited and accountable for their actions—let alone willing to quickly resolve the inevitable litany of ticky-tack disputes—can be a daunting task. When that group consists of twenty-five athletes, many of them Type A personalities who have six months of proximity every year during which to drive each other batty, harmony can take some coercion.

Not surprisingly, baseball clubhouses are laden with unwritten rules that govern the behavior of their citizenry. There are systems to keep rookies in line, to ensure that veterans are afforded their due perks, and to bring a combination of levity and cohesion to a group that could otherwise be dominated by the intensely focused and mirthless among them.

Just as regular society operates within a hierarchical system—some people issue orders, some carry them out, and the rest of us are merely affected by it all—so too does a clubhouse. A careful concoction of veteran status and on-field performance helps determine the upper end of any pecking order, and clubhouse culture rewards those at the top of the food chain. It's the stars who are afforded choice seats on team transportation—"We all knew where Carlton Fisk's seat was," said Jack McDowell. "He was third from the back on the left side. You just knew that"—with veterans afforded the next selections, and younger players forced to accept whatever's left over. (Once, when Tony Gwynn spied Rickey Henderson sitting with the rookies on the team bus, he called him over to the veterans' section, reminding him that as one of the game's elder statesmen he had tenure. The future Hall of Famer's classic response: "Rickey don't have ten year. Rickey have eighteen year!") The system dates back to train travel, when a team's starting lineup was assigned berths in the middle of the sleeper car while the reserves were placed over the wheel wells. "Bobby Brown says that anybody that rode over wheels for his whole career deserves whatever he got," said Charlie Silvera, who spent virtually all of his ten-year career backing up Yogi Berra on the Yankees and sleeping in the most rattly section of every train car in which he rode.

The order extends to locker placement, with the team's biggest stars usually located away from the high-traffic areas of the locker room. In Milwaukee, the visitors' clubhouse manager organized players in order of experience, so the most seasoned veterans went to the far side of the room, away from the door. "It was kind of neat," said Bert Blyleven. "Your goal was to get near the toilet, because that was near the shower. So you always felt like, if you got closer to the toilet, then you were really something. It's not often that people want to get real close to a toilet."

When Dusty Baker first came to the Braves as a nineteen-year-old September call-up in 1968, he learned a quick and important lesson in big-league hierarchy. The Braves were in San Francisco, staying at the Jack Tar Hotel, and manager Lum Harris had implemented a midnight curfew. Baker was at a nearby bar with teammates Hank Aaron, Joe Torre, and Felipe Alou, who at ten minutes to midnight instructed him to return to the hotel. "I said, 'What about you guys?' " recalled Baker. "They said, 'Don't worry, we'll get there in time.' "

Baker made it back with two minutes to spare, and immediately ran into Braves coach Jim Busby, who was checking off players' names as they arrived. When Baker scanned the list, he saw that Aaron, Torre, and Alou had already been checked in. "I'm being a dumb rookie and asked the guys the next day, 'Damn, how'd you get back so quick?' " Baker said. "It didn't take me long to figure out that there's certain things you have to earn. They knew those guys were going to be ready and would come prepared to play."

Ascending the clubhouse hierarchy is not so different from climbing the corporate ladder at a Fortune 500 company. The more that people in power see demonstrations of competence and responsibility in a person, the more trust they feel and the more leeway they grant. It's why thirty-nine-year-old Jack Morris, eighteen years and 244 wins into his major-league career, was openly allowed to return to his Montana farm to tend to his wheat crop between starts with the Cleveland Indians in 1994, though no similar privileges were extended to others on the staff. (The tactic ended up backfiring on the Indians when Morris decided that he cared more about his wheat than his pitching and effectively gave up on a one-million-dollar contract when he refused to alter what the team felt had become an untenable travel schedule.) A decade or so later, Roger Clemens had a similar deal with the Houston Astros, in which he was allowed to skip road trips where he wasn't scheduled to pitch.

But it's more than travel arrangements. When Ted Williams refused to wear a necktie in the late 1940s, he got scant argument from Red Sox manager Joe McCarthy, even though the skipper insisted that everyone else on the club be so attired. When a sportswriter asked McCarthy why he let Williams get away with it, the manager offered a simple answer. "I want to be fair," he said. "Any other gentleman on this club hits .390, he won't have to wear a necktie either." Just down the Eastern Seaboard, Joe DiMaggio had a perk in the form of an on-field caddy—backup outfielder Hank Workman, who was devoted to making sure a lit Chesterfield cigarette was ready when DiMaggio came in from the field.

"You staked out your turf, and you worked around those who had it," said Cecil Cooper, who played seventeen years for the Red Sox and Brewers. "If I'm a star, I get the first shot at seating and you get what's left. I get premium time with the trainer and you work around it. That's how it worked when I was a player. Superstars came first and the rest of us brought up the rear. And that's the way it should be."

"Let's put it this way," said former Giants reliever Matt Herges. "If Barry [Bonds] calls down to get his luggage at the hotel and I call down at the same time, there's a pretty good chance Barry is getting his first."

When players rebel against the established order—or even when they simply mess something up—there are systems in place to right the ship quickly. The most noteworthy is the kangaroo court, baseball's informal clubhouse version of the judicial system—regular convenings of the team in which ballpark justice is meted out to any reprobate member by a jury of his peers. Players are kept in line for both on-field and off-field indiscretions through a system of small fines and good-natured ridicule from their teammates. No offense is too small.

Take, for example, Jay Mazzone, the Baltimore Orioles' batboy in 1967. He was an ordinary kid except for one thing—hooks where his hands should have been, the result of a childhood accident. Some players were understandably confused about how to act around the boy, unsure what to do or say, until a single moment in kangaroo court brought everybody together.

Baltimore's court was enthusiastically led by star outfielder Frank Robinson, who on the day in question was calling for a decision on some long-forgotten offense. He put it to the court to decide whether a fine should be levied via a thumbs-up, thumbs-down vote. As soon as the result was tallied, Robinson affixed his gaze directly on the batboy. "Jay," he said, "you're fined for not voting." Amid the gales of laughter, it became clear that Mazzone needed no special treatment, and he was quickly accepted for what he was, not for what he wasn't. "Somebody even made a big cardboard hand with a thumb," he said, "so I could take part in future votes."

Robinson presided over his court like few others, donning a mop-head wig and using a bat for a gavel. He kept players in line for legitimate mistakes and lightened the tension with outrageous accusations, such as the one against Mazzone. Another of his victims was Brooks Robinson, whose performance in the 1970 World Series was so spectacular—he hit .429 and played consistently wondrous defense—that Frank Robinson eventually fined him for showboating.

Courts are generally made up of a judge (who must be blessed with a strong personality and quick wit), a secretary (who records the charges, which can be brought up by any member of the team against any other member of the team, as long as a witness is procured), and a treasurer (who collects and holds the fine money—traditionally between five and a hundred dollars a pop—which at the end of the season is sometimes donated to charity and sometimes used for a blowout party).

Typically, all charges can be challenged, but if the defendant is overruled, the fine doubles. Of course, the defendant almost never prevails. "That's the kangaroo code," said Oscar Gamble. "You never win." (With the Mets in 2006, David Wright got thrown out at first base after he rounded the bag following a single, and when it was later brought up in kangaroo court he pleaded not guilty, under the auspice that "being a spoiled athlete of this modern era, the player is never wrong and the coach is always wrong." He then accused first-base coach Jerry Manuel of dereliction of duties, but Manuel's argument successfully convinced judge Tom Glavine to clear his name. Wright's fine was subsequently doubled, in addition to his being publicly presented with the Tom Emanski instructional baserunning videotape. "Jerry can only suggest that David run hard through the bag," said Glavine. "If David doesn't listen, that's hardly Jerry's fault.")

In the Orioles clubhouse, Frank Robinson initiated rookie Don Baylor into the system after the twenty-one-year-old boasted to a reporter that he'd break into the starting lineup as soon as he got "in the groove." Baylor was fined for the infraction, tagged with the nickname "Groove" (which stuck with him through his career), and then had to suffer the indignity of spending virtually the entire season in the minors. Baylor, however, had learned a valuable lesson about the power of the court, and quickly stepped into the judge's role after leaving the Orioles. One of his victims was Red Sox utility man Steve Lyons, who was fined by Baylor in 1986 for wearing eye black even though he was not in the starting lineup. Lyons knew better than to fight the ruling, despite having what he felt was a quality explanation. "I played a bunch of different positions, and once they wanted me to go play third base for an inning," he said. "I didn't have my third baseman's glove with me, so I had to run back into the locker room to get it. Baylor fined me for that. Later, I thought there's no way that I wasn't going to be prepared. I made sure I had everything. It was a day game, so that included eye black. If I had to pinch-hit, or if someone got hurt and they ran me out to center field, I didn't want to have to go put eye black on. I became a favorite target for Don."

When Baylor was the judge in the Yankees court, fines were levied against pitchers who gave up hits on 0-2 counts. Ron Guidry reacted by giving Baylor a hundred-dollar deposit in advance of fines he knew would be coming, since, he said, "I throw strikes even on 0-2 counts." Phil Niekro gave Baylor similar advances for the weekly fines he knew he'd accrue when, out of superstition, he refused to stand on the top step of the dugout for the national anthem.

It wasn't just Baylor, of course—courts across baseball pile up fines. After Ken Griffey, Jr., had a rough first month in Cincinnati, batting .217

in April 2000, after the Reds acquired him from Seattle, he was fined by a mop-wig-bedecked Barry Larkin for "imitating an All-Century Player." As a member of the Pittsburgh Pirates, Barry Bonds was fined for standing next to a batting-cage tee so he could practice *taking* pitches. Yankees coach Don Zimmer was once fined for simply being Don Zimmer. Jim Eisenreich was so perfect in Kansas City—he didn't drink, wasn't loud, and never embarrassed himself—that judge Jamie Quirk fined him for his lack of previous fines. Guys are dinged for poor wardrobe selection and for failing to pick up the tab frequently enough. On-field infractions include failing to hit the cutoff man and forgetting how many outs have been recorded. Fred Stanley was fined in the Oakland A's court for overacting his shock and pain in response to a pitch that didn't actually hit him, before eventually taking first base.

With the Mets in 1991, Vince Coleman once took pity on former Cardinals teammate Willie McGee, whose equipment had been stolen from the visitors' locker room at Shea Stadium, and loaned him a glove. He was subsequently fined for aiding the enemy—ten dollars for each ball McGee caught.

Although they're usually good-natured, kangaroo courts have been known to get uncomfortable. In the Pittsburgh Pirates clubhouse in the 1980s, one player felt the need to bring up a teammate on the relatively typical charge of being seen out on the town with an ugly woman. (Former Tiger Jim Price recalled a teammate who was once similarly fined because his date "could eat corn through a picket fence.") The case on the Pirates was so egregious, insisted the player, the woman so ugly, that the fine *must* be doubled. "We're all sitting around listening, and when he brought up the player's name we all got real quiet and said, 'Sit down, sit down!' as quickly as we could," said one member of the team. That's because, unlike the plaintiff, most of the guys in the room knew that the player—who was sitting there among them—hadn't just been out with this woman on the night in question, he had asked for her hand in marriage. "Usually there's razzing going on, but instead there was this dead silence," said the player. "It was pretty awkward."

There were also awards handed out. In the 1970s, the Orioles presented the Don Buford Red-Ass Award, a red-painted toilet seat, to players who grew exceptionally angry during a game. The Indians had a similar totem, with the winner being responsible for transporting the seat from town to town until he was finally able to pass it along to the next red-ass. The offending member of the Kansas City Royals would find a large gong (which wasn't just similar to the one on *The Gong Show*—it *was* the one from *The Gong Show*, courtesy of first baseman Pete LaCock, whose father was Peter Marshall of *Hollywood Squares* fame) in his locker after the game. The Houston version involved a stuffed skunk, which would stay in the player's locker through media interviews and the ensuing questions about why on earth he had a stuffed skunk in his locker.

For a time, the Milwaukee Brewers awarded their star of the game a three-foot rubber phallus, which was placed inside his locker for the duration of the post-game activity. It didn't garner much notice until 1987, when Juan Nieves threw a no-hitter. "He has this thing hanging in his locker, just dangling there," said Brewers catcher Bill Schroeder. "So here's ESPN and everybody interviewing him, and you see this thing hanging over his shoulder. Then you see a hand reach in and grab it and pull it away. It was [general manager] Harry Dalton! That was our kangaroo court, and it was the funniest thing in the world."

Kangaroo courts are just one of many venues in which a ballplayer can express his feelings; most others are far less group-oriented, and virtually all involve a mechanism for blowing off steam. These are men who must regularly handle the pressure of high expectations and public scrutiny. Normal people have therapy; ballplayers have the practical joke.

In a big-league clubhouse, pranks are afforded more than a passing fancy—they're the basis on which much of a team's communication is built. The one most associated with baseball is the time-tested hotfoot, which at its essence involves the simple act of setting fire to a pair of shoes, with the condition that their owner's feet must still be inside them.

Giving a hotfoot can be as simple as igniting some shoelaces, but the classic version involves attaching a lit cigarette to a book of matches, then taping the package to the heel of an unsuspecting victim. The cigarette acts as a fuse, giving everyone in the dugout time to prepare for the impending show as it burns down. When ember hits match, the flame startles (if not scars) the target, who inevitably vows revenge. If he's lucky, his shoes haven't been presoaked in rubbing alcohol to augment the flame. "It hurts," said David Cone, who gave better than he got over the course of his career. "It burns. Baseball players are very fastidious about their shoes, their spikes, their footwear, and it gets ruined, absolutely ruined by a hotfoot. And it hurts. It burns your ankle, it burns your calf."

Ambitious players are known to crawl under the dugout bench in order to set flame to someone's dangling shoes; more frequently than one would imagine, there's also someone behind *them*, returning the favor before the original act can even be perpetrated. Pitcher Moe Drabowsky would wait under a tarp at Tiger Stadium for his teammates to line up for the national anthem, then get them in bunches as they faced the flag. (Drabowsky was so relentless in hotfooting a particular member of the Baltimore media that the guy eventually spent most of his time in the clubhouse staring down at his shoes; Drabowsky responded by setting fire to his notes.) Dick Bosman laid absolute waste to his teammates' footwear during a 1966 doubleheader at Washington's RFK Stadium: "In eighteen innings of baseball I got every guy out there," he said. "And that's quite a challenge." In the 1970s, the New York Yankees made a habit of crawling between rows on their airplane to set fire to the shoes of teammates who slept. In the 1980s, pitcher Ray Searage attached an alligator clip to the end of a car antenna, which he used to extend his reach when surreptitiously applying flame to shoe.

The undisputed master of the craft, however, was pitcher Bert Blyleven. The right-hander pitched in the major leagues for twenty-two years, and if Cooperstown applied the instigation of podiatric discomfort as one of its entry criteria, he would have been enshrined five years after his 1992 retirement. How good was he? For a time, the fire extinguisher in the Angels' clubhouse read "In case of Blyleven. Pull."

Ordinary hotfoot artists settle for wrecking their teammates' cleats, but Blyleven was so good that he took the rare step of drawing the opposition into his line of fire. In 1990, the pitcher, then with the Angels, set his sights on Seattle manager Jim Lefebvre, who made the mistake of conducting an interview near the Anaheim dugout. Never mind that Lefebvre was there at the request of Angels analyst Joe Torre; Blyleven was deeply offended. There was, in the pitcher's mind, only one appropriate response.

"I crawled behind him on my hands and knees," Blyleven said. "And I not only lit one shoe on fire, I lit them both on fire." Torre saw it all, but continued the interview as if nothing was happening. As Blyleven retreated to the dugout to enjoy the fruits of his labor, he was dismayed to see that Lefebvre refused to play along. "We all stood there and watched the flames starting," said Blyleven. "The smoke was starting to come in front of [Lefebvre's] face, but he was not going to back down. By God, he was going to continue this interview. And Joe was laughing, trying not to roll."

Torre offered up an apology as soon as the interview wrapped, but Lefebvre was too busy trying to extinguish his feet to pay much attention. He also knew exactly whom to blame. Blyleven, the following day's starter for the Angels, found out later that Lefebvre offered a hundred dollars to anyone on his team who could hit a line drive off the pitcher's face. Part of the reason the manager was so angry was that he was deeply superstitious about his shoes; in fact, he continued to wear the scorched pair for several weeks, despite the damage.

In the end, Lefebvre wasn't the prank's only dupe. "Bert really screwed me up with that one, because Lefebvre thought I was in on it, and I wasn't," said Torre. "Lefebvre didn't think it was very funny—they were brand-new shoes and he got embarrassed in public. Blyleven was nuts—absolutely nuts."

Hotfoots are a staple, but the pantheon of great baseball pranks extends far beyond fire. Babe Ruth once took a teammate to a woman's house on a blind double date, and in a prearranged skit pretended to be shot by the husband of his "date" while urging his teammate, pitcher Ed Wells, to flee. When a thoroughly disoriented Wells eventually returned to the team hotel, he was greeted by numerous mournful players and told that Ruth was upstairs. "Ed, Babe's been shot. He's in bad shape and asking for you," said second baseman Tony Lazzeri. Wells was taken to Ruth's darkened room, where the slugger lay on his bed with ketchup smeared across his shirt. All it took was outfielder Earle Combs to say, "He's dying," and Wells fainted where he stood. It wasn't until Ruth himself began laughing that his victim believed it to truly be a joke.

Pepper Martin and Dizzy Dean once passed pre-game hours by donning workmen's clothes and redecorating a hall at the upscale Bellevue-Stratford Hotel in Philadelphia with whatever tools they could find—in the middle of a banquet. Cardinals pitcher Joe Hoerner took advantage of a tardy post-game bus driver and leaped behind the wheel to ferry his teammates back to their hotel at high speed, whereupon he parked the carriage in a flower bed atop the Marriott sign. In the early 1980s, an intrepid band of Yankees spent an evening with a high-powered slingshot, shooting water balloons two city blocks from the roof of their Boston hotel. The list goes on and on.

A full examination of the lengths to which players will go for a good prank is impossible, so one will serve here as an example for the rest. It began in Milwaukee in the 1970s, and features at its core a pig, a hotel room, and an enduring mystery. Whenever the Brewers of that era stage a reunion, it's not long before the pig story is retold. The only detail left out has been the name of the culprit, because he never stepped forward. While members of the team have their suspicions, nobody ever found him out . . . until now.

Bob McClure was a fun-loving reliever for those Brewers clubs, someone who proved, if nothing else, that he could take as good as he gave. The story started with his Sunday routine before day games, for which he holed up with a newspaper in the long cinderblock outhouse behind the outfield fence at Milwaukee County Stadium. It was a cool place for an American League pitcher to pass the morning in the shade of the bleachers, escaping the summer heat while his teammates took batting practice.

When the door slammed shut on McClure in the middle of one of these siestas, the pitcher attributed it to a gust of wind. But when he tried to exit, the door wouldn't budge, even though it had no lock. With just a hint of panic, the pitcher pushed again . . . and again. Soon he was exerting so much energy in his frantic bid to escape that he had to stop for periodic breathers. The day was growing hotter, and McClure worked up a sweat; eventually he kicked the air vents from the walls and stripped down to his underwear. "I bet I lost about seven or eight pounds in there," he said. "It was *hot*."

After a half-hour, the pitcher was able to wedge the door open just enough to squeeze through ("I still remember the scrapes across my chest"), whereupon he saw that someone had taken the rope from a flagpole on the other side of the outhouse and pulled it so taut to reach the doorknob that the pole had bowed under the pressure. Once it was affixed to the handle, the rope's tension kept the door from opening; it was only as the fibers started to give that McClure was able, finally, to free himself. (He found out later that members of the visiting Minnesota Twins, coming out for their own batting practice, had been told by his mystery assailant to watch the flagpole, that someone was locked in the lavatory and it would bounce every time he tried to get out.) He put on his clothes and returned directly to the clubhouse, as if nothing had ever happened. "I would say that, if someone gets you, never let them know that they got you," he said. "I think it's inappropriate, if someone really gets you good, to overreact. Don't get mad, just get even." The problem was that he had no idea upon whom to visit his revenge.

Before a game several days later, McClure got his answer. As the pitcher loitered in the outfield before a game, a fan called him over to the bleachers. "Do you want to know who locked you in that room?" she asked. His instinct was to play dumb, but when the woman told him she had pictures, he couldn't resist. She handed them over in exchange for a ball autographed by Robin Yount, and McClure saw exactly what happened: It had taken two men to pull the flagpole rope tight enough to trap him, and their uniforms were clearly visible. It was pitchers Mike Caldwell and Reggie Cleveland.

McClure immediately set to plotting. Six weeks later, when the Brewers had an off-day in Kansas City before a series with the Royals, he struck.

While many players, including Caldwell and Cleveland, spent the afternoon golfing, McClure opted for a hunting trip with a local friend. On the way back they stopped by a farm, where the pitcher bought a small, live—and exceptionally filthy—pig. "It had so much pig dung on it that you couldn't even hardly tell it was a pig," McClure said. "It was perfect. We put it in a burlap sack in the back of my buddy's pickup."

When the pitcher returned to the hotel, he saw that his teammates hadn't returned, and figured they'd be out until the wee hours. McClure bribed his way into the room that Caldwell and Cleveland conveniently shared, and let the pig loose atop the bed. "When that pig hit the sheet, it looked up at me and started projectile shitting everywhere, like a shotgun," he said. "That pig was *alive*. It jumps off the bed, and it's squealing and going nutty. There's shit on the bed, on the floor, on the curtains. It was so loud that I had to get out of the room."

He was staying just across the hall, and hours later was roused by the sounds of his returning teammates. Caldwell was the first to enter, and nearly as quickly lit back into the hallway, shouting, "There's someone in there!" As McClure listened with delight, his teammates rushed the room, then spent the better part of an hour trying to corner the pig. Finally, the noise quieted and McClure went back to sleep.

The next morning, the pitcher veritably bounced across the hall to see how his victims had held up. He entered the room under the pretense of rounding up breakfast companionship, but wasn't at all prepared for what he saw. The place was spotless. The walls, the drapes, the bedspread, and the carpet had all been cleaned. Caldwell was lying on his back in bed, shirtless. Also on its back, in the crook of Caldwell's right arm, was a freshly washed pig. It sported a red dog collar. Caldwell was feeding it French fries dipped in ketchup.

Feigning ignorance, McClure asked why there was a pig in the room and was told the entire story, up to and including an early-morning trip to a nearby pet store, where Caldwell bought collar, leash, and industrial-grade pet shampoo. The pig joined the team at the ballpark that day, serving as the Brewers' mascot. It ended up living on Cleveland's farm, of all places, dreaming recurrently, no doubt, of room service and burlap.

By their nature, practical jokes are random acts, their sporadic occurrence serving to add an element of surprise to an otherwise structured environment. Their closest cousin in clubhouse culture, however, is built less on shock value than on sheer abuse. The unfortunate targets: rookies.

Upon their initial entry through the clubhouse door, first-year players immediately become, in the minds of many teammates, lightning rods for criticism, punishment, and flat-out abuse. They're forced to run clubhouse errands (both real and imagined, sometimes searching in vain for things like the key to the batter's box or a bucket of steam); find their clothes shredded, frozen inside ice buckets, or replaced entirely with garish costumes; and serve as the primary butt of locker-room jokes. Sixto Lezcano was given an all-green wardrobe for one of his team's West Coast swings—green pants, shirt, coat, socks, shoes. ("I looked like a fucking grasshopper," he said.) Minnesota's Eddie Guardado had everything in his locker—glove, cleats, uniform—fastened down with Torx-head screws, for which he couldn't find an appropriate screwdriver, which left him scrambling to find alternate gear to simply take the field on time.

Once, rookie treatment consisted primarily of silence. This extended as far as freezing a young player out of infield or batting practice, the better to protect the job of the veteran ahead of him on the depth chart (as Indians third baseman Ken Keltner and other of the team's tenured players did to a young Al Rosen, who was forced to show up hours before the rest of the team just to receive batting practice from fellow rookie Ray Boone). Jim Davenport estimates that in the 1950s a player had to accumulate at least four hundred at-bats before he was allowed so much as to speak up in the presence of veterans.

Modern rookies have it different, to the point where some would prefer the silent treatment. Rather than being ignored they're assigned such duties as carrying beer onto the plane and doing various clubhouse errands for the veterans. Rookie relievers stock and transport the bullpen's candy bag, which is often an embarrassing children's backpack. Dan Ford made John Shelby give him haircuts. Gaylord Perry made rookie Duane Kuiper fetch cups of coffee from the clubhouse during games, after which he'd take a sip and order one that was hotter . . . or colder . . . or sweeter—again and again. "It was a long way from the dugout to the clubhouse in Municipal Stadium," said Kuiper. "I got to know those corridors very well." Once Kuiper reached veteran status with the Giants he made rookie Mark Grant do the same thing at Candlestick Park.

Jeffrey Leonard summed up the sentiment as a veteran in Seattle's clubhouse in 1989, when he greeted highly touted rookie Ken Griffey, Jr., with the immortal declaration, "There's going to be a lot of people kissing your ass. I won't be one of them."

The ones who get it worst are those who either resist or act somehow entitled, a state of being that any veteran will happily inform them must be earned through tenure. On Lenny Dykstra's first day in the big leagues, he called a batboy to his locker and said, "Kid, how 'bout lacing my shoes?" Veteran pitcher Ron Darling wasted no time responding, quickly approaching the rookie with a pair of scissors and snipping his laces in half.

Dodgers rookie Chan Ho Park went ballistic in response to veteran teammates shredding the suit that was hanging in his locker. It wasn't an unusual practice, but Park took it badly, he said, because the clothes had been given to him in Korea by his mother as a good-luck totem. No matter; his reaction cost him support from many Dodgers. So did that of Armando Benitez, who, after teammates on the Orioles replaced his clothes with a dress on getaway day, refused to don the outfit and, screaming for the return of his wardrobe, pinned down a number of veterans against the far wall of the shower room with a steady barrage of baseballs picked out of a nearby bucket. In the end, the pitcher refused to capitulate, even after being told that his clothes had been packed and were already en route to the airport. "He wore a T-shirt and a pair of shorts on the frickin' plane," said one team member. "That didn't sit too well with the veterans, I can tell you that."

"The guys who make a big fuss about it, who get mad at it, they're usually the ones who don't last too long," said Doug Mientkiewicz, who was forced into female clothing by his Twins teammates as a rookie in 1998. "If you can't be mentally strong enough to wear a dress for one day when every other rookie is, too, then you're probably not going to be mentally strong enough to handle an 0-for-35 stretch in four different cities."

"Of course there were guys who took it the wrong way," said Cubs star Mark Grace. "Then [pitcher Rick] Sutcliffe would take you aside and tell you, 'If you've got a problem with it I'll be glad to beat the ever-lovin' shit out of you.' You learned quick."

There are traditions built around a rookie's first hit (a dummy ball is marked up either with mistaken statistics and misspelled names, or with an abundance of curse words, then presented as the real thing), first home run (upon a rookie's return to the dugout, he's greeted by an impregnable front of silence), and even a rookie's first outstanding play in the field (such as a spectacular catch made by Willie Mays, after which Giants manager Leo Durocher ordered the rest of the Giants to remain silent).

It's not all bad, though. Checks are often picked up by veteran players, as are bills for items such as suits and luggage that can help a rookie look more "big-league." When Brewers rookie Bill Schroeder tried to buy a round of drinks for a group of veterans seated across the bar, one of the players, pitcher Mike Caldwell, marched every glass over to Schroeder, instructed him to finish them all, and left explicit instructions that rookies were to pay for nothing when in the presence of a veteran. "Needless to say," said Schroeder, "I finished the beers, staggered to my room, and never bought them another drink."

It's pretty typical of a veteran's approach to looking out for rookies—a pat on the back alternating with a kick in the rear. Ivan Calderon looked out for Craig Grebeck both on and off the field during the latter's rookie season with the White Sox, serving a role that Grebeck described as "my bodyguard." "If I ever had a problem and I said something to him about it, I didn't have a problem anymore," he said. At the same time, however, Calderon made a habit of confiscating Grebeck's shoes in every airport through which the team passed, refusing to return them until they checked in to the team hotel.

Or take Angels utility man Rex Hudler, who in 1996 viciously lit into rookie Todd Greene for boarding the team plane ahead of some veterans. It didn't make much difference to Hudler that Greene couldn't have been greener—it was his first day as a major-leaguer—but the following evening, when the young catcher connected for his first home run, Hudler atoned. The game was at Detroit's Tiger Stadium, and as soon as the inning ended, Hudler—out of the game and with a baseball in each hand—dashed to the outfield fence near the bleachers where the ball had landed and offered a two-for-one deal to whoever caught Greene's homer. Before he could get a response, though, the inning break ended, and Hudler found himself urged back to the dugout by center fielder Jim Edmonds. Rather than give up his quest, the player vaulted into the stands and watched the Tigers' half of the inning from the bleachers. It was more than enough to win over the locals, and Greene's ball was offered up in short order. "When I came back in, everyone was going, 'What the hell were you doing out there?' " said Hudler. "I went up to Greene and said, 'Greenie, I got your ball for you, man!' You'd have thought I gave him a ten-carat diamond. And now every time I see him he tells someone, 'Hud went out into the center-field stands and got my ball for me.' He never forgets—it's a form of love."

Love is one way of looking at it. If the word contains any accuracy in describing the source of most rookies' treatment, there's never been more collective affection shown than in Chicago. It's the location of one of the most enduring rookie traditions in big-league history, which manages to connect pride, art, and the Civil War.

On the city's North Side, a statue honors Philip Sheridan (1831–88), the fourth general in U.S. history to earn four stars, and the subject of poet Thomas Buchanan Read's "Sheridan's Ride." He is depicted atop his horse, Rienzi, at the intersection of North Lakeshore Drive and West Belmont Avenue, along the route between Wrigley Field and the downtown hotels at which visiting teams stay. Over the years, it became known as bad luck for players to look at the bronze testicles of the prancing and anatomically correct horse when the team bus passed by, for fear of prolonged slumps. Jose Cruz referred to it as the Balls Horse and yelled for his teammates to avert their collective gaze, screaming, "You gonna take an oh-fer every time!"

Somewhere along the line, the legend expanded to something more than simply looking at the horse's genitalia. An example from 1984 serves to illustrate the point. That season, the moribund Giants closed their April schedule with a nine-game losing streak, at which point they were already nine games behind the Dodgers. When the club rolled into Chicago in early May, several veterans had seen enough.

In the bus on the way to Wrigley Field, Mike Krukow, Duane Kuiper, and Steve Nicosia spun an off-the-cuff tale of tradition, passion, and paint, informing the team's impressionable rookies about how ballplayers had been sneaking out at night for decades to paint the horse's testicles in team colors. Krukow had done it with the Phillies, Nicosia with the Pirates, Mays and McCovey with the Giants. "We told them that if they got caught they'd go downtown to sign the police register," said Krukow, "and they'd be signing underneath the names of Billy Williams and Ernie Banks. Lou Gehrig's in there—he got caught." Not a word of it was true.

"We didn't think anything of it," said Kuiper, "until the next day, when we drove by and the horse was painted orange."

Rookies Frank Williams and Jeff Cornell had taken it upon themselves to complete the fictional task, and their teammates were suitably impressed. "There were about nine layers of paint on it," said Krukow. "It was a beautiful job."

Two years later, the Giants featured so many first-year players—

fourteen rookies suited up for them over the course of the season—that traveling secretary Dirk Smith had to arrange a bus to transport the masses to the horse. "You try climbing a bronze horse in pouring-down rain armed with spray paint," said Jeff Brantley, who took his turn in 1989. "That was very difficult."

For a long while, it was possible to tell which team had most recently visited Wrigley Field by the color of the horse's undercarriage—Dodgers blue, Pirates yellow, Cincinnati red. Chris Speier not only painted the horse during his rookie season, but made sure he was sitting atop it when the bus passed by.

This is how pranks evolve. As the paint-heavy response to the Sheridan curse became commonplace among visiting teams, a Chicago police officer—a lifelong Cubs fan stationed at Wrigley Field—got into the act. The day following a given team's late-night escapades, the officer (sometimes accompanied by one or more colleagues) would march into the visitors' clubhouse and "arrest" the offending parties, sometimes going so far as to put them in cuffs and lead them away, while their teammates tried to stifle their laughter. (According to Andy Van Slyke, Pirates rookie Dan Miceli told the police to "go fuck themselves" under interrogation, rather than give up the names of his cohorts. "He got our respect for that," said Van Slyke, "which is worth its weight in gold.")

In 1989, San Francisco's Charlie Hayes was the victim of the clubhouse police, and was especially terrified after having already been warned against painting the statue. He was the only person in the room who didn't know what was actually going on and, upon being threatened with jail time, quickly sold out his accomplices. "I swear I thought Charlie was going to start crying," said Brantley. "He jumped out of that chair and ratted out everybody who was there, the veteran who took them—everybody. We were crying, laughing so hard. It was funny. He heard a lot about it after that."

If the collective rookie experience regarding General Sheridan can be summed up in a single sentiment, no one has come closer to it than Kevin Mitchell, whose turn came with the New York Mets in 1986. Said Mitchell: "Painting nuts ain't fun."

Conclusion

Deion Sanders came to the major leagues in 1989 as a fully formed personality. Noteworthy primarily for his excellence as a defensive back and kick returner with the Atlanta Falcons, he made a habit of scrawling dollar signs into the batter's-box dirt before at-bats and did his best to carry over the personality that led to his NFL nicknames, "Prime Time" and "Neon Deion."

Batting for the Yankees in a game against the White Sox in 1990, Sanders popped up to shortstop and did little to hide his lack of interest in heading toward first. The move would increasingly become the mark of major-league superstars over the coming years, and even then it wouldn't have drawn much attention—on most days.

Unfortunately for Sanders, Chicago's catcher was Carlton Fisk, forty-two years old and entrenched at the time as one of the premier members of baseball's old guard. Watching Sanders's lackadaisical display, the future Hall of Famer could barely contain himself. "Run the fucking ball out, you piece of shit—that's not the way we do things up here!" he screamed at the startled hitter, two decades his junior and playing in just his twenty-fourth big-league game. By that point, of course, it was too late; the ball was already settling into the shortstop's glove, and Sanders had nowhere to go but back to the dugout.

When Neon Deion came to the plate two innings later, he took the time to inform Fisk that "the days of slavery are over." The catcher responded in kind, and the dugouts quickly emptied. "I just told him I thought that there was a right way and a wrong way to play the game, and he was playing it wrong, because it offended guys like me," said Fisk. "And if he didn't care to play it right, let's go at it, right here."

Intentionally or not, Fisk's actions represented a desperate grab at the unraveling thread of the unwritten rules, a selfless effort to restore balance to a sport that even then was forgetting many lessons from its own history. Though there's no debating the Code's importance, neither can we deny that its vitality has recently waned. Many players, particularly those born in the 1980s and later, have little idea what many of the rules even mean.

The reasons for this aren't difficult to pinpoint. Baseball is now more than ever an individualistic sport, with many players more beholden to their agents than to the teams that employ them. The increased frequency of franchise-hopping means that more players have friends and acquaintances on rosters around the league, which results in the inevitable erosion of the us–versus–them ethos that once permeated clubhouses. The situation was described by Bob Gibson in his book, *Stranger to the Game;* even though the author was speaking specifically about pitcher-hitter relationships, he might as well have been addressing the primary reason why, on the whole, ballplayers no longer burn as hot as they once did.

> Modern trends have made [pitchers and hitters] allies in many important respects. Many share an agent. They play golf together and consort in business affairs, subscribing to the same source of career advice. Meanwhile, they are well aware that their confrontations on the field will be closely monitored by the umpires, and, consequently, one has no reason to regard the other, his professional cohort, as an immediate threat to his livelihood. The real gamesmanship in which they participate is conducted largely off the field, in strategy sessions at the agent's office. The rules promote this sort of congeniality. They ensure that major-league baseball does not become personally adversarial to the point of being fierce. The rancor between the pitcher and the hitter, which characterized the game in my time and Ruth's and Cobb's and Musial's, has been legislated out in favor of a kinder, gentler game in which there is more cheap offense for the paying customer.

Logic dictates that if players are more civil to each other across the field of play, the need to enact unwritten rules to maintain civility becomes increasingly marginalized. When the baseline for opposing players was enmity (at best), the Code was vital; now that they glad-hand each other around the batting cage and catch up in the winter over Caribbean vacations, it becomes far less prevalent.

Intra-sport civility, however, is far from the only culprit in the Code's diminishment. The unwritten rules are under a multi-pronged attack from forces that have become inextricably intertwined with the fabric of the game.

Money

"The overall respect for the game has declined," said Pete Rose. "The only thing the guys respect now is money." He has a point. Money is said to ruin everything, and though baseball's ruination is not yet upon us, there's no denying the pervasive impact of modern finances. The day when the average major-league player found himself residing among the nation's gilded gentry was the day that the status quo of the unwritten rules could no longer support itself. No owner wants to see a player in whom he's invested seven, eight, or nine figures disabled by a head-hunting scrub who should be toiling in Triple-A. Neither do they want to see a star infielder injured by a baserunner with vengeance on his mind.

This came to the forefront of public attention during Game 2 of the 1977 ALCS, when Kansas City's Hal McRae roll-blocked Yankees second baseman Willie Randolph on national television. It was a brutal (and legal) slide that immediately sent the Yankees—especially manager Billy Martin—into a tizzy. Randolph said it was the second time that season McRae had given him such treatment; he had nearly broken his wrist upon landing after the first one. Said Martin: "I told Randolph later, the next time he comes down there, if he's out by five feet even, don't tag him—hit him right in the mouth with the ball."

Randolph, just twenty-three, had been an All-Star in both his full big-league seasons to that point, and was a face of the future in the sport's biggest market. Owners quickly hedged their bets with rules changes, ostensibly aimed at safety, to remove aggressive tactics and strip away players' power to police each other on the field. Lost vigilance would serve as collateral damage in the quest for the greater good.

So what's replaced it? Now that major-league tenure equals financial solvency—often for multiple generations of family members—the love of the game has been replaced in some unknowable percentage of players by love of the paycheck. It's hardly a leap to see that players with dollar signs in their eyes have little reason to care about baseball's past, choosing instead to focus on lifestyle possibilities without considering the historical foundation on which those possibilities were built.

"There are players now who, if you ask them about guys even ten years ago, they'll say, 'Who?' " said former Red Sox pitcher Al Nipper. "You've got to be shitting me. When you don't know the history of the game, you're going to repeat history. When you don't know what's happened and why the game has reached this point, then you disrespect it.

"The old-timers played for the love of the game. Shit, they didn't get paid. There are still players now who play for the love of the game, but money is part of the equation. There's nothing wrong with being paid, but you can still have a great love and desire and dedication and passion for the game. And that's the thing—have a passion for the game. It's an honor to wear a frickin' major-league uniform. It's an honor."

Media

The financial aspect of baseball is inherently tied to the ESPN effect, in that those who get paid are inevitably those who frequent the nightly highlight reels.

Players regularly describe the game as entertainment, and themselves as entertainers, essentially seeing their primary job as putting on a good show for the fans. These are especially grievous concepts for baseball's traditional set, who, while accepting the sport's status as public diversion, also see it as something more. These men are infuriated by the modern player whose concern with appearing on *SportsCenter* is as great as his concern for winning the game.

Also part of the picture is the twenty-four-hour news cycle, in which cable television endeavors to slake a constant thirst for content. This is one area in which the concept of sports-as-entertainment is beyond debate, with invasive reporting tactics making lives as miserable for many professional athletes as they have for movie stars and pop singers. It's easy to forget that the news bombshell about Alex Rodriguez's use of performance-enhancing drugs, dropped just before spring training in 2009, hardly reintroduced him to recent headlines. He'd been there all winter, with speculation raging about whether his alleged affair with Madonna had ruined his marriage, and gossip about who his soon-to-be ex-wife was romping around with.

A by-product of this mentality is a relatively newfound focus on the sensational acts that take place during a game—dustups and temper tantrums among them. If retaliation is involved, that piece of drama is immediately elevated to the front of the story.

"Things are under such a microscope on TV," said Jason Schmidt. "You hit a guy and the announcers are analyzing it and the fans are getting into it. You didn't have all that, back in the day. What happened on the field was part of the ballpark and it ended right there. Now it's like somebody gets hit and, even though the guy who hit him is just wild, he gets a reputation and he needs to be dealt with."

"That stuff shouldn't even be brought up," said Doug Mientkiewicz. "Let's talk about the 2-2 ball that was hit down the line that scored two runs. Let's not talk about stuff that shouldn't involve the public. The game can take care of itself if it's allowed to."

Fundamentals

There's one more factor in the diminishment of the Code: Baseball itself has fundamentally changed. Shifting from a station-to-station game to one more beholden to the three-run homer; replacing vast stadiums such as the Polo Grounds and the old Yankee Stadium with bandboxes like those in Cincinnati and Philadelphia; watching a parade of meatball-serving pitchers who wouldn't have sniffed the major leagues in the era before expansion; seeing steroids and supplements and tightly wound baseballs have an undeniable effect on the offensive game—there's no denying that the action on the field is wildly different from what it was in generations past. And if the game is no longer the same, what about its moral compass?

"How in the hell do you even say exactly what the unwritten rules are, because they've changed over the years," said reliever Al Hrabosky. "What was once a safe lead no longer is a safe lead. Everything's different."

And yet nothing's different. An ill-timed stolen-base attempt still draws ire from the opposing dugout, just as an overt showboat still elicits glares and the occasional warning shot across his bow. The pitchers responsible for policing Code violations are still active, and hitters still respond accordingly. Players flood from dugouts in fight situations, and rookies continue to get hazed. No matter a player's motivation, it's all just baseball, and there's no other way to treat it.

"The name of the game is trying to win, but you have to keep it in perspective," said third baseman David Bell. "Show people respect. You want to walk away from a game or a career saying, 'I feel good about the way I treated people, about the way I competed.' It's nice to say you won, but I think, in the long run, those are the things that you are going to feel best about."

Bell is a great example of the legacy of the unwritten rules. His father, Buddy, was a five-time All-Star and managed the Tigers, Rockies, and Royals; Buddy's father, Gus, was a four-time All-Star. David Bell was raised in the game by both men, and came to the major leagues with a better understanding of the Code than is held by many veterans. It's a clear example of the power that clubhouse leadership (or, in this case, household leadership) can possess. It's Pee Wee Reese publicly accepting Jackie Robinson as his teammate on the Dodgers. It's Mike Krukow challenging a malingering teammate in front of the entire clubhouse to step up his game, for the simple reason that nothing the coaches had tried seemed to work. Just as a child can be ruined if his parents instill in him the wrong ideals and motivations, so too can a ballplayer be ruined in terms of the unwritten rules if he comes up with managers, coaches, and mentors who teach him the wrong thing or nothing at all.

"As players and coaches, our obligation is to pass the game on the way it's supposed to be played, just like we're supposed to pass on our names to our children," said Nipper. "We're supposed to pass this game on with respect and honor. There's a right way to hit somebody and there's a wrong way to do it. There's a right way to take someone out at second base and a wrong way. There's dirty players and clean players, head-hunters and people who know how to pitch in. These are fine lines, and you don't want to go past them. It's our obligation to do things right—respect the game and pass it on."

When Nipper arrived in Boston in 1983, he picked up cues from clubhouse leaders like Dwight Evans. When Evans arrived in Boston eleven years earlier, he emulated clubhouse leaders like Carl Yastrzemski. When Yastrzemski arrived in Boston in 1961, it was to an organization that had been dominated since 1939 by Ted Williams. This is how the leadership cycle is passed down through a half-century of baseball.

Examples can even be set from outside the boundaries of one's own team. When Mientkiewicz was a struggling rookie first baseman with Minnesota in 1999, he found himself in a clubhouse devoid of veterans at his position on whom he felt comfortable leaning. He was so visibly disoriented, in fact, that he was noticed by a member of the opposition, who reached out in an effort to set him straight. It happened before a game against Oakland, and A's first baseman Jason Giambi—in his fifth year as a big-leaguer and in the middle of his first truly monstrous offensive season—ventured across the aisle, for no reason other than to make sure an overwhelmed young player was properly equipped to right himself emotionally.

"Jason told me, 'It's not the end of the world—you're not the only guy who's come up your rookie year and struggled,' " said Mientkiewicz. "He took the time to talk to me—about hitting, about life. He told me how to act, how to be. He became my friend."

The irony of the gesture is that a generation earlier such an act would have been considered tantamount to treason; the Code—not to mention Giambi's first big-league manager, Tony La Russa—strictly kept opposing players from fraternizing on the field, let alone offering advice to complete strangers on the other team. Giambi's effort represented a sea change, and though he was breaking an unwritten rule, his action—intentionally or otherwise—was aimed at the larger purpose of preserving the Code. He cast aside one rule to ensure the propagation of the rest.

Giambi did it because he saw a young, struggling player with nowhere to turn. He did it because he had been in a similar place himself as a rookie. He did it because, from one ballplayer to another, it was the right thing to do.

Like so many before him, Giambi saw the continuum that exists between generations, and realized that, if left unchecked, unhealthy tendencies can quickly permeate the game. He wasn't a teacher, he was a ballplayer—and he understood that every player in possession of the proper attitude was another cog in the line of defense against encroaching apathy for the Code. "When I was coming up, guys had taken me under their wing, and I just wanted to do the same for somebody who needed it," he said, looking back on his interaction with Mientkiewicz. "That's the transition of the game. That's how it keeps going." (Sure enough, seven years later, when various members of the Royals were approached about who among their ranks would be a good spokesman for the unwritten rules, one name was universally brought up: Doug Mientkiewicz.) It's a self-perpetuation of the Code that invariably lights up someone in every clubhouse when he sees how powerful it can be.

"I honestly believe that what you learn in this game is not yours to possess, but yours to pass on," said Dusty Baker. "I believe that, whether it's equipment, knowledge, or philosophy, that's the only way the game shall carry on. I believe that you have to talk, communicate, and pass on what was given to you. You can't harbor it. You can't run off to the woods and keep it for yourself, because it isn't yours to keep. And what you teach other guys is the torch you pass. I don't make this up—it was passed to me."

Take Rex Hudler, who in 1998 had been relegated to finishing what would be his last professional season, with the Triple-A Buffalo Bisons. At age thirty-seven, however, Hudler, struggling even in the minor leagues, decided to hang it up mid-season. He informed Bisons manager Jeff Datz of his decision, along with two requests: He wanted to play for the final time in the following day's game, and he wanted to address the team beforehand. Hudler—known around baseball for his unbridled enthusiasm—was keenly aware of everything that two decades in baseball had done for him, and understood that his ability to hold a room's attention had not diminished nearly as much as his ability to get around on a fastball.

The next day, when everyone was assembled before him, Hudler bared his soul. A roomful of minor-leaguers sat rapt before the fervor on display from a man who, to judge by the lines on his face, had less business being their teammate than he did being their coach. He spoke about the fulfillment baseball gave him. He talked about playing hard, being aggressive, fostering noble work habits. Mostly, he talked about respect. It was respect learned over time, ever since he had signed with the Yankees as a teenager in 1978. He talked about giving respect to the other team, expecting it in return, and how to react should it fail to be reciprocated. Hudler's fervor was his paean to baseball, his tribute to the sport he loved.

When the game began, Hudler started at second base, the position he played when he made it to the major leagues. It was a perfect send-off to a fulfilling career . . . until Hudler's third at-bat, when a pitch from Indianapolis reliever Scott Ruffcorn hit him on the neck, just below his helmet. Hudler pitched forward into the batter's box, landing on his knees. It was the first time in a career that spanned two decades that he had absorbed a blow above his shoulders from a pitched baseball. But there he was, less than an hour away from retirement, in the dirt. A knot swelled behind his ear as Datz squatted next to him, trying gently to nudge him toward the dugout, out of the game and away from baseball. Hudler needed a moment to collect his senses enough even to look up and address the last manager he would ever have, but once he could, all he said, quietly, was "Step aside." Then, even though play had stopped, he struggled to his feet and took off in a dead sprint to first base.

Three thousand people sat in the stands, baffled. To Hudler, though, the answer was simple. He had to play it out. It was the final time he'd leave a batter's box as a professional ballplayer. He pulled himself from the game before his next turn at bat, his enthusiasm and his respect firmly intact.

He couldn't have been happier.

ACKNOWLEDGMENTS

This project would not have been possible without help and support from dozens, if not hundreds, of people, starting with our agent, Christy Fletcher. Christy took us through seemingly endless revisions of the initial proposal; once it hit all the right notes, she sold the book within days. She knows her stuff, and we are fortunate to have her representing us.

That we met Christy is thanks to Pulitzer Prize–winning journalist and good friend Craig Wolff. Craig didn't have to recommend us, or our idea, to his agent, but he did. His encouragement was essential in getting past the "Can we really do this?" phase of the process. We're eagerly anticipating the completion of his book about Willie Mays.

Our editor at Random House, Andrew Miller, helped us figure out which 25 percent of our original manuscript presented the very best material—a difficult and time-consuming job. He does excellent work for a Mets fan; the book would look nothing like it does without his stewardship.

We must also thank the media relations departments of our two home teams: Blake Rhodes, Jim Morehead, and Matt Hodson of the San Francisco Giants, and their counterparts with the Oakland Athletics, Debbie Gallas and Jim Young.

The research staff at the National Baseball Hall of Fame in Cooperstown, N.Y., was invaluable, as were the librarians at the Village Library of Cooperstown, who gave us a place to camp out when the Hall of Fame was closed due to flooding concerns during our stay.

261

Other media relations people of note: Josh Rawitch of the Los Angeles Dodgers, Jason Zillo of the New York Yankees, David Holtzman of the Kansas City Royals, Brian Bartow of the St. Louis Cardinals, Matt Chisholm of the Colorado Rockies, and Rob Butcher of the Cincinnati Reds, as well as the helpful folks with the Iowa Cubs and various other minor league teams who we peppered with phone calls over the course of multiple seasons.

The reporting of this book would not have been possible without input from those who have played, coached, and described the game for a living. Special mention goes to Jack McDowell, our first official interview, who sat down with us for burgers and Guinness at Lefty O'Doul's restaurant in San Francisco, in the middle of a random weekday afternoon in 2004. His candor enabled us to get the ball rolling significantly more quickly than we otherwise might have been able.

Other interviewees who merit special mention for the amount of time they were willing to spend with us both at and away from the ballpark include Dusty Baker, Mike Krukow, Bip Roberts, and Charlie Silvera. They had no reason to do so, save for genuine decency and an abiding love of baseball's Code.

We compiled literally hundreds of interviews for this book, both in person and on the phone. We spoke to people in dugouts, clubhouses, bullpens, dining rooms, broadcast booths, offices, luxury boxes, and on the fields of ballparks across five states. Conversations ranged from a few minutes stolen before batting practice to long-form chats that over the course of multiple hours delved as deeply into the psyche of the American ballplayer as one could hope to travel.

We offer sincere thanks to the complete list of our interview subjects for taking whatever time they did: Mike Aldrete, Rod Allen, Felipe Alou, Larry Andersen, Sparky Anderson, Tony Armas Jr., Rich Aurilia, Mack "Shooty" Babitt, Harold Baines, Dusty Baker, Paul Bako, Ernie Banks, Brian Bannister, Jim Barr, Bill Bavasi, Billy Beane, Buddy Bell, David Bell, Don Biebel, Craig Biggio, Bud Black, Vida Blue, Bert Blyleven, Bruce Bochy, Kevin Bootay, Dick Bosman, Jim Bouton, Larry Bowa, Ron Brand, Jeff Brantley, Bob Brenly, Marty Brennaman, George Brett, Jim Brower, Mike Butcher, Brett Butler, Mike Caldwell, Dave Campbell, Tom Candiotti, Jamey Carroll, Sean Casey, Bill Castro, Frank Catalanotto, Orlando Cepeda, Will Clark, Gene Clines, Jim Colborn, Jerry Coleman, Dave Collins, David Cone, Cecil Cooper, Chuck Cottier, Bobby Cox, Jose Cruz Jr., Jose Cruz Sr., Jimmy Davenport, Jim Deshaies, Pat Dobson, Rich Donnelly, Bill Doran, Al Downing, Shawon Dunston, Ryne Duren, Jim Dwyer, Damian Easley, Shawn Estes, Ron Fairly, Prince Fielder, Brad Fischer, Mike Flanagan, Tim Flannery, Tim Foli, Ray Fosse, Paul Foytack, Terry Francona, George Frazier, Bill Freehan, Oscar Gamble, Ron Gardenhire, Mark Gardner, Phil Garner, Jason Giambi, Dan Gladden, Tom Glavine, Luis Gonzalez, Mark Grace, Mark Grant, Craig Grebeck, Ken Griffey Jr., Jason Grilli, Ozzie Guillen, Tony Gwynn Jr., Chris Haft, Brad Halsey, Mike Hargrove, Mike Harkey, Ken Harrelson, Ron Hassey, Mike Hegan, Wes Helms, Dave Henderson, Brad Hennessey, Matt Herges, Greg Hibbard, Steve Hinton, Rick Honeycutt, Al Hrabosky, Rex Hudler, Torii Hunter, Tadahito Iguchi, Darrin Jackson, Ron Jackson, Bruce Jenkins, Derek Jeter, Von Joshua, Harry Kalas, Gabe Kapler, George Kell, Fred Kendall, Charlie Kerfeld, Ryan Klesko, Steve Kline, Randy Knorr, Mike Krukow, Duane Kuiper, Marcel Lacheman, Rene Lacheman, Pete LaCock, Gene Lamont, Dave LaRoche, Tony La Russa, Don Larsen, Jeffrey Leonard, Jim Leyland, Sixto Lezcano, Davey Lopes, Mark Loretta, Noah Lowry, Ed Lynch, Steve Lyons, Ken Macha, Greg Maddux, Mike Maddux, Rick Manning, Charlie Manuel, Jerry Manuel, Gary Matthews Sr., Gary Matthews Jr., Tim McCarver, Steve McCatty, Greg McClain, Lloyd McClendon, Bob McClure, Mike McCormick, Hal McCoy, Jack McDowell, Roger McDowell, Hal McRae, Bob Melvin, Orlando Mercado, Doug Mientkiewicz, Jon Miller, Joe Moeller, Rick Monday, Ed Montague, Rance Mulliniks, Jerry Narron, Lance Niekro, Dave Nelson, Bob Nightengale, Al Nipper, Dickie Noles, Bill North, Mike Norris, Buck O'Neil, Jose Oquendo, Gregg Orr, Russ Ortiz, Tom Paciorek, Mitchell Page, Jim Palmer, Terry Pendleton, Ron Perranoski, Johnny Pesky, Rick Petersen, Joe Pettini, Mike Piazza, Jim Price, Jamie Quirk, Tim Raines, Gary Rajsich, Jerry Remy, Dave Righetti, Jose Rijo, Tracy Ringolsby, Bip Roberts, Dave Roberts, Ron Roenicke, Al Rosen, Brian Sabean, Randy St. Clair, Billy Sample, Reggie Sanders, F. P. Santangelo, Ron Santo, Curt Schilling, Jason Schmidt, Bill Schroeder, Henry Schulman, Mike Scioscia, Richie Sexson, Mike Shannon, John Shelby, Charlie Silvera, Chris Singleton, Jim Slaton, Don Slaught, Chris

Speier, Justin Speier, Paul Splitorff, Mike Stanton, Charlie Steiner, Dave Stewart, Bill Stoneman, Jim Sundberg, Mac Suzuki, Dale Sveum, Mark Sweeney, Nick Swisher, Chuck Tanner, Frank Thomas, Milt Thompson, Dick Tidrow, Mike Timlin, Joe Torre, Jim Tracy, Del Unser, Bobby Valentine, Andy Van Slyke, Gary Varsho, Omar Vizquel, Bob Walk, Ron Washington, John Wathan, D'Jon Watson, John Wehner, Don Werner, Jerry White, Ed Whitson, Ernie Whitt, Bob Wickman, Mark Wiley, Billy Williams, Jerome Williams, Stan Williams, Tim Worrell, Al Worthington, David Wright, Ned Yost, Robin Yount, Greg Zaun, and Don Zimmer.

Jason must start by thanking his wife, Laura, who put more of a premium on this project's success than anybody. She served as cheerleader, director, and inspirational speaker throughout the process, not to mention as babysitter for a little girl while Daddy was at the ballpark into the wee hours of many long nights. It was Laura who without fail sat little Mozi down with a copy of *The Big Red Barn* and the telephone just before bedtime, allowing me to sneak into a back press-box office to recite the text by heart. To say that Laura deserves significant credit for my accomplishment here is an understatement of immense magnitude. Thank you for all you have done and all you continue to do.

Thanks must also be given to my parents, Mike and Ellen, whose love and support over the years have allowed me to chase this and other dreams; and to my in-laws, Michael and Simma, who continually helped me keep perspective through the book-writing process. Thanks also to Esther "The Woj" Wojcicki and Conn Hallinan, whose mentorship and inspiration through various levels of schooling were absolutely key to where I ended up. Thanks to my friends, who stuck with me through the many months I spent underground trying to get this thing finished, and to Nealus, for years' worth of glaringly perverse inspiration. He shows surprising agility for a fat man.

Finally, a mention to Reuben, who wasn't yet born when this book was being written but has since made his presence unmistakably felt.

·   ·   ·

Michael's reflections:

Books don't just happen. The time between having an idea and seeing a book with your name on the cover is measured in years, or even decades. And the list of people deserving of thanks might well be another whole book itself.

This book started as an idea I had in 2002. In 2004, Jason and I began to develop it, Craig Wolff offered input and an introduction to Christy Fletcher, and it became serious.

Jason took my idea and made it real, working tirelessly to make prose out of my half-baked concepts and on-the-fly interviews while adding much of his own creativity. I can't think of anyone who could have done better.

From 2002 to 2010 is a long time. It requires a lot of trust, confidence, patience, and belief to stick with something that long. Those are attributes that would have been in short supply in my life were it not for my wife, Kelli, who remained relentlessly positive through the process. Even as a writer, I have no words to adequately thank her, or my children, Ryan, Arthur, Stephen, AD, and Maureen.

Finally, to my father, Joe, now ninety-one years old, a twenty-plus-year survivor of lung cancer, who always believed I could do this, and much more. Thank you for, literally, everything.

NOTES

Unannotated quotes are from oral interviews conducted by the authors.

Introduction

3   "The way [people] carry on": *Chicago Sun-Times*, Aug. 10, 1993.
4   "cow-mugging": Ibid.
4   "the first guy ever to get": *Austin American-Statesman*, May 19, 2001.
7   "He's been throwing at batters": *Chicago Sun-Times*, Aug. 5, 1993.
8   "When someone comes out to the mound": Associated Press, Aug. 6, 1993.
8   "felt it was necessary": *Chicago Sun-Times*, Aug. 26, 1993.
8   "You learn what's acceptable": Tom House, *The Jock's Itch: The Fast-Track Private World of the Professional Ballplayer* (Lincolnwood, Ill.: NTC Publishing Group, 1989).
11   "Baseball protects its own": Ibid.
12   fought in the clubhouse: Bill Werber, *Memories of a Ballplayer: Bill Werber and Baseball in the 1930s* (Cleveland: Society for American Baseball Research, 2000).
12   Johnson, reluctant at first: *Baltimore Sun*, Feb. 18, 1996.
12   "Everybody had at least one black eye": House, *Jock's Itch*.
13   "You can ask Hank Aaron": *Baltimore Sun*, Feb. 18, 1996.
13   "You might not like everybody": *New York Daily News*, Feb. 20, 2005.

1   Know When to Steal 'Em

17   "I didn't appreciate": *Milwaukee Journal Sentinel*, July 30, 2001.
18   "Davey and I argued": *San Diego Union Tribune*, July 30, 2001.
18   "To be blunt, what he did": *Milwaukee Journal Sentinel*, July 30, 2001.
19   "All of those people": *Milwaukee Journal Sentinel*, Aug. 7, 2001.
19   Yankees third-base coach Larry Bowa: *Baltimore Sun*, June 5, 2006.
21   "The biggest message": *Akron Beacon Journal*, Aug. 6, 2001.
21   "There's a difference in trying": *Milwaukee Journal Sentinel*, Aug. 7, 2001.
22   "You never know about baseball": *Seattle Times*, Aug. 6, 2001.
23   "We weren't trying to incite": *Chicago Sun-Times*, May 11, 2003.

24 "I was trying to figure": *Los Angeles Daily News,* April 18, 1996.

25 "If he's that confused": Ibid.

26 "I lose respect": *Boston Herald,* June 28, 2003.

26 "I can see why": Ibid.

27 "I don't know what I'm supposed to do": *Dayton Daily News,* June 14, 2003.

29 "You don't cherry-pick": *New York Times,* May 16, 1993.

32 "When Brock would keep stealing": Bob Gibson with Lonnie Wheeler, *Stranger to the Game: The Autobiography of Bob Gibson* (New York: Viking, 1994).

2 Running into the Catcher

33 "Gallagher had every right": *Sporting News,* June 23, 1973.

34 "Look, I'm the winning run": Roger Kahn, *Pete Rose: My Story* (New York: Macmillan, 1989).

3 Tag Appropriately

36 Negro Leagues shortstop Willie Wells: Richard Scheinin, *Field of Screams: The Dark Underside of America's National Pastime* (New York: Norton, 1994).

4 Intimidation

38 "The pitcher has to find out": *New York Times,* July 9, 1979.

39 "He was mean": Bob Cairns, *Pen Men* (Boston: World Publications, 1995).

39 Casey even went so far: Daniel Okrent and Steve Wulf, *Baseball Anecdotes* (New York: Oxford University Press, 1989).

40 "[Other teams used to] say, 'Here come' ": Donald Hall with Dock Ellis, *Dock Ellis in the Country of Baseball* (New York: Simon & Schuster, 1989).

40 "That's what our team was starting to do": Ibid.

41 "[Ellis's] point was not to hit": Ibid.

41 The Hall of Famer proceeded: Charles Alexander, *Breaking the Slump: Baseball in the Depression Era* (New York: Columbia University Press, 2004).

41 "The Giants went up and down": *New York Times,* May 20, 1937.

41 Durocher said: Leo Durocher, *Nice Guys Finish Last* (New York: Simon & Schuster, 1975).

42 "frequent 'duster' pitches": *New York Times,* June 9, 1940.

42 "I was mad inside at Drysdale": Russell Schneider, *Frank Robinson: The Making of a Manager* (New York: Penguin, 1980).

43 "brushback pitch with attitude": Bob Gibson with Lonnie Wheeler, *Stranger to the Game: The Autobiography of Bob Gibson* (New York: Viking, 1994).

44 "I want to jiggle their eyeballs": *New York Times Magazine,* March 4, 2001.

47 "I don't think you can say": *Philadelphia Inquirer,* June 18, 2004.

48 "That's the first time the thought": *Providence Journal,* May 5, 1989.

48 "trauma": *Boston Globe,* April 25, 1992.

49 "Intimidate and kill are different": *Boston Globe,* May 2, 1989.

49 "I had to block out what had happened": Nolan Ryan, *Throwing Heat* (New York: Doubleday Religious Publishing, 1988).

49 "Baseball is a business": Ibid.

49 "Show me a guy": Don Drysdale with Bob Verdi, *Once a Bum, Always a Dodger: My Life in Baseball* (New York: St. Martin's, 1990).

5 On Being Intimidated

50 "The catcher warns the rookie": Christy Mathewson, *Pitching in a Pinch, or Baseball from the Inside* (Lincoln: University of Nebraska Press, 1994 [reprint]).

52 Don Drysdale went so far: *New York Times*, July 9, 1979.

52 When Ted Williams was a twenty-year-old rookie: David Halberstam, *The Summer of '49* (New York: HarperCollins, 2002).

53 "because my head ain't gonna be here": *Saturday Evening Post*, Sept. 14, 1963.

53 "He threw a pitch close to Jim's chin": Bill Lee with Richard Lally, *The Wrong Stuff* (New York: Random House, 2006 [reprint]).

54 "I took your best shot": Sparky Lyle with Peter Golenbock, *The Bronx Zoo: The Astonishing Inside Story of the 1978 World Champion New York Yankees* (Chicago: Triumph Books, 2005 [reprint]).

54 "You could hear the thud": Don Drysdale with Bob Verdi, *Once a Bum, Always a Dodger: My Life in Baseball* (New York: St. Martin's, 1990).

6 Slide into Bases Properly

57 "about to tackle" Kingman: *New York Times*, May 26, 1985.

58 "I don't know what I was doing": Ibid.

58 "I think we'll make sure": Ibid.

7 Don't Show Players Up

59 "What's that crazy bastard": Whitey Ford with Phil Pepe, *Slick* (New York: Dell, 1988).

60 "from his chin to his knees": *Hartford Courant*, Aug. 21, 2000.

60 Stoneham had gone out of his way: *Newsday*, July 12, 1995.

61 "I hated to lose a sucker bet": Mickey Mantle with Mickey Herskowitz, *All My Octobers: My Memories of 12 World Series When the Yankees Ruled Baseball* (New York: HarperCollins, 2006).

61 "Here it was only the end": *New York Times*, April 3, 1977.

61 "It didn't dawn on me right away": Mantle with Herskowitz, *All My Octobers*.

61 it did for Goose Gossage: *Boston Herald*, May 2, 2000.

62 "Play to win against Villanova": *Newsday*, Feb. 26, 2008.

62 "Killebrew was the first one I saw": *Boston Globe*, April 5, 1991.

62 "The pause at this moment": ESPN.com, n.d.

63 "That's fucking Little League shit": *St. Louis Post-Dispatch*, May 19, 2001.

65 "Seeing Howell and his curveball": New York *Daily News*, Oct. 5, 1988.

66 "won enough times": *New York Times*, Oct. 10, 2001.

67 "So he's dropping the past tense": Buster Olney, *The Last Night of the Yankee Dynasty: The Game, the Team, and the Cost of Greatness* (New York: HarperCollins, 2008 [reprint]).

68 "If my daddy was managing": Associated Press, May 25, 2006.

69 "It's not LeCroy's fault": *Washington Post*, May 26, 2006.

69 "When a player shows the club up": *New York Times*, June 19, 1977.

69 "Without an injury": Cleon Jones with Ed Hershey, *Cleon* (New York: Penguin, 1970).

69 "If you're not running good": Ibid.

70 "Look in that mirror": *New York Times*, Sept. 27, 1990.

70 Jones's opinion was that Hodges's message: *Newsday*, Oct. 3, 1985.
70 "Gil once told me": *New York Times*, Sept. 27, 1990.
70 "Gil wasn't the type of man": Transcript, "A Tribute to Gil Hodges," at Brooklyn Baseball Gallery, KeySpan Park, April 27, 2003.
71 "I've seen you guys talk people": Bruce Nash and Allan Zullo, *Baseball Hall of Shame 4* (New York: Simon & Schuster, 1991).
71 "After they talked me off second": Ibid.

8 Responding to Records

72 "Denny told me, 'Let him hit one' ": *Baseball Digest*, March 2002.
72 "Denny stood out there on the mound": Ibid.
73 "just make it close": Bill Madden, *Pride of October: What It Was to Be Young and a Yankee* (New York: Grand Central, 2004).
73 "There couldn't have been a more complete fix": Ibid.
73 "Say, Ed": *Sport*, October 1948.
74 In 1961, Roger Maris was denied: *Washington Post*, June 10, 2001.
76 "didn't let me finish": Associated Press, Oct. 2, 1992.
77 "I don't know why he did that": Interview with Tim Keown, ESPN; also in *Chicago Sun-Times*, June 17, 2001.
77 "I would rather earn it": Ralph Berger, SABR Baseball Biography Project.
78 "The first hit of a no-hitter": *Orange County Register*, Oct. 2, 1986.
78 "has a lot to learn": *San Diego Union Tribune*, May 27, 2001.
78 "I don't know if you saw my swings": Associated Press, May 27, 2001.
78 "What if it's the seventh game": Ibid.
78 "drop our weapons": *Chicago Sun-Times*, May 28, 2001.
79 "If it was the eighth or ninth": *Tacoma News Tribune*, Aug. 10, 2006.

9 Gamesmanship

81 "If I did think Knoblauch": *Sports Illustrated*, March 31, 2003.
82 In 1892, with Cleveland's Jesse Burkett: Bruce Nash and Allan Zullo, *Baseball Hall of Shame 4* (New York: Simon & Schuster, 1991).
83 "You could make a great video": *New York Times*, Jan. 26, 2008.
84 "Dick gets there": Bob Cairns, *Pen Men* (Boston: World Publications, 1995).
84 "Bench told me later": Ibid.
86 "could clean the bag off": *San Francisco Chronicle*, June 29, 1994.
86 "The intent was not to embarrass": *Cleveland Plain Dealer*, Sept. 21, 1997.
87 Philadelphia infielder Steve Jeltz: *Philadelphia Daily News*, Aug. 6, 1986.

10 Mound Conference Etiquette

89 Hall of Famer Early Wynn: Jonathan Fraser Light, *The Cultural Encyclopedia of Baseball* (Jefferson, N.C.: McFarland, 2005).
89 St. Louis Cardinals manager Eddie Dyer: Ibid.
92 "I don't want to hear you": *New York Times*, June 23, 1985.
92 "Okay, so I'm the manager of Nolan Ryan": *Sports Illustrated*, April 6, 1992.
92 "They're starting pitchers": Buzz Bissinger, *Three Nights in August: Strategy, Heartbreak, and Joy Inside the Mind of a Manager* (New York: Houghton Mifflin, 2006).

11 Retaliation

98 "One of the best pitches": *New York Times*, March 9, 1992.

101 "I can promise you as long as I'm general manager": *Kansas City Star*, April 4, 2004.

102 "dirty baseball": *Cleveland Plain Dealer*, April 23, 1994.

102 "that slide wasn't good, hard baseball": *Dallas Morning News*, April 24, 1994.

103 "I thought this was finished in Cleveland": *Cleveland Plain Dealer*, July 7, 1994.

105 "Well," said Messersmith: *New York Times*, Aug. 20, 1985.

105 " 'If you had eight hits in a row' ": *Newsday*, June 15, 2002.

108 "If I have any advice": *New York Post*, May 28, 2000.

109 "It infuriated [Blyleven]": *Sporting News*, June 17, 1991.

110 "Thomas got his priorities mixed up": *Seattle Post-Intelligencer*, May 12, 2006.

110 "That's for looking through my goddamn shaving kit": Don Drysdale with Bob Verdi, *Once a Bum, Always a Dodger: My Life in Baseball* (New York: St. Martin's, 1990).

110 " 'Mr. Craig, I think that fellow' ": *Playboy*, Oct. 1988.

111 "I will order it": Russell Schneider, *Frank Robinson: The Making of a Manager* (New York: Penguin, 1980).

112 Martin: "Goose, when you get in the game": Richard "Goose" Gossage with Russ Pate, *The Goose Is Loose: An Autobiography* (New York: Random House, 2000).

112 "The message was, we will not tolerate": *Chicago Tribune*, March 6, 1998.

114 "learned from it": *Sports Illustrated*, July 3, 2006.

114 "If Padilla hits somebody": *Chicago Sun-Times*, July 21, 2006.

114 "I make it clear, I won't wait": *New York Sun*, July 26, 2006.

116 "What's your problem?": *Playboy*, June 2003.

116 "[Clemens] was obviously jacked up": Ibid.

116 found him sobbing: *New Yorker*, March 9, 2009.

117 fighting "someone else's battle": *New York Times*, June 14, 2002.

121 "If Jon Lieber hits Craig Biggio": *Chicago Tribune*, May 7, 2000.

123 "future Hall of Famer": *Toronto Globe and Mail*, Oct. 3, 1987.

124 "It was better when we didn't have helmets": *Houston Chronicle*, June 20, 1988.

125 "I threw at him": *Cincinnati Post*, Sept. 10, 1991.

125 "What he said was a disgrace": *Los Angeles Times*, Sept. 11, 1991.

125 "stupid," "dumb," and "idiotic": Ibid.

125 "If I were a pitcher and I hit someone": Ibid.

126 when Mickey Lolich of the Tigers: Bill Freehan, *Behind the Mask: An Inside Baseball Diary* (New York: Popular Library, 1970).

127 "I don't want to talk about that": Buster Olney, *The Last Night of the Yankee Dynasty: The Game, the Team, and the Cost of Greatness* (New York: HarperCollins, 2008 [reprint]).

127 "On the record?": *Los Angeles Times*, July 5, 2006.

127 "I don't have any bad blood with those guys": Associated Press, June 3, 1998.

128 "When I was about 15 feet from home plate": *Detroit Free Press*, Aug. 18, 1997.

130 "Know you!" shouted Lasorda: *Los Angeles Times*, March 9, 1997.

12 The Wars

132 "the Desert Storm of baseball fights": *Seattle Times*, May 16, 1999.

132 "It took baseball down 50 years": Associated Press, Aug. 13, 1984.

133 "We can't be intimidated": Ibid.

135 "It was the wildest thing": Scripps Howard News Service, May 18, 2000.

136 "The donnybrook . . . was the best": Richard "Goose" Gossage with Russ Pate, *The Goose Is Loose: An Autobiography* (New York: Random House, 2000).

136 After Atlanta finally closed out the 5–3 victory: Associated Press, Aug. 13, 1984.

136 "with a capital 'I' ": Ibid.

137 "It would've been a lot simpler": *Sports Illustrated*, Aug. 27, 1984.

137 "The only problem": *Sports Illustrated*, Oct. 20, 2008.

138 "There will be another day": *St. Petersburg Times*, Aug. 30, 2000.

138 Afterward, he sneaked out a rear exit: *Sports Illustrated*, Oct. 20, 2008.

139 "You can't act like what happened never happened": *Boston Herald*, July 23, 2002.

139 "Players on that team are saying": *Boston Globe*, April 27, 2005.

139 "I have forgot more baseball": Associated Press, April 28, 2005.

140 "throw a punch at me right away": Associated Press, March 28, 2006.

140 "hits like a woman": *Boston Globe*, March 28, 2006.

140 Carl Crawford subsequently challenges: *Sports Illustrated*, Oct. 20, 2008.

140 with seventeen knockouts: *Boston Herald*, June 6, 2008.

140 "little girls, trying to scratch": *Boston Globe*, June 6, 2008.

141 "With the way we hate them": *Sports Illustrated*, Oct. 20, 2008.

13 Hitters

143 "The first time I could have crushed him": Associated Press, June 1, 1996.

143 "professional courtesy": Ibid.

145 "I have dozens of spike scars": Ty Cobb, *Memoirs of Twenty Years in Baseball*, ed. William R. Cobb (Marietta, Ga.: William R. Cobb, 2002).

145 "The next thing I know": Bill Werber, *Memories of a Ballplayer: Bill Werber and Baseball in the 1930s* (Cleveland: Society for American Baseball Research, 2000).

145 "had it coming": Scripps Howard News Service, May 30, 2001.

145 "I remembered in Cobb's book": *Centre Daily Times*, July 26, 2003.

146 "I had to hold the bag down": Ibid.

146 pulling "the cork out of the bottle": Maury Wills and Mike Celizic, *On the Run: The Never Dull and Often Shocking Life of Maury Wills* (New York: Carroll & Graf, 1991).

147 "all sitting back on the bench": Ibid.

148 "did it deliberately": *Sport* magazine, Oct. 1951.

148 Robinson "even slowed down": *New York Times*, April 7, 1997.

148 "a crushing shoulder block": *New York Times*, April 24, 1955.

148 "[Manager Leo Durocher] used to tell us": *Sport* magazine, Oct. 1951.

148 "Like a streak of murderous slaughter": *Baseball Magazine*, June 1913.

149 "little Dago son of a bitch": *Sports Illustrated*, June 2, 1979.

150 "Of course Martin was throwing at Campy": Ron Bergman, *Mustache Gang* (New York: Dell, 1973).

150 "I think he had too much pine tar": *Orange County Register*, May 23, 1988.

14 Off the Field

152 Finley waited until the A's: Ron Bergman, *Mustache Gang* (New York: Dell, 1973).

153 "Thanks for saying something to me": *New York Daily News,* July 17, 1976.

153 "things like this happen in baseball": Ibid.

153 "No way I was going to give Gaylord": Russell Schneider, *Frank Robinson: The Making of a Manager* (New York: Penguin, 1980).

153 "stick a ball in his fucking ear": Ibid.

154 "What time does the blimp go up?": John Snyder, *Cubs Journal: Year by Year and Day by Day with the Chicago Cubs Since 1876* (Cincinnati: Emmis Books, 2005).

154 "You'll hear from me all summer": Dick Bartell, Norman L. Macht, and Fred Stein, *Rowdy Richard: A Firsthand Account of the National League Baseball Wars of the 1930s and the Men Who Fought Them* (Berkeley, Calif.: North Atlantic Books, 1987).

154 "the biggest hit I made all year": Ibid.

154 "for coming down so hard on me": Ibid.

15 Sign Stealing

158 Charlie Dressen: *Sacramento Bee,* May 25, 1997.

158 "somebody's going to get killed": *Montreal Gazette,* May 8, 1997.

158 "Maybe they were pissed": Ibid. Expletives deleted by newspaper and reinstated by author.

159 "Hey, if you're dumb enough": *San Jose Mercury News,* May 8, 1997.

159 Yankees stars Joe DiMaggio and Mickey Mantle: Frank Crosetti, in *Saturday Evening Post,* Aug. 8, 1959.

160 "We were the best [sign-stealing] team": *Baseball Digest,* Aug. 2002.

160 Hank Greenberg proclaimed himself the "greatest hitter in the world": Lawrence Ritter, *The Glory of Their Times: The Story of the Early Days of Baseball Told by the Men Who Played It* (New York: HarperCollins, 1992).

160 "All right, Hank": Ibid.

161 "I guess we'll never know, huh?": *Riverside Press Enterprise,* May 9, 2005.

162 "As I did it, I'm thinking": *San Diego Union-Tribune,* May 8, 2005.

162 "a semi–power hitter": *National Post,* May 10, 2005.

162 "I started watching the pitchers": *Baseball Digest,* Aug. 2002.

163 "Here comes curveball. . . .": Ibid.

163 "probably called the pitch on half": Ibid.

163 Hitters would start every at-bat: *San Diego Union-Tribune,* June 18, 2001.

163 The pitcher was so good: Associated Press, March 20, 1988.

163 Roger Maris: *St. Petersburg Times,* May 8, 2001.

163 "Jim, he's whistling": Mike Shannon, *Tales from the Dugout: The Greatest True Baseball Stories Ever Told* (New York: McGraw-Hill, 1997).

164 "Haywood Sullivan came down": *Richmond Times-Dispatch,* June 29, 1997.

164 Toronto "had every pitch": Ibid.

164 In 1973, Nolan Ryan responded: Nolan Ryan, *Throwing Heat* (New York: Doubleday Religious Publishing, 1988).

165 Once he pinpointed the trouble: *St. Louis Post-Dispatch,* Aug. 3, 2002.

165 When Babe Ruth first came: Babe Ruth as told to Bob Considine, *The Babe Ruth Story* (New York: Penguin, 1992 [reprint]).

165 "When Andy Benes pitched": Todd Jones, in *Sporting News,* Aug. 23, 2004.

165 In 1986, Toronto slugger George Bell: *Sports Illustrated,* April 15, 1991.

166 "If he saw our catcher signal": *New York Times,* April 25, 1952.

167 "Frank, Billy said he wants": *Sports Illustrated,* April 15, 1991.

16 Don't Peek

169 "What are you doing?": *Sports Illustrated,* April 4, 1988.

169 "Okay," he said. "What pitch do you want?": Ibid.

169 "Did you see me swing?": *Toronto Star,* March 7, 1988.

169 "You do that," said Mark Grace: *Fort Lauderdale Sun-Sentinel,* June 13, 2004.

169 "I hit .350": *Los Angeles Times,* Sept. 12, 1991.

170 "I have to say he was throwing at me": *Toronto Globe and Mail,* May 11, 1979.

170 "[Cowens] thinks I'm guilty": Ibid.

170 "It's a fine line out there": *Chicago Tribune,* Sept. 17, 1989.

17 Sign Stealing (Stadiums)

173 "As a player it was none of his business": *Saturday Evening Post,* May 2, 1964.

174 "Baseball is a game": Ibid.

174 "It was hump city": Bob Cairns, *Pen Men* (Boston: World Publications, 1995).

175 "I doubt there is one club": Bill Veeck with Ed Linn, *Veeck—As in Wreck* (New York: Putnam, 1962).

175 "Sounds impossible": *Los Angeles Times,* Sept. 12, 1991.

175 "Bootling information to the batter": *Wall Street Journal,* June 6, 2003.

175 "You know the two vertical dots": *Jerusalem Post,* May 6, 1997.

177 Philadelphia went so far as to have Murphy: Paul Dickson, *The Hidden Language of Baseball* (New York: Walker, 2005).

177 In one noteworthy instance, the 1948 Indians: Newhouse News Service, Sept. 24, 1999.

178 "I myself called a grand-slam homer": *Cleveland Plain Dealer,* Sept. 24, 1999.

178 Among the inflammatory items O'Neill found: *New York Times,* Aug. 27, 1950.

178 "out and out cheating": *Baseball Digest,* Aug. 1, 2003.

180 "It was easy to spot them": *Sports Illustrated,* April 15, 1991.

18 If You're Not Cheating, You're Not Trying

182 "We do not play baseball": Thomas Boswell, *How Life Imitates the World Series: An Inquiry into the Game* (New York: Doubleday, 1982).

182 "Some of that stuff": Copley News Service, June 9, 2003.

183 "Our television announcers are aware": *Houston Chronicle,* June 8, 2003.

183 "George," Piniella responded: Ibid.

184 "There is a culture of deception": Copley News Service, June 9, 2003.

184 "Everyone cheats": *South Florida Sun-Sentinel,* Nov. 5, 2003.

184 Tigers star Norm Cash: *Baseball Digest,* Sept. 2001.

184 Or take the time in 1941: Jonathan Fraser Light, *The Cultural Encyclopedia of Baseball* (Jefferson, N.C.: McFarland, 2005).

185 "I've been in baseball since 1914": *True* magazine, 1961.

185 "If you know how to cheat": *Washington Post,* Feb. 1, 2001.

185 It's why the Yankees allegedly made: *New York Times,* June 17, 1990.

185 "Anything short of murder": *Seattle Times,* Sept. 19, 1999.

186 "Pitchers have always cheated": *Allentown Morning Call,* Aug. 13, 1987.

186 "He stuck [the pine tar] on": Dick Dobbins, *The Grand Minor League: An Oral History of the Old Pacific Coast League* (Riverside, N.J.: Andrews McMeel, 1999).

187 "the whole Yankee staff": *San Francisco Examiner,* Aug. 7, 1983.

187 "No player shall intentionally": *2008 Official Rules of Major League Baseball* (Chicago: Triumph Books, 2008).

187 "The advantage to K-Y Jelly": *Chicago Tribune,* Feb. 24, 1985.

188 Dodgers manager Charlie Dressen: *Palm Beach Post,* Aug. 24, 1997.

188 Pirates pitcher Dock Ellis: Donald Hall with Dock Ellis, *Dock Ellis in the Country of Baseball* (New York: Simon & Schuster, 1989).

188 In the 1980s, several of Billy Martin's pitchers: *Newsday,* July 27, 2003.

188 "During a game I'd just reach back": Ibid.

188 A's closer John Wyatt: *New York Times,* June 25, 1979.

188 Phonney Martin: *Baseball Magazine,* July 1931.

188 White Sox star Ed Walsh: *Vero Beach Press Journal,* March 3, 2000.

189 "Yes it was": *New York Times,* March 14, 1989.

189 "the [decade] of the spitter": *San Antonio Express News,* Aug. 25, 2002.

189 only 30 percent of 120 players: *New York Times,* April 24, 1955.

189 "Restore the spitter?": Ibid.

189 After Yogi Berra grabbed the wrong container: *New York Times,* April 3, 1977.

189 "He looked up, rubbed his knee": *New York Times,* July 26, 1973.

189 "Just about everything he throws": *New York Times,* April 12, 1973.

189 "gutless": Ibid.

190 "fastballs and sliders": Ibid.

190 "off-speed stuff": Ibid.

190 Thurman Munson asked to see the ball: *New York Times,* July 1, 1973.

190 "I just want to lead the league": Gaylord Perry with Bob Sudyk, *Me & the Spitter: An Autobiographical Confession* (New York: Saturday Review Press, 1974).

190 "Perry's big right hand": *New York Times,* July 1, 1973.

191 It didn't take long—all of six innings: *New York Times,* April 7, 1974.

191 "It's a hard slider": Light, *Cultural Encyclopedia of Baseball.*

191 "But he doesn't throw it any less": *New York Times,* June 25, 1979.

191 "When Rod Carew was inducted": *San Francisco Chronicle,* July 31, 1991.

192 to inadvertently prick Kunkel: Light, *Cultural Encyclopedia of Baseball.*

192 "The evidence at that point": *Myrtle Beach Sun-News,* Oct. 28, 2006.

192 "You might as well get the whole kit": Boswell, *How Life Imitates the World Series.*

192 "Sometimes you can be so frustrated": *Myrtle Beach Sun-News,* Oct. 28, 2006.

193 "It's a huge difference": *Detroit News,* May 4, 1999.

193 a sharpened belt buckle: *New York Times,* June 25, 1979.

193 A pitcher for the Milwaukee Brewers: *Palm Beach Post,* Aug. 24, 1997.

193 "It looked believable": *Newsday,* July 27, 2003.

193 "more than three and fewer than 10": *Washington Post,* Aug. 5, 1987.

194 "Rick Rhoden and Tommy John": *Washington Post,* Aug. 6, 1987.

194 "On occasion I've pitched": Nolan Ryan, *Throwing Heat* (New York: Doubleday Religious Publishing, 1998).

194 "If you covered the rubber up with dirt": Whitey Ford with Phil Pepe, *Slick* (New York: Dell Paperback, 1988).

195 "I played with a guy": Nick Peters, *Tales from the San Francisco Giants Dugout* (Champaign, Ill.: Sports Publishing, 2003).

195 Lighter bats equal faster swings: L. P. Fallon and J. A. Sherwood, "A Study of the

Barrel Construction of Baseball Bats," *Proceedings of the 4th International Conference on the Engineering of Sport,* Kyoto, Japan, Sept. 2002.

196 "Very funny": *Montreal Gazette,* Aug. 4, 1987.

197 mixed soap flakes into the downslope: Burt Solomon, *Where They Ain't: The Fabled Life and Untimely Death of the Original Baltimore Orioles, the Team That Gave Birth to Modern Baseball* (New York: Simon & Schuster, 2000).

197 The Orioles even went so far: *Los Angeles Times,* May 31, 1990.

197 "I think the majority of teams": *Seattle Times,* Sept. 19, 1999.

198 "I'm shocked and dumfounded": *Toronto Globe and Mail,* April 29, 1981.

19 Caught Brown-Handed

201 "an example of bullshit baseball": World Series Game 2, post-game press conference, Sunday, Oct. 22, 2006.

201 "There was a time": Ibid.

201 "I said, 'I don't like this' ": Ibid.

201 "Tony's been through a lot himself": *Detroit Free Press,* Oct. 24, 2006.

202 threatened to "undress" Nationals pitchers: *Washington Post,* June 23, 2005.

202 "There's etiquette and there's lack of etiquette": Ibid.

202 "Pine tar is accepted practice for pitchers": Mark Thomas, MLB.com, June 15, 2005.

202 "I don't put anything on the baseball": World Series Game 2, post-game press conference.

202 "Better grip means better spin": *New York Times,* July 5, 1987.

203 Davey Johnson grew suspicious: Darryl Strawberry with Art Rust, *Darryl!* (New York: Bantam Dell, 1992).

204 "I don't think he was cheating": *Chicago Tribune,* Oct. 9, 1988.

204 "It was a big clump of dirt": World Series Game 2, post-game press conference.

204 "I don't believe": Ibid.

204 "get down in the tunnel": Ibid.

204 "If it wasn't illegal": Ibid.

205 "What they're doing": Ibid.

205 "Pine tar in North Carolina is clean": *San Francisco Chronicle,* Oct. 24, 2006.

20 Don't Talk About a No-Hitter in Progress

210 "There's no way he can't know": Rex Barney with Norman L. Macht, *Rex Barney's Thank You for 50 Years in Baseball from Brooklyn to Baltimore* (Centreville, Md.: Cornell Maritime/Tidewater, 1993).

211 "Wow!" said Wells: *Syracuse Post Standard,* May 19, 1998.

211 "like he was going to kill": Ibid.

212 "Rule number one in baseball": David Wells with Chris Kreski, *Perfect I'm Not: Boomer on Beer, Brawls, Backaches, and Baseball* (New York: Harper Paperbacks, 2004).

213 "Well, Mick, do you think I'll make it?": Mickey Mantle with Mickey Herskowitz, *All My Octobers: My Memories of 12 World Series When the Yankees Ruled Baseball* (New York: HarperCollins, 2006).

215 "You don't ever mess with the lineup": Wells with Kreski, *Perfect I'm Not.*

215 "My father was there": *St. Petersburg Times,* July 21, 1988.

216 "I looked over there from first base": *Sporting News,* Aug. 8, 1994.

216 "I like that": *Palm Beach Post,* Aug. 7, 1994.

216 "Obviously, what I said": Curt Smith, *Voices of the Game: The First Full-Scale Overview of Baseball Broadcasting, 1921 to the Present* (South Bend, Ind.: Diamond Communications, 1987).

216 "Dodgers: one run": *Christian Science Monitor,* Oct. 31, 1988.

217 "Well, I'll be a suck-egg mule": *New York Times,* January 13, 2008.

217 "There was a hue and cry that night": *Christian Science Monitor,* Oct. 31, 1988.

217 "I broadcast Warneke's mastery": Ibid.

217 "In those days people did not mention 'no-hitter' ": *Arizona Republic,* Oct. 8, 2006.

218 "I thought that if I ever did a no-hitter": *Newsday,* June 25, 2006.

218 "It's just those three words": Stephen Borelli, *How About That! The Life of Mel Allen* (Champaign, Ill.: Sports Publishing, 2005).

218 "I usually make a couple pit stops": *Newsday,* May 16, 1996.

218 "Listen to me": *Philadelphia Inquirer,* April 29, 2003.

219 "Parrish, needless to say, is not superstitious": *New York Times,* April 10, 1984.

219 "I'm not a big believer in jinxes": *New York Post,* July 20, 1999.

220 "Coleman didn't reply": *New York Post,* Sept. 16, 2003.

21 Protect Yourself and Each Other

222 Moore outlasted sixteen play-by-play partners: Curt Smith, *Voices of Summer* (New York: Carroll & Graf, 2005).

222 "It's an automatic $500": *New York Times,* July 15, 1973.

222 when the Mets hired Allan Lans: *Sports Illustrated,* Feb. 27, 1995.

223 "It's a good example": Sparky Lyle, *The Bronx Zoo: The Astonishing Inside Story of the 1978 World Champion New York Yankees* (Chicago: Triumph Books, 2005 [reprint]).

223 "He kept his own book": *New York Daily News,* Oct. 29, 1995.

223 Joe Kerrigan was purported: Fox Sports (specific information unavailable).

225 Mets pitcher Doug Sisk: Jeff Pearlman, *The Bad Guys Won* (New York: Harper-Collins, 2005).

226 Negro Leagues star Buck O'Neil: Lecture given at Oakland Museum of California, Jan. 2006.

22 Everybody Joins a Fight

228 "a Little League move": *Los Angeles Times,* Sept. 1, 1999.

229 "I gained respect for certain people": Ibid.

229 "Gary DiSarcina, Darin Erstad, [Troy] Glaus": Ibid.

229 "I'm sick and fucking tired of this shit!": *Riverside Press Enterprise,* Sept. 2, 1999. Expletives deleted by newspaper and reinstated by author.

229 "I've been telling these assholes": Ibid.

229 "I've been getting drilled all year": Ibid.

230 "I have three guys on me": Jeff Pearlman, *The Bad Guys Won* (New York: Harper-Collins, 2005).

230 "I know what was expected of me": *New York Times,* Aug. 14, 1986.

232 "I raced toward the infield": Richard "Goose" Gossage with Russ Pate, *The Goose Is Loose: An Autobiography* (New York: Random House, 2000).

234 "It wasn't a pretty sight": *Milwaukee Journal Sentinel,* Aug. 2, 2001.

23 The Clubhouse Police

237 "I want to be fair": Mickey McDermott with Howard Eisenberg, *A Funny Thing Happened on the Way to Cooperstown* (Chicago: Triumph Books, 2003).

237 Joe DiMaggio had a perk: Richard Ben Cramer, *Joe DiMaggio: The Hero's Life* (New York: Simon & Schuster, 2002).

238 "Jay," he said: Associated Press, July 6, 1991.

238 "Somebody even made a big cardboard hand": Ibid.

238 Another of his victims was Brooks Robinson: *USA Today,* April 3, 2002.

239 as soon as he got "in the groove": *Sports Illustrated,* June 16, 1986.

239 "I throw strikes even on 0–2 counts": Associated Press, July 6, 1991.

240 fined for aiding the enemy: Ibid.

242 Pitcher Moe Drabowsky: Bob Cairns, *Pen Men* (Boston: World Publications, 1995).

242 "In case of Blyleven": *Los Angeles Times,* Nov. 29, 1993.

243 "Ed, Babe's been shot": Werber, *Memories of a Ballplayer: Bill Werber and Baseball in the 1930s* (Cleveland: Society for American Baseball Research, 2000).

244 Cardinals pitcher Joe Hoerner: Peter Golenbock, *The Spirit of St. Louis* (New York: HarperCollins, 2000).

244 shooting water balloons two city blocks: Richard "Goose" Gossage with Russ Pate, *The Goose Is Loose: An Autobiography* (New York: Random House, 2000).

247 On Lenny Dykstra's first day: Jeff Pearlman, *The Bad Guys Won* (New York: HarperCollins, 2005).

250 "You gonna take an oh-fer": Larry Dierker, *This Ain't Brain Surgery* (Lincoln, Neb.: Bison Books, 2005).

251 "You try climbing a bronze horse": Nick Peters, *Tales from the San Francisco Giants Dugout* (Champaign, Ill.: Sports Publishing, 2003).

251 "Painting nuts ain't fun": Pearlman, *The Bad Guys Won.*

Conclusion

252 "Run the fucking ball out": *Sporting News,* April 15, 1991.

252 "the days of slavery are over": *Chicago Sun-Times,* May 27, 1990.

252 "I just told him I thought": ESPN's *SportsCentury* biography.

253 "Modern trends have made": Bob Gibson with Lonnie Wheeler, *Stranger to the Game: The Autobiography of Bob Gibson* (New York: Viking, 1999).

254 "The overall respect for the game": *Orange County Register,* June 23, 2002.

254 "I told Randolph later": *New York Times,* Oct. 7, 1977.

INDEX

Baldwin, James, 112
Balfour, Grant, 140
balks, 39, 41, 162
Ball Four (Bouton), 10–11
Baltimore chop, 197
Baltimore Orioles, 19, 73, 74, 196–7
    kangaroo court of, 238, 239
Bamberger, George, 182
Banks, Ernie, 42, 230, 250
Barber, Red, 216–17, 218
Barnett, Larry, 150
Barney, Rex, 39, 210
Barr, George, 41
Barr, Jim, 88–9, 93, 106, 150
barrel rolls, 56–7
Barrett, Marty, 163–4
Barrow, Ed, 73
Bartell, Dick, 41, 154
Bartlett, Jason, 140
baseball
    as entertainment, 255–6
    fundamental changes in, 253–60
Baseball Magazine, 148, 188
baseballs
    cutting and scuffing of, 183, 192–4, 200
    foreign substances applied to, 60, 184, 186–91, 199–205
baserunners
    aggressive play by, 56–7, 102–3, 127–8, 140, 254
    base stealing by, *see* stolen bases
    dekes by, 84
    sliding by, 55–8, 102, 140, 142–7, 254
bats
    corking of, 184, 185, 194–6, 201
    flipping of, 62–3
    letting go of, 128, 138, 149
    pine tar on, 203
    throwing of, 115–20, 148–51
batters
    in blowout games, 27–31
    charging the mound by, 3–4, 7–8, 27, 103–4, 108, 122, 135, 137, 140, 147, 228
    crowding the plate by, 38, 39, 42
    peeking at signs by, 168–71
    reactions to knockdown pitches, 123–4, 147–51

see also hit batters
batter's box
    alterations to, 197–8
    digging into, 4, 5, 8, 62
    stepping out of, 61
batting helmets, 124
Bavasi, Bill, 234
Baylor, Don, 55, 105, 239
beanballs, 29, 39, 42, 47, 52, 111, 122–4, 126, 127, 128, 129, 137, 139, 148
Bedrosian, Steve, 135–6
Bell, Buddy, 257
Bell, David, 257
Bell, George, 144, 165, 234
Bell, Gus, 257
Bell, Jay, 77
Bell, Wally, 119
Belle, Albert, 142–4, 151, 185, 196
Beltre, Adrian, 107–8
Bench, Johnny, 41, 84
Benes, Andy, 165
Benitez, Armando, 248
Berra, Dale, 57–8
Berra, Yogi, 38, 163, 165–6, 189, 236
Bevacqua, Kurt, 132, 134, 136
Bevens, Bill, 216–17, 218
Biebel, Don, 179–80
Biggio, Craig, 57, 98, 121
big lead, changing definition of, 19–20
Billingham, Jack, 84
binoculars, sign stealing with, 172–3, 175–80
Bird, Doug, 128–9
Blair, Willie, 112
Blalock, Hank, 112–13
Blanchard, Johnny, 163
Blanton, Joe, 100
blowout games, aggressive play in, 7, 9, 17–32
Blue, Vida, 152
Blyleven, Bert, 109, 236
    no-hitter of, 209–10, 212
    as practical joker, 209, 242–3
Bochy, Bruce, 18, 19, 78, 232
Bonds, Barry, 9–10, 12, 62, 101, 107–8, 237, 240
Bonds, Bobby, 160
Booker, Greg, 134, 232
Boone, Bret, 44

A Note About the Authors

Jason Turbow's writing has appeared in the *New York Times*, the *Wall Street Journal*, SI.com, *Slam* magazine, *Popular Science*, and the *San Francisco Chronicle*, and he is a regular contributor to *Giants Magazine* and *Athletics* magazine. He lives in the Bay Area with his wife and two children.

Michael Duca was the first chairman of the board of Bill James's Project Scoresheet and has written for SportsTicker, "Giants Today" in the *San Francisco Chronicle*, and the Associated Press. He works for the Office of the Commissioner as an official scorer, and for MLB.com.

A Note on the Type

The text of this book was set in Ehrhardt, a typeface based on the specimens of "Dutch" types found at the Ehrhardt foundry in Leipzig. The original design of the face was the work of Nicholas Kis, a Hungarian punch cutter known to have worked in Amsterdam from 1680 to 1689. The modern version of Ehrhardt was cut by the Monotype Corporation of London in 1937.

Composed by Creative Graphics, Allentown, Pennsylvania
Printed and bound by Berryville Graphics, Berryville, Virginia
Designed by Wesley Gott